Also by P. J. O'Rourke

Modern Manners
Holidays in Hell
Republican Party Reptile
Give War a Chance

P. J. O'Rourke
PARLIAMENT OF WHORES

P. J. O'Rourke is currently the White House correspondent for *Rolling Stone* magazine. He is the author of, among other books, *Holidays in Hell* and *Give War a Chance.*

PARLIAMENT OF WHORES

*A Lone Humorist Attempts
to Explain the Entire
U.S. Government*

P. J. O'Rourke

Vintage Books
A Division of Random House, Inc.
New York

To Amy

FIRST VINTAGE BOOKS EDITION, MAY 1992

Copyright © 1991 by P. J. O'Rourke

All rights reserved under International and Pan-American Copyright Conventions. Published in the United States by Vintage Books, a division of Random House, Inc., New York, and simultaneously in Canada by Random House of Canada Limited, Toronto. Originally published in hardcover by Atlantic Monthly Press, New York, in 1991.

Library of Congress Cataloging-in-Publication Data
O'Rourke, P. J.
Parliament of whores: a lone humorist attempts to explain the entire U.S. government / by P. J. O'Rourke.—1st Vintage Books ed.
p. cm.
Originally published: New York : Atlantic Monthly Press, c1991.
ISBN 0-679-73789-8 (pbk.)
1. United States—Politics and government—Humor. 2. Politics, Practical—United States—Humor. I. Title.
[JK34.074 1992]
320.973'0207—dc20   91-50710
CIP

Manufactured in the United States of America
10 9 8 7 6 5 4 3 2 1

ACKNOWLEDGMENTS

I'm sure nobody wants credit for my political opinions, so let me say that the influence exercised on me by the people and institutions mentioned below was exercised unintentionally.

The foremost of these unintentional exercisers was Andy Ferguson, former Assistant Managing Editor of the *American Spectator* and presently an editorial writer of great merit for the Scripps-Howard newspaper chain. Andy's knowledge of politics is encyclopedic, his understanding of political behavior is complete and his judgment of man as a political animal is fair and even kind. I have learned a great deal from Andy—when he could get a word in edgewise.

Not long after Andy and I met, we were driving down Pennsylvania Avenue and encountered some or another noisy pinko demonstration. "How come," I asked Andy, "whenever something upsets the Left, you see immediate marches and parades and rallies with signs already printed and rhyming slogans already composed, whereas whenever something upsets the Right, you see two members of the Young Americans for Freedom waving a six-inch American flag?"

"We have jobs," said Andy.

This book owes whatever virtues it has (the vices it acquired while I

Acknowledgments

wasn't looking) to long, pleasant sessions of cocktail drinking with Andy and his wife, Denise, who, until sidetracked by motherhood, was Production Manager of the *American Spectator*, and with Mary Eberstadt, former speech writer for George Shultz and Executive Editor of the *National Interest*, and her husband, Visiting Fellow at the Harvard Center for Population Studies and Visiting Scholar at the American Enterprise Institute, Nick Eberstadt. These four people and my wife, Amy, endured the dress rehearsals, in inebriated monologue form, of everything here. Thanks to their diplomatically proffered critical skills, what I've written is no worse than it is.

I've also spent hours picking the brains and bending the ears of Jim and Marilyn Denton, John Podhoretz, Chris and Lucy Buckley, John and Anna Buckley, Michael and Barbara Ledeen, Peter Collier, David Horowitz, Ed Crane, Grover Norquist, the Honorable Chris Cox, the Honorable Dana Rohrabacher, Paula Dobriansky, Josh Gilder, Jacques and Julie Mariotti, Dave York, Chris Isham, Michael Kinsley, Bob Tyrrell, Wladyslaw Pleszczynski and Ron Burr.

I owe a general and enormous debt of gratitude to Rick Robinson, a paragon among Capitol Hill staffers and maybe the only person on Earth who both understands the civics book chapter on "How a Bill Becomes a Law" and knows how to get good seats at the Kentucky Derby.

Three books that I found invaluable in writing this uninvaluable one were *Losing Ground* and *In Pursuit of Happiness and Good Government* by Charles Murray and *An American Vision*, edited by Ed Crane and David Boaz, President and Executive Vice President, respectively, of the Cato Institute. I commend these tomes to any critic of government seeking serious amelioration rather than comic relief.

I would like to thank Franklin Lavin for helping make the executive branch of government comprehensible, and my former (and, it is to be hoped, future) Congressman Chuck Douglas for doing the same with the judiciary. David E. Davis, Jr., Editor and Publisher of *Automobile* magazine, provided me with all the necessary information about the Department of Transportation for my chapter on the bureaucracy. It would have been impossible to write the chapter on drug policy without the aid and intellect of Dick Weart, Special Agent, U.S. Customs Service.

Acknowledgments

Curtis Sliwa and the Guardian Angels were just what their name says they are while I researched the poverty chapter. And Meg Hunt, Robert Rector and all the people at the Heritage Foundation likewise watched over me when I ventured into the bad neighborhoods of political economy.

I wrote the chapter on agriculture with the help of Mary Anne Gee's legislative expertise, James Bovard's book *Farm Fiasco* and the Honorable Dick Armey's angry speeches in Congress. My thanks also go to Peter Davis, who actually farms.

Steve Masty, Dick Hoagland and Lisa Schiffren gave me the "Frontierland Tour" of the Afghanistan border.

Captin David Bill III kindly hosted me aboard his ship the USS *Mobile Bay* and showed me some things the Iraqis have since seen close up.

Kathleen Day's article "S&L Hell" in the March 20, 1989, *New Republic* is almost the only sensible thing I've read about the savings-and-loan crisis, and it gave me a starting point for a less sensible thing of my own. Fellow Toledoan Debbie Shannon explained banking to me as well as any mortal could and also taught me how lobbying really works (it turns out to be less distasteful than most voting).

I owe various boons and favors to the following people and organizations: the Honorable Jim Bunning, Russ Hodge, Bob Beckel, Tony Snow, the Honorable Susan Molinari, Ken Walker, Mona Charen, Walter Gottlieb, Fox TV's "Off the Record," the National Forum Foundation, the Heritage Foundation, the American Enterprise Institute, Americans for Tax Reform, the Political Economy Research Center, the Manhattan Institute, the Cato Institute and a thousand people in Washington, some of whom I'm forgetting and some of whom would rather not be remembered here.

And I especially want to thank Lee Atwater for his political and spiritual inspiration—and for providing a great sound track.

Fully half of this book has appeared, in article form, in *Rolling Stone* magazine. Authors are forever saying, "This book could not have been written without blah, blah, blah." But this particular book really couldn't have been written if it hadn't first been *under*written by *Rolling Stone.* I thank *Rolling Stone* editors Robert Vare, Bob Wallace and Eric Etheridge for their necessary and welcome blue-penciling. And I thank Jann Wenner for his super-necessary and extra-welcome paychecks.

Acknowledgments

A large part of the "Protectors of a Blameless Citizenry" chapter appeared in *Automobile* magazine, and "Among the Compassion Fascists" was originally published in the *American Spectator*. I'd like to thank those publications for the permission (which, it occurs to me, I've probably forgotten to request) to reprint this material.

Finally, I must thank my publisher, Morgan Entrekin. He gave this project patience, money and hard work and even stood up as best man at my wedding. What can I say, Morgan? I promise my next book will be *Madonna's Illegitimate UFO Diet to Cure AIDS and Find Elvis*.

P. J. O'ROURKE
Dhahran, Saudi Arabia, 1991

A Note on the Arithmetic Herein

The numbers in this book are correct to the best of the author's ability to make them so. But the statistics presented here are for illustrative, not statistical, purposes. Some figures are disputable, some will be out-of-date by the time this is published and a few were probably wrong from the get-go. Humor is, by its nature, more truthful than factual. Don't bet the ranch on my math.

What stops a man who can laugh from speaking the truth?

—Horace

CONTENTS

Contents

THE THREE BRANCHES OF GOVERNMENT: MONEY, TELEVISION AND BULLSHIT

OUR GOVERNMENT: WHAT THE FUCK DO THEY DO ALL DAY, AND WHY DOES IT COST SO GODDAMNED MUCH MONEY?

Contents

PREFACE

Why God Is a Republican and Santa Claus Is a Democrat

The subject of this book is government because I don't have to do anything about it.

I am a journalist and, under the modern journalist's code of Olympian objectivity (and total purity of motive), I am absolved of responsibility. We journalists don't have to step on roaches. All we have to do is turn on the kitchen light and watch the critters scurry. If I were a decent citizen instead of a journalist, I would have a patriotic duty to become involved in the American political system and try to reform or improve it. In that case I would probably do my patriotic duty about the way I did in the 1960s, before I was a journalist, when my involvement with the American political system consisted of dodging the draft. All this is by way of saying that if you are a nonjournalistic American and don't want to read this book because it's about government, just buy it and let it lie around your house like *A Brief History of Time*.

I decided to write about the United States government after I had spent some years writing about awful things that happen to foreigners overseas. It occurred to me that some pretty awful things happen to us right here. Furthermore, they happen in English, so that I could ask people why they were doing the awful things or getting the awful things done to them. Then, when the people told me and I didn't understand, at least I'd know that I didn't understand and wouldn't get confused by the language barrier and maybe think I did.

I also found the sheer, boring, gray dullness of government a challenge to my pride as a reporter. "I," I thought, "I alone—master that I am of the piquant adverbial phrase and the subordinate clause *juste*—can make this interesting. Why, combine my keen eye for detail with my sharp nose for the telling particular, and the reader will get . . . a faceful of minute observations. Yes, I can paint the drab corridors of power in the party hues of lively prose, dress the dull politicos in motley and cause the Mrs. O'Leary's cow of governmental insipidity to kick over the lantern of public indignation and set the town ablaze." I am not the first journalist to make this mistake.

Anyway, I thought I'd observe the 1988 presidential race and then go to Washington for the first six months of the new administration, learn everything there is to know about government and write a book. But the six months turned into two years. I'm not sure I learned anything except that giving money and power to government is like giving whiskey and car keys to teenage boys. And what resulted was not so much a book as a great digest of ignorance.

Grant me at least that it is an ambitious failure. In the following volume I have tried to do a number of things. I have tried to write a kind of Devil's Civics Text in which, like a voodoo doctor teaching poli-sci, I give unnatural life to a description of American government. I have also tried to present a factual—data-filled, at any rate—account of how this government works. Which is complicated by the fact that it doesn't. So I've tried to present a factual account of how the government fails, too. Finally, I've attempted to compose a dissertation on what we Americans expect from our government and how—like parents or fans of certain sports teams—we intend to maintain those expectations even if it kills us. And, several times in the past, it has.

I have tried to keep the book reasonably free of personalities. Not that this was possible in a political system (a socioeconomic system, for that matter) as fame-driven as ours. I had to mention the president by name, though I was tempted not to. I've always admired the way the movies of the 1930s and 1940s would only show the president character from the back. It was more respectful. Either that or movies were made by Republicans in those days.

I preferred to concentrate on systems and institutions, not because people aren't important, but because people are important, in Washington, so briefly. There was a time not long ago when day could hardly break without asking permission from Don Regan, and now, for all I know, he's hosting a talk radio show in Anaheim. I concentrated on institutions because in order to concentrate on persons I'd have had to keep revising and revising until the moment these pages went to press, and I'd still wind up with a book as dated as a Jody Powell joke.

Having said that, I was reading my manuscript (book buyers may not realize it, but we writers often do read what we write, although some of us just wait for the movie version), and I noticed that Senator Daniel Patrick Moynihan is singled out for criticism in three different chapters. I have nothing in particular against the senator from New York. There are plenty worse in the nation's upper house—John Kerry, Edward Kennedy, Christopher Dodd, Claiborne Pell, Alan Cranston and the appalling Howard Metzenbaum, to name just six. Senator Moynihan's triplicate appearance is mostly coincidental. He wrote something pertinent to the chapter about poverty, said something pertinent about the Social Security tax and happened to be in Pakistan at the same time I was. So—Paddy to Paddy—I apologize, Senator. On the other hand, Daniel Patrick Moynihan is the archetypal extremely smart person who went into politics anyway instead of doing something worthwhile for his country. So maybe he owes all of us an apology, too.

This book is written, of course, from a conservative point of view. Conservatism favors the restraint of government. A little government and a little luck are necessary in life, but only a fool trusts either of them. Also, conservatism is, at least in its American form, a philosophy that relies upon personal responsibility and promotes private liberty. It is an ideology of individuals. Everyone with any sense and experience in life would rather take his fellows one by one than in a crowd. Crowds are noisy, unreasonable and impatient. They can trample you easier than a single person can. And a crowd will never buy you lunch.

But although this is a conservative book, it is not informed by any very elaborate political theory. I have only one firm belief about the American political system, and that is this: God is a Republican and Santa Claus is a Democrat.

God is an elderly or, at any rate, middle-aged male, a stern fellow, patriarchal rather than paternal and a great believer in rules and regulations. He holds men strictly accountable for their actions. He has little apparent concern for the material well-being of the disadvantaged. He is politically connected, socially powerful and holds the mortgage on literally everything in the world. God is difficult. God is unsentimental. It is very hard to get into God's heavenly country club.

Santa Claus is another matter. He's cute. He's nonthreatening. He's always cheerful. And he loves animals. He may know who's been naughty and who's been nice, but he never does anything about it. He gives everyone everything they want without thought of a quid pro quo. He works hard for charities, and he's famously generous to the poor. Santa Claus is preferable to God in every way but one: There is no such thing as Santa Claus.

THE MYSTERY
OF GOVERNMENT

Good laws derive from evil habits.
—Macrobius

$\mathbf{W}$hat *is* this oozing behemoth, this fibrous tumor, this monster of power and expense hatched from the simple human desire for civic order? How did an allegedly free people spawn a vast, rampant cuttlefish of dominion with its tentacles in every orifice of the body politic?

The federal government of the United States of America takes away between a fifth and a quarter of all our money every year. That is eight times the Islamic zakat, the almsgiving required of believers by the Koran; it is double the tithe of the medieval church and twice the royal tribute that the prophet Samuel warned the Israelites against when they wanted him to anoint a ruler:

> This will be the manner of the king that shall reign over you. . . . He
> will take the tenth of your seed, and of your vineyards. . . . He will
> take the tenth of your sheep. . . . And ye shall cry out in that day
> because of your king. . . .

Our government gets more than thugs in a protection racket demand, more even than discarded first wives of famous rich men receive in divorce court. Then this government, swollen and arrogant with pelf, goes butting into our business. It checks the amount of tropical oils in our snack foods, tells us what kind of gasoline we can buy for our cars and how fast we can drive them, bosses us around about retirement, education and what's on TV; counts our noses and asks fresh questions about who's still living at home and how many bathrooms we have; decides whether the door to our office or shop should have steps or a wheelchair ramp; decrees the gender and complexion of the people to be hired there; lectures us on safe sex; dictates what we can sniff, smoke and swallow; and waylays young men, ships them to distant places and tells them to shoot people they don't even know.

The government is huge, stupid, greedy and makes nosy, officious and dangerous intrusions into the smallest corners of life—this much we can stand. But the real problem is that government is boring. We could cure or mitigate the other ills Washington visits on us if we could only bring ourselves to pay attention to Washington itself. But we cannot.

During the last presidential campaign deep-thinking do-gooders at some tax dodge called the John and Mary R. Markle Foundation set up a commission to study the electorate and discovered that 49 percent of the public didn't know Lloyd Bentsen was the Democratic vice-presidential nominee. That is good news for Lloyd Bentsen—he now only has to make 51 percent of the public forget he was ever on the Dukakis ticket. But the Markle commission members were not so pleased. They called the information "astonishing" and claimed it "suggests a wide-spread, glacial indifference" to elections.

This is an insult to glaciers. An Ice Age would be fascinating compared with government. We'd be wondering whether to update our snowblowers and trying to figure out if using rock salt to keep ice floes off our driveways would kill the herbaceous borders. We'd be *interested* if glaciers were the problem. "American voters today do not seem to understand their rightful places in the operation of a democracy," said the Markle commission. Wrong again. It's democracy that doesn't understand its rightful place in the operation of us—to shut up and get out of our faces.

Government is boring because political careers are based on the most tepid kind of lie: "I'll balance the budget, sort of." "I won't raise taxes, if I can help it." Of course politicians don't tell the truth: "I am running for the U.S. Senate in order to even the score with those grade-school classmates of mine who, thirty-five years ago, gave me the nickname Fish Face," or, "Please elect me to Congress so that I can get out of the Midwest and meet bigwigs and cute babes." But neither do politicians tell huge, entertaining whoppers: "Why, send yours truly to Capitol Hill, and I'll ship the swag home in boxcar lots. You'll be paving the roads with bacon around here when I get done shoveling out the pork barrel. There'll be government jobs for your dog. Leave your garden hose running for fifteen minutes, and I'll have the Department of Transportation build an eight-lane suspension bridge across the puddle. Show me a wet basement, and I'll get you a naval base and make your Roto-Rooter man an admiral of the fleet. There'll be farm subsidies for every geranium you've got in a pot, defense contracts for Junior's spitballs and free day care for Sister's dolls. You'll get unemployment for the sixteen hours every day when you're not at your job, full disability benefits if you have to get up in the night to take a leak, and Social Security checks will come in the mail not just when you retire at sixty-five but when you retire each night to bed. Taxes? Hell, I'll have the government go around every week putting money *back* in your paycheck, and I'll make the IRS hire chimpanzees from the zoo to audit your tax returns. Vote for me, folks, and you'll be farting through silk."

Government is also boring because in a democracy government is a matter of majority rule. Now, majority rule is a precious, sacred thing worth dying for. But—like other precious, sacred things, such as the home and family—it's not only worth dying for; it can make you wish you were dead. Imagine if all of life were determined by majority rule. Every meal would be a pizza. Every pair of pants, even those in a Brooks Brothers suit, would be stone-washed denim. Celebrity diet and exercise books would be the only thing on the shelves at the library. And—since women are a majority of the population—we'd all be married to Mel Gibson.

Furthermore, government is boring because what's in it for us? Sure, if we own an aerospace contracting company, a five-thousand-acre sugar-beet farm or a savings and loan with the president's son on the board of directors, we can soak Uncle Sucker for millions. But most of us failed to plan ahead and buy McDonnell Douglas, and now the only thing we can get out of government is government benefits—measly VA checks and Medicare. We won't get far on the French Riviera on this kind of chump change. Besides, the French look at us funny when we try to buy *pâté de foie gras* and Château Margaux '61 with American food stamps.

Government is so tedious that sometimes you wonder if the government isn't being boring on purpose. Maybe they're *trying* to put us to sleep so we won't notice what they're doing. Every aspect of our existence is affected by government, so naturally we want to keep an eye on the thing. Yet whenever we regular citizens try to read a book on government or watch one of those TV public affairs programs about government or listen to anything anybody who's in the government is saying, we feel like high-school students who've fallen two weeks behind in their algebra class. Then we grow drowsy and torpid, and the next thing you know we are snoring like a gas-powered weed whacker. This could be intentional. Our government could be attempting to establish a Dictatorship of Boredom in this country. The last person left awake gets to spend all the tax money.

Boredom isn't the only problem, of course. American lack of interest in government is well developed, but American ignorance of government is perfect. Almost everything we know about the workings of Congress, the presidency, the Supreme Court and so forth comes from one high-school civics course and one spring vacation when Dad took the family to Washington, DC. On the trip to Washington we learned that the three branches of government are the White House, the top of the Washington Monument and the tour of the FBI Building. In the high-school civics class we learned just how long an afternoon can be made to seem with the help of modern educational methods.

I can remember everything about my civics course—what classroom it was in, who taught it, which of my friends were in the class with me, where I sat and what the brassiere of the girl who sat next to me looked like when I peeked down the armhole of her sleeveless blouse. About the civics I remember nothing. There must have been tiny subliminal messages printed between the lines of my textbook saying, "Go ahead, take another look, she must be a 42D."

That was twenty-six years ago, but things have not changed much. I got a copy of a current high-school civics book, *American Civics*, published by Harcourt Brace Jovanovich. I'm told it is one of the nation's most widely used texts. The heft of the thing, its awkward shape and inept cover art, the glossy, teen-resistant paper—all of this gave me what I can only describe as a backup of the memory's septic system. I was all of a sudden swamped with powerful, involuntary recollections of dreary class discussions, irksome pop quizzes and desiccated spring afternoons.

American Civics is, of course, completely up-to-date. Its blurry, stilted photographs of people in unfashionable clothes are printed in color instead of black and white. Its page layouts have been tarted up with cartoons, pastel type and *USA Today*–style lists of "fun facts" to suit the attention span of the "Sesame Street" generation. And, dispersed throughout the book, are little boxed items such as this:

CAN YOU GUESS?
One of our Presidents had a serious physical handicap. Who was he?

Answer is on page 578.

(The answer is not, by the way, "Ronald Reagan and his handicap was Nancy.")

American Civics has also trimmed its sails to the prevailing ideological winds. It has a section with the infelicitous title "Upsetting America's Ecology" and another section that says, "The Reverend Jesse Jackson ran a strong campaign for the 1984 and 1988 Democratic Presidential nominations." There's a photo of a man in a wheelchair above the caption, "Disabled doesn't mean unable," and in the "Living Documents" appendix at the end—tossed in with the Mayflower Compact, the Gettysburg Address and the Emancipation Proclamation—is some screed from a women's rights conference in 1848 called the Seneca Falls Declaration.

What's more, the authors of *American Civics* assume their students are as ignorant of everything as they are of government. Thus, among such traditional chapter headings as "How a Bill Becomes a Law" and "Our Federal Court System," we find "Your Family and You" and—I'm not

7

kidding—"Using Television as a Resource" and—I'm still not kidding—
"Civics Skills: Reading a Help Wanted Ad." (Though I suppose ignorance
is relative. Few seventeen-year-olds today need to peek into the armhole of
a sleeveless blouse to find out what a brassiere looks like.)

Underneath the moral and typographical frills and lessons in how to
use a phone, however, *American Civics* is the same font of monotony, the
same bible of ennui that civics books have always been. I defy anyone to
read two paragraphs of it without incurring a strong desire to join Posse
Comitatus or the Symbionese Liberation Army or some other group that
promises to kill high-school civics teachers. I also defy anyone to read two
paragraphs of it and tell me what he just read.

There are, of course, other sources of information on government
available to literate adults. I have in my hand—or, rather, in both my
hands, because it is 793 pages long and weighs more than a cinder block—
The Power Game: How Washington Works by Hedrick Smith. This comes
with a gold-foil sticker on its cover saying, "AS SEEN ON PBS." Just four little
words, yet oh how they catch the heart.

The Power Game seems to contain everything that Hedrick Smith, in
his long career as a *New York Times* reporter, has ever heard or seen in
Washington, including—I'm not sure about this, but the literary styles are
similar—the entire District of Columbia phone book. *The Power Game*
is—and I'm quoting the dust-flap copy so you know I'm telling the truth—
"an eye-opening inside portrait of how Washington, D.C., really works
today." It's a very different kind of book from *American Civics.* Where
American Civics is amazingly boring, *The Power Game* is . . . words fail me
. . . an eye-opening inside portrait of how Washington, D.C., really works
today.

Our Founding Fathers lacked the special literary skills with which
modern writers on the subject of government are so richly endowed. When
they wrote the Declaration of Independence, the Constitution and the Bill
of Rights, they found themselves more or less forced to come to the point.
So clumsy of thought and pen were the Founders that even today, seven
generations later, we can tell what they were talking about.

They were talking about having a good time:

> We hold these Truths to be self-evident, that all Men are created equal,
> that they are endowed by their Creator with certain unalienable Rights,
> that among these are Life, Liberty and the Pursuit of happiness. . . .

"This is living!" "I gotta be me!" "Ain't we got fun!" It's all there
in the Declaration of Independence. We are the only nation in the world
based on happiness. Search as you will the sacred creeds of other nations
and peoples, read the Magna Carta, the *Communist Manifesto,* the Ten
Commandments, the *Analects* of Confucius, Plato's *Republic,* the New
Testament or the UN Charter, and find me any happiness at all. America
is the Happy Kingdom. And that is one good reason why we who live here
can't bring ourselves to read *American Civics* or *The Power Game* or even
the daily paper.

As it is with us, so it was with the Original Dads. Their beef with Triple
George? He was *no fun:*

> He is, at this Time, transporting large Armies of foreign Mercenaries
> to complete the works of Death, Desolation, and Tyranny, already
> begun with circumstances of Cruelty and Perfidity, scarcely paralleled
> in the most barbarous Ages, and totally unworthy the Head of a
> civilized Nation.

Totally.

There are twenty-seven specific complaints against the British Crown
set forth in the Declaration of Independence. To modern ears they still
sound reasonable. They still sound reasonable, in large part, because so
many of them can be leveled against the present federal government of the
United States. Maybe not the "Death, Desolation, and Tyranny" complaint
(unless you're deeply opposed, on fight-for-your-right-to-party grounds, to
coca-plant eradication in Bolivia and Peru), but how about:

> . . . has erected a Multitude of new Offices, and sent hither Swarms
> of Officers to harass our People, and eat out their Substance.

George III was a piker compared with FDR or LBJ.

Or:

. . . has called together Legislative Bodies at Places unusual, uncomfortable, and distant . . . for the sole Purpose of fatiguing them into Compliance with his Measures.

Every American president does that to the House and the Senate.

. . . has refused his Assent to Laws, the most wholesome and necessary for the public Good.

Our Congress won't pass a balanced-budget constitutional amendment or any legislation banning people over thirty from wearing spandex bicycle shorts.

. . . has endeavored to prevent the Population of these States; for that Purpose obstructing the Laws for Naturalization of Foreigners; refusing . . . to encourage their Migrations hither. . . .

Tell a Vietnamese boat person, a Hong Kong shopkeeper or a migrant worker from Mexico that this doesn't describe U.S. immigration policy.

. . . has kept among us, in Times of Peace, Standing Armies. . . .

Certainly.

. . . has combined with others to subject us to a Jurisdiction foreign to our Constitution, and unacknowledged by our Laws, . . .

Federal regulatory agencies, for instance.

. . . Depriving us, in many Cases, of the Benefits of Trial by Jury.

If we cross one of those regulatory agencies.

. . . Cutting off our Trade with all Parts of the World

is what our trade quotas and tariffs do.

. . . Imposing Taxes on us without our Consent.

Nobody asked me if I wanted a 1040 Form.

. . . Taking away our Charters, abolishing our most valuable Laws, and altering fundamentally the Forms of our Governments.

So say states rights conservatives.

. . . has plundered our Seas, ravaged our Coasts . . . and destroyed the Lives of our People.

All the tree huggers believe this.
And lastly:

. . . has excited domestic Insurrections amongst us. . . .

In Watts, Bensonhurst, that Mohawk reservation in upstate New York and my house since I married into a family full of Democrats.

American Civics calls the Declaration of Independence a "living document." All too true.

The Constitution is an equally forthright piece of work and quite succinct—twenty-one pages (in the *American Civics* E-Z-reader large-type version) giving the complete operating instructions for a nation of 250 million people. The manual for a Toyota Camry, which only seats five, is four times as long. And, thanks to the pro-growth economic policies of the vigorously libertarian—not to say completely impotent—Continental Congress, the Constitution is not translated from Japanese.

An hour's perusal of our national charter makes it hard to understand what the argle-bargle is about. The First Amendment forbids any law "abridging the freedom of speech." It doesn't say, "except for commercials on children's television" or "unless somebody says 'cunt' in a rap song or 'chick' on a college campus."

The Second Amendment states that "the right of the people to keep and bear arms, shall not be infringed," period. There is no mention of magazine size, rate of fire or to what extent these arms may resemble assault rifles. All rifles were assault rifles in those days. Furthermore, if the gun laws that Massachusetts has now had been in force in 1776, we'd all be Canadians, and you know what kind of weather Canada has.

There is no reference to abortion whatsoever in the Constitution, not so much as an "I'll pull out in time, honey, honest." The Tenth Amendment tells us that "the powers not delegated to the United States by the Constitution, nor prohibited by it to the States, are reserved to the States respectively, or to the people." This means the power to drive the nation crazy over a gob of meiotic cells that wouldn't fill a coke spoon and, on the other hand, the power to murder innocent babies that haven't even been born yet are—just as the amendment says—"reserved to the States respectively, or to the people."

The Constitution is not hard to understand. Although the quality of reasoning degenerates in the later amendments. The Sixteenth Amendment is particularly awful:

> The Congress shall have the power to lay and collect taxes on incomes, from whatever source derived. . . .

And Section 4 of the Fourteenth is very silly:

> The validity of the public debt of the United States, authorized by law, . . . shall not be questioned.

The Twenty-Sixth Amendment, giving the vote to eighteen-year-olds, must have been drafted by people who'd never met any eighteen-year-olds or, worse, by people who were eighteen.

And then there is the—from a male point of view—tactically foolish Nineteenth Amendment:

> The right of citizens of the United States to vote shall not be denied or abridged by the United States or any State on account of sex.

This made women stop protesting a trivial wrong to their gender—exclusion from the electoral process—and allowed them to focus their indignation on more serious forms of injustice, such as the fact that women suffer discrimination and harassment in the workplace, are paid less than men, are rarely promoted to the highest levels of corporate or professional responsibility and this year's hemlines make their legs look fat.

There are also a few gimmicks and dodges in the Constitution, such as Section 4 of the presidential disability and succession amendment, which says that the vice president "and a majority of either the principal officers of the executive departments *or of such other body as Congress may by law provide*" (italics my own) can declare the president incompetent. If I'm reading this right, it means that with the help of pals in the House and Senate, Dan Quayle and the principal officers of the Fort Wayne, Indiana, Elks Club can send George Bush to the bughouse and declare a national golf emergency.

But, on the whole, the text is easily glossed. The single exception being Article Two, Section 1:

> The electors shall . . . vote by ballot for two persons. . . . The person having the greatest number of votes shall be the President; . . . and if there be more than one who have such majority, and have an equal number of votes, then the House of Representatives shall immediately choose by ballot one of them. . . .

This was later modified by the rather more confusing Twelfth Amendment:

> . . . The person having the greatest number of votes for President, shall be the President, if such number be a majority of the whole number of Electors appointed; and if no person have such majority, then from the persons having the highest numbers not exceeding three on the list of those voted for as President, the House of Representatives shall choose immediately, by ballot, the President.

The idea seems to be to make the election of a president so complicated and annoying that no one with an important job or a serious avocation—that is, no one presently making any substantial contribution to society—would be tempted to run for the office. So far, it's worked.

Otherwise, only one important question is raised by the Constitution, a question implicit in its preamble:

> We the people of the United States, in order to form a more perfect Union, establish justice, insure domestic tranquility, provide for the common defense, promote the general welfare, and secure the blessings of liberty to ourselves and our posterity . . .

The question being, "Are we done yet?"

The first objective was achieved in 1865 when we squashed the rednecks and peckerwoods. The result was a definitely more perfect union. Compare it, for example, with the Union of Soviet Socialist Republics or the AFL-CIO. We've established about as much justice as the country can stand—maybe more, to judge by the verdict in the Marion Barry trial and some of the sentences handed to the Iran-contra conspirators. (Perfect justice being a thing none of us would care to confront.) Domestic tranquility we don't have, but how we'd get any without violating every clause of this document that is supposed to ensure it I can't imagine. The common defense is so well provided for that even such uncommon things as Saudi Arabians are defended by it. In the matter of promoting the general welfare, we have—to judge by the welfare rolls—done it too well. The blessings of liberty are so manifestly secured to ourselves that we seem weighed down by the things, and lately are attending AA meetings, joining religious congregations and formulating personal diet and exercise regimens to ease the burden. And, as for posterity, that's why birth control was invented.

So when can we quit passing laws and raising taxes? When can we say of our political system, "Stick a fork in it, it's done"? When will our officers, officials and magistrates realize their jobs are finished and return, like Cincinnatus, to the plow or, as it were, to the law practice or the car dealership? The mystery of government is not how Washington works but how to make it stop.

THE DICTATORSHIP
OF BOREDOM

Be silent, wretch, and think not here allow'd
That worst of tyrants, an usurping crowd
                              —Alexander Pope, trans., *The Iliad*

ON THE BLANDWAGON

A Political Convention

The American political system is like a gigantic Mexican Christmas fiesta. Each political party is a huge piñata—a papier-mâché donkey, for example. The donkey is filled with full employment, low interest rates, affordable housing, comprehensive medical benefits, a balanced budget and other goodies. The American voter is blindfolded and given a stick. The voter then swings the stick wildly in every direction, trying to hit a political candidate on the head and knock some sense into the silly bastard.

In July 1988 I attended the specious, entropic, criminally trivial, boring, stupid Democratic National Convention—a numb suckhole stuffed with political bulk filler held in that place where bad malls go when they die, Atlanta, a city with a midsummer climate like the inside of a locked van stalled in the Sahara at noon. Then—with barely time to hose the Dukakis sludge out of my tape recorder and scrape the talk of Democratic-party unity off the bottom of my loafers—I flew to that other oleo-high colonic, the Republican convention, an event with the intellectual content of a Guns n' Roses lyric attended by every ofay insurance broker in America who owns a pair of white shoes and which was held in New Orleans, a summertime visit to which is like taking a sauna in a high-crime drainage ditch.

These are shameful affairs, our political party conclaves. We have a government of, by and for the people. We're supposed to be ruling ourselves. We have to decide how much of this ruling we want to do to each other and by what means we're going to do it. Is the president supposed to be a big Nosenheimer or not? When should Congress monkey around with things, and when should it buzz off? What about the Supreme Court—solemn defenders of constitutional integrity or nine old nags in black muumuus? And how much is all this going to cost?

A lot of public noodling and citizen knitting of brows would be called for, you'd think. Yet when our country's only two political parties with more than one hundred members not under psychiatric care get together, the delegates act like Shriners on a toot. I'm exaggerating. Shriners ride tiny motorcycles around in circles, which is more useful than anything political-convention delegates do, and Shriner hats aren't as funny.

A political convention is another of the innumerable special-occasion events that litter the American calendar. What is it, Annual Old Yodelers Week in Minneapolis? Recovering Alcoholic Single Mothers Olympics? Grammies for the Deaf? Or free citizens exercising their precious rights of political liberty? As long as it's got a light show, a celebrity who sings and Bryant Gumbel in the broadcast booth, it could be practically anything.

Conventions no longer even determine who's going to run for president. Unvoted-in primaries at weird times of the year in states you've never heard of take care of that. And the real political debate at conventions—debate that could change anybody's mind or put anything in that mind to change—wouldn't fill a bumper sticker. Party platforms are as bland as club-soda soup, vague as a TV commercial for condoms. The 1988 Democratic platform contained such ringing declarations and tough-minded statements of principle as these:

> We believe that it is time for America, within a strong commitment to fiscal responsibility, to reassert progressive values and reinvest in its people. . . .
>
> We believe that this nation needs to invest in its children. . . .
>
> We believe that we can rebuild America, creating good jobs at good wages through a national reinvestment strategy. . . .

(You'll note that politicians no longer spend money, they invest it. Don't worry about paying more to the Internal Revenue Service. You aren't being taxed; you're taking a plunge on a fly-by-night stock issue.)

> We further believe that no person should go to bed hungry. . . .
>
> We believe it is time for America to change and move forward again in the interest of all its families. . . .
>
> We believe the American dream of opportunity for every citizen can be a reality for all Americans willing to meet their own responsibilities to help it come true. . . .

Hell, you could run anybody on that platform—Mother Cabrini, Sagegh Ghotbzadeh, Salvador Allende, Pat Paulsen, Ronald Reagan. Even Communists have more respect for their electorate than this. The Soviet Communists had just spent half of June 1988 in a party congress where people actually spoke their minds, had real arguments and made genuine plans. Mikhail Gorbachev and Yegor Ligachev didn't lock themselves up in a secret logrolling session and then come out doing the bunny hug while their supporters waved their nicknames on sticks.

Both Democrats and Republicans are guilty of mindless sports-fan behavior, rat-gagging gluttony for political office and ideology without ideas. But there was something especially unattractive about the Democratic vagueness in 1988. Republicans were, after all, a defined term—something we'd been using (or vice versa) since 1980. If we liked the Reagan administration, we could vote for Bush and, presumably, get seconds. If we didn't like the Reagan administration or couldn't bring ourselves to admit that we did, we could vote for Dukakis and get something different—but God knew what.

Democrats are also the party of government activism, the party that says government can make you richer, smarter, taller and get the chickweed out of your lawn. Republicans are the party that says government doesn't work, and then they get elected and prove it. One philosophy is not necessarily an improvement on the other, but if you want the tooth fairy to come, you've got to have some teeth under your pillow.

Furthermore, the Democratic party is, to be polite about it, broad based. It's the Cat-Canary Love Association, Dogs and Mailmen United. Some people say the only reason Lloyd Bentsen is a Democrat is to keep Republicans from being embarrassed by his ties to big business. And Jesse Jackson—if you listen to what he says rather than how he says it—sounds like Fidel Castro's Jiminy Cricket. Jackson told the 1988 Atlanta convention that the Democratic party "needs both its left wing and its right wing to fly." But putting Bentsen out on the tip of one primary feather and Jackson way over on the other makes for a bird the size of the Chicago Merchandise Mart. Don't stand out in the yard when it flies overhead.

Then there was Michael Dukakis. Dukakis wasn't a right-winger or a left-winger. He was . . . Well, he was sort of . . . I mean . . . um . . . mmmm . . .

Excuse me, I dozed off for a moment and went face down into the typewriter keys.

Jesse Jackson was the only Democrat who came to Atlanta with real ideas. This is because, in the American political system, you're only allowed to have real ideas if it's absolutely guaranteed that you can't win an election. Thus the only substantive political platforms belong to candidates such as Norman Thomas, Henry Wallace, George Wallace and Eugene McCarthy, and—as you can see by that list—saying a candidate has real ideas is no compliment.

Anyway, Jackson wanted a five-year freeze on military spending, a 100-percent, mandated-by-law increase in educational funding, a no-first-use A-bomb promise, a Palestinian homeland, etc., etc.—all easily demanded since they'd never have to be delivered. And he admitted he would raise taxes.

This at least *sounded* courageous. But even courageous sounds don't last long at a Democratic National Convention. Jackson had been in Atlanta for all of about five minutes before he cuddled up to Michael Dukakis in return for some unspecified role in a never-never administration.

Jesse and Mike emerged from the strange-bedfellow room on Monday morning of convention week claiming to still respect each other. They then engaged in a kind of lukewarm political necking that *New Republic* editor Fred Barnes called "kiss on the lips but no tongue."

So much for an exciting convention-floor fight. Smart reporters—of whom there were none in attendance, as you may have noticed if you watched any of this on TV—packed their bags and flew back to their summer shore rentals. What remained of the Democratic convention (which is to say all of it) was a four-day greased-liberal catching contest. Herewith a few of the dramatic highlights:

Monday night everybody packed into the Democratic convention hall, which in real life is the Atlanta Hawks basketball arena and is shaped approximately like a toilet but isn't as comfortable. There was an overblown podium that could be moved up and down to make Michael Dukakis look shorter. The convention's production designers thought, according to Maureen Dowd of the *New York Times,* that red, white and blue would look "cheap" on television. Therefore, they painted this vast ziggurat salmon, eggshell and azure. A nice patriotic touch. *O say does that pastel-spangled banner yet sit / O'er the land of block grants and of fed benefits?*

The keynote speaker was Ann Richards, the state treasurer of Texas, and that says something about how many high-powered women government officials the pro-ERA Democrats had managed to elect. (Richards would, however, in the elect-a-fool year of 1990, become governor of Texas.)

Richards had had a few good lines scripted for her about George Bush, e.g.: "Poor George, he can't help it. He was born with a silver foot in his mouth." She could tell a joke and wax as folksy as a wine-cooler spokesperson. And she was a champion performer in the Reagan-blaming competition, branding the chief executive as the cause of every single national ill. (You remember how President Reagan used to slip out of the White House at night and get teenage girls pregnant and sell crack.) For a moment it seemed as though the convention would rise in a body and nominate

Richards for president, she had so much more pep than Lickpenny Mike. But they didn't.

The centerpiece of Richard's address was a querulous letter from one of her constituents: "Our worries go from payday to payday. . . . I worry how I'm going to pay the rising car insurance and food. . . . I pray my kids don't have a growth spurt from August to December so I have to buy new jeans. . . . We don't take vacations or go out to eat. . . . I believe people like us have been forgotten in America." Good sob-sister stuff. But there was a biographical note about the letter-writer on the speech transcript handed out by the Democratic press office. The anonymous correspondent and her husband and kids lived in a small town outside Waco and had a combined family income of $50,000. Now, I know $50,000 doesn't sound like much to somebody in a lucrative field such as Texas politics. But, honestly, Ms. Richards, there are some of us who consider that to be a halfway decent income.

Richards talked about the homeless, too, of course. A Democrat who didn't talk about the homeless in 1988 would have been dumber than a Republican who didn't talk about the Iran hostages in 1980. "And there is no city in America where you cannot see homeless men . . . ," said Richards.

Except Atlanta. There was not a recumbent bum, importunate panhandler or cardboard pied-à-terre visible within parking distance of downtown. Walking toward the convention center on that Monday afternoon, *American Spectator* editor Andy Ferguson and I had been approached by three scruffy guys. Were we reporters? Could we interview them? They didn't look any more boneheaded than the rest of the people we'd been interviewing.

"Notice how you haven't seen any homeless around?" said one. "They've been locking them up. They were all run off last week. They started hassling us three or four days before the convention. We got kicked out of the bus station. Police won't even let us back in to get our stuff out of the lockers. There's usually seventy-five to a hundred of us in the park over there, sleeping every night. We tried to sleep in there like usual, and they turned the sprinklers on at 3:00 A.M."

After Ann Richards, Garrison Keillor came out onstage and, in his terrifyingly unthreatening way, read a batch of "If I Were President" essays by children. Jolene Dann Barkley, a first-grader from Lander, Wyoming, was apparently one of the people who helped draft the 1988 Democratic party platform:

> If I was the president I would tell people how to get somewhere and help people in homes with children. If there was a snow blizzard I would help the animals get food. If a family's mom or dad die they could come and live with me. If there was a war I would stop it because I love people. I would keep people away from mean people. I would wear a black and dark purple dress.

Ex-President Carter spoke last. I hadn't known he was in reruns.

Tuesday night Ted Kennedy gave the "Where Was George?" speech, which was supposed to provide the Democratic campaign with a much-needed T-shirt slogan. T-shirt slogans being as close as American political parties come to argument of hypotheses by logical inference.

> . . . As the administration secretly plotted to sell arms to Iran, . . . where was George?

> . . . When the administration tried repeatedly to slash Social Security, . . . where was George?

This speech backfired and ended up, instead, giving the Republicans *their* T-shirt slogan: "DRY, SOBER AND HOME WITH HIS WIFE." You can—with a certain amount of post hoc reasoning and license taking with popularity poll data—trace George Bush's victory in the November elections to that moment in July when Ted Kennedy asked, "Where was George?"

Various corporations operated hospitality suites at the Democratic convention—hedging their free-market bets with some drinks on the house for corporate statism. Truly mossbacked Democrats and what few conservative political journalists there are gathered at the ARCO suite. It was here, brimming with ARCO hospitality, that I watched Kennedy's speech on closed-circuit TV:

. . . When the administration was planning to weaken voting rights
. . . and veto the Civil Rights Restoration Act of 1988, . . . where was
George?

The catcalls started immediately. "He wasn't out drowning campaign volunteers in a car." "He was in Kennebunkport with the woman he's married to." And suchlike. I can't claim I heard anything as neatly phrased as "DRY, SOBER AND HOME WITH HIS WIFE." But the people in the ARCO suite were getting close. Being present at the conception of a minor quip was the most interesting thing that happened to me at the Democratic convention.

Then there were the political videos the Democrats kept showing on the convention hall's giant screen. Try to imagine something fully as stupid as MTV but without the sex or the violence or the music.

Even the state delegation tank-ups and other booze soirees were a frost. Delegates everywhere. Appointment as a convention delegate is a puppy treat thrown to the kind of people who hang around Wal-Mart parking lots with campaign literature, tape Dukakis posters to their lawn ornaments and come to your door with questionnaires right in the middle of dinner. Put a bunch of these around a cash bar, and it's like partying with Hare Krishnas who drink.

By Wednesday of convention week I was pretty much confined to my hotel room with a case of the six-pack flu. I wasn't even watching the convention on television. And neither were you. Sixty-eight percent of prime-time viewers were tuned to something—anything—else. In the Los Angeles area "Three's Company," "Family Ties" and "M*A*S*H" reruns topped the ratings. And in Chicago as many people watched "Wheel of Fortune" as watched all three network convention shows combined.

I did, however, want to hear Jesse Jackson speak. He is the only living American politician with a mastery of classical rhetoric. Assonance, alliteration, litotes, pleonasm, parallelism, exclamation, climax and epigram—to listen to Jesse Jackson is to hear everything mankind has learned about public speaking since Demosthenes. Thus Jackson, the advocate for people who believe themselves to be excluded from Western culture, was the only 1988 presidential candidate to exhibit any of it.

I watched Jackson's speech, "A Call to Common Ground" on CNN in my hotel. It was a fair example of his oratory:

> . . . So many guided missiles and so much misguided leadership, the stakes are very high. Our choice? Full participation in a democratic government or more abandonment and neglect. So this night, we choose not a false sense of independence. . . . Tonight we choose interdependency. . . .

And I was touched by it. Not just because I was drunk. And not by Jackson's political ideas, which serve to do nothing but work 10 or 15 percent of the nation into useless enthusiasms. But here was this firebrand, this radical, this leader of an alienated and angry minority. And was he in jail? Was he in exile? Was he dead? He certainly would have been one of the three in any other nation-state in history. But, no. He was being absorbed whole—daft notions, vexed supporters and all—by the largest political organization in the United States. He was turning into a pol, another spoils-mongering highbinder and wire-puller, one more bum on the plush. And this was heartwarming.

The American fanaticism for turning everything harmless and bland, our orthodoxy of co-option, lets nothing stand in its way—not race, not ideology, not even being bigger and better looking than your own party's presidential nominee.

One more beer and I was reconciled to the Democratic National Convention. Our democracy, our culture, our whole way of life is a spectacular triumph of the blah. Why *not* have a political convention without politics to nominate a leader who's out in front of nobody? Maybe the American political system isn't like a Mexican Christmas fiesta. Maybe it's like fast food—mushy, insipid, made out of disgusting parts of things and everybody wants some. Maybe our national mindlessness is the very thing that keeps us from turning into one of those smelly European countries full of pseudo-reds and crypto-fascists and greens who dress like forest elves. So what if

P. J. O'Rourke

I don't agree with the Democrats? What's to disagree with? They believe everything. And what they don't believe, the Republicans do. Neither of them stands for anything they believe in, anyway.

And from this, we've built a great nation.

ATTACK OF THE MIDGET
VOTE-SUCKERS

The Presidential Election

The inevitable result of choosing candidates is an election, in this case the 1988 presidential one. To drag ourselves back through the events of that drab contest is as bad as going to our high-school reunion and standing around for hours in the kind of motel "banquet facility" where both high-school reunions and campaign events are held while we're bored silly by that—Is it Rick? Is it Nick? Is it Billy?—Gephardt fellow we could never stand in the first place. Once upon a time the people described below had some relevance to our lives, and even then they weren't very interesting. Now, remembering what they did and said is like trying to read yearbook inscriptions. We don't recall the person. The message is saccharine and hackneyed. And whoever wrote it is over the hill.

Still, for reportorial purposes, there's no choice. As of this writing another presidential election has not been held. Unless George Bush gets caught in bed with a naked American business depression, there probably won't be a presidential election of significance until 1996. And there are important lessons to be learned from the 1988 election. Lessons such as "Those who fail to learn history are fated to repeat it." Which is ridiculous. Of course we're fated to repeat it. We're supposed to repeat elections. That's what they're there for. Or lessons such as "Those who fail to learn history usually aren't doing so well in English or practical math either." Or some kind of lesson, anyway.

So there we were in the fall of 1988 with the field of presidential contenders winnowed to two, one of whom you can probably recall—he's in the White House now—and the other was the husband of the best-selling author of an unauthorized biography of herself, Kitty Dukakis.

Michael Dukakis's pitch to the voters was that Massachusetts (a state where he was governor when he had a moment) possessed a swell economy. Never mind that the Massachusetts high-tech boom was about to collapse like a Red Sox pennant race. And never mind that the boom, when it did exist, was the result of hog-wild defense spending and hard work, two things Democrats are not known for promoting. Furthermore, never mind that the small, homely state of Massachusetts had an awful deficit, nasty drug and race problems, no housing at any price and the filthiest harbor and worst traffic jams this side of Lagos, Nigeria. If elected, Pinchgut Micky promised to stand around and take credit for anything good that happened. He also promised to look under the couch cushions for new sources of revenue.

Dukakis was considering Danny Ortega as a running mate, but Ortega's Central American peace plan proved too similar to Ronald Reagan's. So Mike went with the high-concept ticket-balancing choice of Lloyd Bentsen, who was two hundred fifty years old and a little to the right of Albert Speer. Actually, Dukakis wanted a Texan who was slightly more liberal, but George Bush was busy.

There you had them, the Odd Couple—two funny guys who were divorced (from reality) would be sharing an administration in Washington. Mike's a fussbudget neatness fanatic, always cleaning and tidying the political machine, and Lloyd (that slob!) keeps leaving huge piles of corporate campaign contributions lying around the White House. It's a riot.

Then, over there on the other ballot, wearing the colorful rich-guy pants, we had George Bush and Bob Duck or Ned Bird Dog or whatever his name is. To the public George Bush was known only as a wealthy playboy. Little did the world suspect that when night cast its inky cloak across the sky, he donned the fearsome costume of Republicanman and ventured forth to do battle with . . . with labor unions or something, accompanied by his ward, Dan, better known as Chicken, the Goy Wonder.

George ran one of the great room-temperature political campaigns of all time, saying, basically, "America's had a great eight years. Maybe a vague president and an incompetent and somewhat corrupt administration is what the nation *needs.*"

Bush also claimed to be the only person in the Western Hemisphere who didn't know there was an Iran-contra scandal. Not that the public gave a hoot. The Iranians didn't fire those missiles at anything but other hankie-heads, and *contra* graft was used to kill Communists or people who would have become Communists if they'd lived to adulthood. This did not spill much beer down at the VFW hall, no matter how much it worried the *Boston Globe.*

And George was closely identified with Reagan's heartless social programs. This gave him a boost with eighties-style social activists who wanted to do something about drug-addled welfare mothers—starve them to death, for instance. What's more, Bush used to be head of the CIA, so he could have us all killed if we didn't vote for him.

As you can see, George was so far ahead of the game that we didn't even need to have an election. But then he went and pulled some wild pledge stunt with a C-average frat boy from DePauw University. "Gosh, I'll get the GOP loyalists together, Dan, and you go pick up some girls." George must have been missing a few strings on his squash racket. Was everybody with a bong in the attic supposed to vote the Bush ticket because Danny was forty-one years old? But baby boomers weren't going to vote for baby boomers. We *know* us. We're nuts. We don't want anyone in our generation anywhere near the ICBM launch codes, he might start channeling Idi Amin. Plus Quayle was a twink. He got all the way through the sixties without dying from an overdose, being institutionalized by his parents or getting arrested for nude violation of the Mann Act on a motorcycle. At least he was a draft dodger—although Dan timidly joined the National Guard instead of bravely going to his physical in panty hose.

Then, along about late September, the Moody-Loners-with-Handguns National Support Group announced they'd be sitting this one out. According to a spokesperson for the organization, "Anyone enthusiastic enough about the 1988 presidential election to kill either of the candidates should seek professional help."

Enough about personalities. Let's talk about issues. What did these men believe in? Where was their vision of America's future? And why didn't somebody stuff leg warmers in their mouths when they started blithering about "family values"? (Whoever started this family-values stuff sure never met my family, with values like secret daytime drinking, beating the stepkids and wrecking the car and saying my sister did it.)

Anyway, the Republicans were running on the Dumb-Old-Dad platform: "You kids today, you don't know how good you've got it. Why, back in 1979 inflation was so bad that nickels cost fifty cents, the Dow was minus a million, they were giving out food stamps as stock dividends and you couldn't walk to your garage without getting held hostage by Iranians." Meanwhile the Democratic platform was pure whining brat: "Like, full employment is *sooooo* boring and I *hate* having a big navy and you *promised* a drug-free America and I want my free drugs *now.*"

The Democrats were for a lot more of something to be named at a later date. The Republicans were for less of whatever it was except the death penalty. The Democrats said, "We don't know what's wrong with America, but we can fix it." The Republicans said, "There's nothing wrong with America, and we can fix *that.*"

We had a choice between Democrats who couldn't learn from the past and Republicans who couldn't stop living in it, between Democrats who wanted to tax us to death and Republicans who preferred to have us die in a foreign war. The Democrats planned to fiddle while Rome burned. The Republicans were going to burn Rome, then fiddle.

When you looked at the Republicans, you saw the scum off the top of business. When you looked at the Democrats, you saw the scum off the top of politics. Personally, I prefer business. A businessman will steal from you directly instead of getting the IRS to do it for him. And when Republicans ruin the environment, destroy the supply of affordable housing and wreck the industrial infrastructure, at least they make a buck off it. The Democrats just do these things for fun. Also, the Democrats wanted the federal government to solve every one of America's problems, from AIDS to making sure the kids wipe their feet before they come in the house. For chrissake, the federal government can't even deliver mail, and how hard is that? The stuff's got our address right on it and everything.

But it was all the same in the end. If you voted for Bush, you'd be robbed blind. If you voted for Dukakis, you'd be too poor to be worth robbing. Besides, there was no telling what either one of these ballot mice would actually do once in office. Bush and Dukakis told us exactly where they stood on only one issue—they were both in favor of getting elected.

Bush or Dukakis? Eeny or Meeny? Miney or Moe? Amazingly enough, after all the polls and primaries and guys in empty suits talking about themselves in the third person and conventions and commercials and other nonsense we'd been through, we still had to go down to a smelly high-school gym and stand in a corner and pull levers until somebody turned up in the Oval Office.

How, in God's name, did we wind up with these two quibbledicks vying for helicopter rides on the South Lawn? Why did this pair of jacklegs follow us home? America is the richest and most powerful nation on earth, with more than a quarter billion native citizens and any number of household pets from which to pick our head of state. And yet when chief-executive open season commenced in March 1988, we found ourselves forced to choose among (Be honest, how many of these names can you put a face to anymore? Paul Simon's ears don't count) Babbit, Biden, Bush, Dole, Dukakis, DuPont, Gephardt, Gore, Haig, Hart, Jackson, Kemp, Robertson, Simon and Lyndon LaRouche. We might as well have gone through the phone book and picked male names at random. Maybe we did—the fingers lingering a bit too long among the Bs and Ds.

To call our system of primaries and party caucuses a beauty contest is to slander the Miss America pageant. No Miss Texas ever had a voice as grating or diction as tangled as George Bush. No Miss Massachusetts ever plucked her eyebrows as incompetently as Michael Dukakis. And neither Mike nor George could twirl a baton. If you want to get really depressed about the quality of our presidential hopefuls, think of it this way: What if you were wrongly accused of murder and *any* of these men showed up as your court-appointed attorney? Hello, lethal injection.

P. J. O'Rourke

*   *   *

Who is to blame for this grim state of electoral affairs? How about the media? Most things seem to be the media's fault. And members of the press did manage—who knows how—to make the '88 election more trivial than it already was. That is, they were a lot better at finding out what Dan Quayle was doing on the golf course with Paula Parkinson than at finding out what Lloyd Bentsen was doing in bed with the entire petroleum industry.

But I don't know if it's fair to blame the media. Newspapers, magazines, television and radio gave exhaustive coverage to the scramble for the presidency. Reporters used everything but torture to get serious position statements out of the would-be denizens of *Air Force One.* In fact, if you watched any of the eleven thousand candidate debates, you'll note that the media *did* use torture. Unfortunately, they used it on us, the viewing audience, instead of on the candidates. The only question answered by the debates was "Which one of you guys is which, anyway?" And we've forgotten the answer to that.

Nor can we blame the candidates themselves. They were just looking for work, something we expect every able-bodied adult to do in this society, at least during Republican administrations. No, the guilty are to be found a bit closer to home, right in our own lap pools and open-plan gourmet kitchens.

We *wanted* a lo-cal, polyunsaturated, salt-free election slate. Otherwise we wouldn't have been out on the lawn rolling in every stinky detail of the candidates' lives. We didn't even try to get the presidential wannabes to tell us what they meant or what they'd do. Instead, we spent election year peeking down Donna Rice's bathing suit, poking Bob Dole's war wound, trying to get Jesse Jackson to say "hymie" again, trading locker-room stories about Jack Kemp and waiting for Kitty Dukakis to explode. Every person in America has done or said *something* that would keep him or her from being president. Maybe a nation that consumes as much booze and dope as we do and has our kind of divorce statistics should pipe down about "character issues." Either that or just go ahead and determine the presidency with three-legged races and pie-eating contests. It would make better TV.

Two of our candidates—Bruce Babbit and Pete DuPont—actually

tried to say something. You'll remember where it got them. Babbit said that if we wanted to get rid of the deficit, we were going to have to pay money to do it; the U.S. Treasury doesn't take Master Charge. DuPont said that farmers should go pound sand with the rest of us. When somebody's muffler shop goes bankrupt, the government doesn't pay him $100,000 to not install mufflers.

But we didn't want to hear any bad news. And Babbit and DuPont couldn't get votes for free drugs in a crack house. We weren't even willing to learn facts, let alone face them. The conservatives among us refused to believe that the homeless were homeless because they didn't have homes. And liberals refused to believe that rent control, bad mores and civil rights for nutties were what turned the homeless out-of-doors. Drugs can be controlled only by military intervention in Latin America, which liberals would never allow, or by legalization of narcotics, which conservatives will always forbid. (And drugs can really be controlled only by putting millions of people in jail, including me.) Federal expenditures will never be reduced until liberals and conservatives both quit shoveling huge middle-class subsidies such as Social Security, Medicare, Keogh plans and mortgage deductions into their own pockets. And so on and so forth. But we wanted a "weather and sports" candidate. We wanted a happy-talk president. We wanted someone familiar and reassuring in the White House, someone like us. In fact, I wouldn't be surprised if we secretly wanted to be president ourselves. What could be more familiar than that? And who's more like us than we are? It's almost what we got. And it's about what we deserve. "Hey, the place really *is* oval. Cool desk. Where do they keep 'the button'? Let's send the helicopter out for Chinese."

THE WINNERS GO TO
WASHINGTON, DC

I, embarking on my attempt to make government comprehensible, and the Bush administration, embarking on its attempt to make government, arrived in Washington at about the same time in early 1989.

Many reporters, when they go to work in the nation's capital, begin thinking of themselves as participants in the political process instead of as glorified stenographers. Washington journalists are seduced by their proximity to power, and that was me. Power had my lipstick smeared and was toying with my corset hooks before I even got off the Trump Shuttle.

Newsmen believe that news is a tacitly acknowledged fourth branch of the federal system. This is why most news about government sounds as if it were federally mandated—serious, bulky and blandly worthwhile, like a high-fiber diet set in type.

All of Washington conspires to make reporters feel important—a savvy thing to do to people who majored in journalism because the TV repair schools advertised on matchbook covers were too hard to get into. The U.S. government, more than any other organization on earth, takes pains to provide journalists with "access" to make the lap-top La Rochefoucaulds feel that they are "present at the making of history." Of course, the same high honor can be had by going around to the back of any animal and "being present at the making of earth."

If you can get accreditation to the Congressional Press Galleries—which, when you're employed by a "major news outlet," is about as difficult as falling asleep in a congressional hearing—you receive a photo ID tag to wear on a chain around your neck. Everybody who's anybody in Washington wears some kind of ID tag on a chain around his neck, so that the place looks like the City of Lost Dogs. I wore mine everywhere until one day in the shower, when I had shampoo in my eyes, the chain caught on the soap dish and I was nearly strangled by my own identity. This happens a lot to members of the Washington press corps.

Within days of getting to Washington I began to write pieces featuring all the access I had and frequently mentioning that real political figures, some of them so important you'd actually heard their names, spoke directly to me in person. Thus, readers were left with an indelible sense of "A politician talked to him? What the hell else does a politician ever do to you except take your money?" I even got a part-time slot on one of those public affairs TV shows that air at 6:00 A.M. on Sunday mornings. It was a sort of farm-team "McLaughlin Group," but it gave me a chance to say things like "Washington journalists are seduced by their proximity to power."

Washington is a fine place for journalists to live as well as to brown-nose. It has plenty of the only kind of people who can stand journalists—other journalists—and plenty of the only kind of people journalists get any real information from—other journalists. It is, like most journalists themselves, not very big (Washington is smaller than Memphis, Tennessee) and not as sophisticated as it thinks. And it's pretty. Washington has lots of those Greek- and Roman-style buildings that practically make you feel like a senator just walking up the steps of them. Senators, in particular, are fond of this feeling, and this is one reason official Washington escaped the worst effects of modern architecture. Also, steel and glass skyscrapers are relatively cheap to build, and cost effectiveness is not a concept here. As Article One, Section 9, paragraph 7 of the U.S. Constitution says, "No money shall be drawn from the Treasury, but in consequence of appropriations made by law. . . ." So it's obvious what the whole point of lawmaking is.

But Washington, though it costs taxpayers a fortune, is itself inexpensive—at least compared with New York or Los Angeles. In Washington journalists can afford to live almost as well as people who work for a living. Those stories about crack wars and the "murder capital of America" are nonsense, of course—as long as you stay in the part of Washington that concerns itself with real wars and being the regular capital. This is the part that extends northwest along Connecticut, Massachusetts and Wisconsin avenues from the tourist attractions on the Mall to the Maryland suburbs—the "white pipeline." People do occasionally venture outside this zone, people who come in to do your cleaning or mow the lawn.

Numerous demonstrations, marches, PR stunts and other staged events are held in Washington to give journalists an excuse for not covering real events, which are much harder to explain. Barely a weekend passes without some group of people parading in the capital to protest the piteous condition of those inevitable victims of injustice, themselves.

One Saturday it's opponents of abortion dragging little children along to show they hadn't been killed. The next Saturday it's advocates of abortion dragging little children along to show they'd been born on purpose. The homeless come and make themselves at home around the Washington Monument. The Vietnam veterans are veteran gatherers at the Vietnam Veterans Memorial. Earth Day organizers litter the streets with posters and pamphlets calling for trash to be recycled. The AIDS Memorial Quilt is unfolded, and the Cancer Sampler and Car-Wreck Duvet are probably coming soon.

For the people in government, rather than the people who pester it, Washington is an early-rising, hard-working city. It is a popular delusion that the government wastes vast amounts of money through inefficiency and sloth. Enormous effort and elaborate planning are required to waste this much money. At 10:30 on weekday nights Washington bars and restaurants are as empty as synagogues in Iraq. I have never gotten up so early in Washington—or stayed up so late, for that matter—that somebody wasn't already awake and jogging by beneath my apartment window. On my first full day in Washington I saw an astonishingly beautiful young woman, slim, doe-eyed and still dewy from a hinterland childhood, the kind of girl who would be streaking like a Tomahawk cruise missile through the New York fashion-model and dance-club world. She was reading "Defense News" on the Metro at 7:45 A.M.

People in government jobs, especially political appointees and high-level bureaucrats, are customarily at their desks by eight in the morning and still there at six at night. They return calls, are courteous over the phone, prompt in their appointments and helpful to the point of obsequiousness.

Government people work so hard for the curious reason that their output can't be measured. There are plenty of ways to determine bad government, but good government is hard to quantify. How can streets be too clean or crime rates too low? A poverty threshold is easy to establish, but nobody's ever too rich. The casualties of war are simpler to count than the augmentations of peace. And that's why government employees work so hard—since output can't be measured, input has to be.

People in government are also a cheerful and indefatigably optimistic bunch. At first I was mystified. Government work would seem to be a run in a hamster wheel. Government can do nothing, at least nothing right. For instance, the deficit is terrible, but lower spending will hurt the poor and higher taxes will lead to a recession causing more people to become poor and get hurt by the lower spending needed to bring taxes down to end the recession, and so on. But since government rarely succeeds, it hardly ever fails. And government programs aren't necessarily designed to go anywhere. Like the joggers beneath my window, who are the people who run those programs, they just go. The results—sweat, ruined knees, America as a second-rate world power—don't matter. It's the effort that makes the action worthy. Frank Lavin, who was the director of the Office of Political Affairs in the Reagan White House (notice my access), told me, "People who believe in government regulation and intervention in life—for them government is a church." And people who are truly committed to government exhibit the same dull self-satisfaction and slightly vapid peace of mind as do devout churchgoers. They also know their business is never going to be bought by Sony.

Washington's optimistic enthusiasm, dreadfully wholesome energy and overabundance of media types is never more evident than when a fresh batch of optimistic enthusiasts and wholesomely energetic dreadfuls is sucked into town by a new presidential administration and all the media types rush there to meet them.

This was particularly true in the case of George Bush. Usually journalists suffer a brief, syrupy infatuation with an incoming chief executive. But everybody had such a crush on George that you began to wonder if the *New York Times* editorial board wasn't maybe driving by George's house in the middle of the night and pining out the car window or sneaking into the Kennebunkport Yacht Club to leave anonymous poems in his locker.

First the jerk disappeared—the tall schmo with the voice up his nose, the one who was running for president but nobody could figure out why because he kept getting his tongue in a clove hitch and calling every whatchamajigger a "thing." He vanished without a trace. You'll remember that until the beginning of January 1989 George Bush was a skinny, inconsequential doofus, an intellectual smurf and moral no-show who'd wound up in the White House by default. Then one day I saw in the newspapers that the president-elect was a seasoned Washington professional, a man who knew where all the levers and pedals and remote-control channel changers of government were located, plus he was a symbol of unity and strength reaching out to Americans of every hue, stripe and polka-dot pattern and gathering us together in an immense bipartisan hug, cuddle and smooch.

Next George was applauded like an Academy Award–winning actor with cancer for his proposed cabinet appointments. (This being before the U.S. Senate decided that former senator John Tower was too drunk and silly to be secretary of defense but not quite drunk and silly enough to be a senator again.) In fact, only two of Bush's nominees were other than mundane. There was William Bennett, who had been so much fun as Reagan's secretary of education. You had to love a man who'd made that many schoolteachers mad. Bennett always seemed about to say, "Anybody who doesn't know what's wrong with America's schools never screwed an el-ed major." However, now Bennett was to be "drug czar." Would his scholastic background help? Would he make dead crack addicts stay after life and write, "I will not be killed by rival gangs of drug dealers" one hundred times on the blackboard? Then there was Jack Kemp, the proposed secretary of Housing and Urban Development. But was it a bold stroke or a mean prank to make the only real conservative in the crowd go down to the ghetto and explain the Laffer curve?

Anyway, for the moment, the media was treating Bush's cabinet picks as if they were the nine worthies, the three wise men and two surefire ways to lose weight without dieting. And this was nothing compared with what had happened to Barbara Bush: apotheosis. Now, Barbara Bush was reputed, on good authority, to be a nice woman, warmhearted, funny, sensible and all the things we usually say about our mothers when they're listening. But it wasn't as though she'd actually done anything or even said much. Barbara Bush, it seemed, was elevated to secular sainthood strictly on the basis of gray hair and a plump figure. And such is the remarkable speed of fashion in Washington that, within hours of the swearing in, snowy bouffants and comfortable tummies appeared everywhere among the politically chic. A few extra pounds were spilling over the waistband of my own boxer shorts, in fact.

Even the Dan Quayle market was—very temporarily—up. This is the fellow who was supposed to answer the question once and for all "Can a person be too dumb for government?" But in February 1989 columnists and commentators were mumbling about what a hard-working senator Dan had always been. The *Wall Street Journal* went so far as to call him "an avid reader . . . not just of newspaper clips or an occasional magazine piece, but of real live books." Quick to note a vogue in toadying, the *New Republic* offered a Quayle Revisionism Award, only to have readers write in suggesting the prize be given to the *New Republic*'s own senior editor, Morton Kondracke, for saying Dan Quayle was "well informed, intelligent, candid and engaging."

There was a giddiness in the District of Columbia during inauguration week, and not just among Republicans dizzy from victory and cheap, warm domestic Inaugural Ball champagne. Liberals were sidling up to each other and confessing profound relief that Puckermug Micky was back in Boston with a huge, poorly balanced Massachusetts state budget about to fall on his head. Garry Trudeau had run out of punchlines for his "Doonesbury" comic strip and was stuck with an "invisible George" joke about a president so hopelessly visible that he seemed to show up everyplace except "The

39

Oprah Winfrey Show." Jesse Jackson and George Bush looked to be on the verge of starting their own two-man Operation PUSH chapter. Jackson said Bush's inaugural speech "set exactly the right tone." And the *Tehran Times*—this is true—welcomed George Bush to the White House and opined that he'd "acted wisely" at the onset of his administration.

On inauguration day anti-Bush demonstrators were thin on the ground. A smattering of ERA signs were held aloft along the parade route. A few devoted peace buffs were camped across from the White House in an antinuke vigil that they'd vowed to continue until the world didn't blow up. The homeless were nowhere to be seen. I suppose the police had told them to go home. The *Washington Post* devoted only fifteen column inches to "alternative" celebrations in its special Saturday inauguration section. And I saw just one protester outside an Inaugural Ball, a lonely flake in pigtail and knapsack with a message about the Super Bowl hand-lettered on notebook paper: "If Joe Montana Passes Like Dan Quayle Speaks, the Bengals Will Win." (They didn't.) The *liberal* liberals, the serious hemorrhaging valentines, the real giveaway-and-guilt bunch, had disappeared into the same black hole as the jokes about Barbara looking like George's mother. Alas, the pinkos—they'd lost to the guy who lost to George. They weren't even ranked anymore.

Of course, in those bastions of GOPery, where you'd expect the welkin to ring, there were rung welkins all over the place. At a Republican National Committee staff party at the Grand Hyatt, the crowd was young, integrated, drunk, loud and seemed to have lost its copy of the "How to Act Like a Republican" manual. A large can of men's hair-styling gel had been discovered in the hotel suite's bathroom, and people were being tackled at random. "Mousse him! Mousse him!" went the cry. Someone would go down in a pile-on and emerge with improbable hair spikes projecting above pin-striped suit jacket.

A clean-cut person in his middle fifties with very good posture walked in. "It's the general!" yelled the RNC staff. "Hey, General! Hi ya doin', General?! MOUSSE HIM!!!" He came out looking pretty good, too. Later I remember somebody, possibly me, weaving down the hotel hall with a large cigar in one hand and a larger drink in the other, shouting, "We had all the money! Then we won all the votes! Now we've got all the fun!" while his wife kicked him and threatened to call security.

* * *

It had been a long while since there was this much good cheer and auld lang syne at a presidential inauguration. You'd have to go back to 1961, when Jackie was a tomato and Jack was giving the world a nudge and a wink, and the New Frontier stretched before us full of challenge, potential and shoving people into swimming pools. (Although it's instructive to remember what happened in the late sixties and early seventies when we reached the unexplored regions of that New Frontier—war, drugs, STDs, disco music and about a billion ruined marriages.)

George Bush looked like he'd be a cozy president, old shoe, *gemutlichkeit*. This wasn't the same as having a smug little wiseacre or a big Hollywood movie star in the White House. The first word of George Bush's inaugural address was *hey*. (That is, of course, after he'd said "Thank you, ladies and gentlemen," because this is a president who minds his manners.) "Hey, Jack, Danny," said George, looking around at Congressmen Jack Brooks and Dan Rostenkowski as though he'd just stepped up to the podium at a Monday Rotary lunch. "Mr. Chief Justice, Mr. President, Vice President Quayle, Senator Mitchell," George continued, "Speaker Wright, Senator Dole, Congressman Michel, fellow citizens, neighbors, friends . . ." For a moment it seemed as though the president might just keep on greeting people for hours, like a little kid trying to include everybody in the God-bless section of his bedtime prayers: ". . . colleagues, compatriots, associates, acquaintances, distant cousins, people who graduated from high school about the same time I did . . ." But he stopped himself, gave the world a goofy smile and delivered a speech we'd all heard a hundred times before but never from a president of the United States. It was a speech we'd all heard a hundred times from our dads:

. . . This country has a meaning beyond what we can see . . . our strength is a force for good. . . .

We are not the sum of our possessions. They are not the measure of our lives. . . .

We have more will than wallet; but will is what we need. . . .

The final lesson of Vietnam is that no great nation can long afford to be sundered by a memory. . . .

41

> A president is neither prince nor pope, and I do not seek "a window on men's souls." In fact I yearn for a greater tolerence, an easy-goingness about each other's attitudes and way of life. . . .

Most dads don't have Peggy Noonan speech writing for them, so their phrases aren't so orotund and rhetorically balanced, but it's the same lecture in the den:

> You should thank your lucky stars you were born in the United States of America.
>
> Money isn't everything.
>
> Hard work never killed anybody.
>
> Family is family so quit picking on your little brother.

and

> I can't follow you around for the rest of your life keeping you out of trouble, so use your common sense and don't do anything stupid; it would break your mother's heart.

Then the Reagans blew out of town. The herds of anchorfolk covering this on TV did their best to make the departure damp-eyed, but you could practically hear the nationwide sigh of relief. They are really lovely, lovely people, the Reagans, and we enjoyed their stay, we really did, but, well, you know . . . They *have* been here quite a while, and they're frankly not getting any younger. And they're a bit—let's be truthful—la-di-da, especially her. When you come right down to it, it's great to have them out of the way so we can spend Sundays padding around in our bathrobes with the funny papers all over the place and can leave the TV on during dinner if we want.

Which is apparently what the Bushes were doing. Twenty-eight members of the Bush family spent the first night of the Bush presidency at the White House. "You kids cut that out! Go to sleep this minute! No pillow fighting in the Green Room, you'll break the gosh-darned antiques!"

During the inaugural parade Bush kept darting in and out of his limousine, and the crowd reacted as if he were the early Beatles. These pop-outs were much better received than the Jimmy Carter business of walking the whole parade route. We Americans like our populism in small doses and preferably from an elitist. A Democrat populist might mean what he says and take our new Toro away because a family down the street can't afford the self-starting kind with the de-thatching attachment. A Republican populist is only going to indulge in the popular types of populism and will then get back in his Cadillac and behave.

Dan Quayle stayed in his Cadillac entirely and broadcast cheery greetings to the parade viewers over the car's built-in PA system: "Section A . . . stand 21, how are you? Hello, Section B." (These are actual quotes.)

It was worth going to the Inaugural Balls on Friday night just to see hundreds of newspaper reporters in bad tuxedos and mortal pain from rented dress shoes. I went to two of the things, which is about all a nonelected human being can bear. Ball procedure consists of standing around chatting amicably in itchy clothes if you're a man, or, if you're a woman, standing around chatting amicably in clothes that parts of you are about to squeeze out of. You can't drink because the bar is two hundred fifty thousand Republicans away from where you are. And you can't dance because the music is being played by marines on sousaphones. This must be what entertainment was like in the nineteenth century, before fun was invented.

The Young Americans Ball at the J. W. Marriott Hotel was particularly crowded, and the Young Americans were horribly well behaved. I'd bet most of them weren't even on drugs. This may be just as well. What kind of hallucinations would these clean-cut juveniles have? "Oh, man, I was staring at these clouds, and they looked just like falling bond yields." Though I'm a conservative myself, I worry about the larval Republicans. They should act up now and get it over with, otherwise misbehavior may come upon them suddenly in middle age, the way it came upon the protagonist of Thomas Mann's *Death in Venice* and, also, Gary Hart.

The Maine and Indiana Ball at Union Station was better, full of the most reassuring kind of grown-ups, who looked like grown-ups used to look thirty years ago—happy, prosperous, solid, sensible, a little boring and not about to turn up in a Bret Easton Ellis novel. It was worth hundreds of hours of transactional analysis and a prescription for Valium just to walk around among their merry, placid faces and ample cummerbunds.

Dan Quayle arrived at Union Station about 10:30 wearing a smile that said—as only an open, honest, corn-fed midwestern smile can say—"Fuck you." Who can blame him? There was terrific press bias against Quayle during the election because most journalists worked harder at college than Dan did and all it got them was jobs as journalists. Marilyn Quayle was there, too, looking—it was indeed a strange week in Washington—great. She had her hair done up in something my wife said was a chignon, and whatever it was, it made Marilyn look considerably less like a Cape buffalo than usual. Though actually I admired the Cape buffalo look. I have an idea that—like the Cape buffalo—if Marilyn Quayle gets furious and charges, you've got only one shot at the skull. You wouldn't want to just wound her.

The next night the president's campaign manager, the supposedly cold-blooded Lee Atwater, staged an immense rhythm-and-blues concert at the Washington Convention Center auditorium. This was more or less Atwater's first official act as the new Republican National Committee chairman—inviting Sam Moore, Percy Sledge, Bo Diddley, Albert Collins, Joe Cocker, Ron Wood, Willie Dixon, Etta James, Dr. John, Stevie Ray Vaughan, Delbert McClinton, Billy Preston and about a dozen other blues musicians to entertain, of all things, the GOP faithful.

I'd like to travel back in time to January 1969, when Richard Nixon was being inaugurated, and Pigasus, the four-footed Yippie candidate, was being inaugurated, too, and the country was a mess, and so was my off-campus apartment. And I'd like to tell the self that I was then: "Twenty years from today you will watch the chairman of the Republican National Committee boogie down on electric guitar. And he's going to duck walk and do the splits and flip over backward and sing "High Heel Sneakers" at the top of his lungs. And when he gets finished, the president of the United States—a Republican president—is going to be pulled up on stage by Sam Moore of Sam and Dave and presented with another electric guitar with THE PREZ painted on the front. And the president of the United States and the chairman of the RNC are going to trade blues licks in front of a crowd of eighty-five hundred Americans very similar to yourself, who are going to go wild with politically motivated glee."

I'd like to know what I would have thought, that is, after I got over the shock of seeing myself come back in time so jowly and with an ROTC haircut.

Anyway, the concert sounded like Jesse Jackson had been elected, except the music was better. Jackson would have felt compelled to have boring Sting there and some Suzanne Vega and Tracy Chapman depressive types and dreary Rainbow Coalition stuff, too, probably featuring "Hava Negilah" played by a marimba band. The Republicans were under no such constraints.

When President Bush entered the auditorium, no one played "Hail to the Chief." Instead, the 1967 Bar-Keys instrumental "Soul Finger" had been chosen as the presidential theme. Bush walked, as he'd have to for at least the next four years, inside a hollow square of stiff-necked fellows with long-distance looks and pistols in their armpits. But within the Secret Service phalanx you could see one bright, white head swaying and nodding to the beat. Barbara Bush didn't sit down all night.

Atwater, whose health problems were still a year away, proved to be an excellent guitar player and a, well, very enthusiastic vocalist. The evening's master of ceremonies, the president's son Marvin, bellowed into a microphone: "They call Frank Sinatra the chairman of the board, but they call Lee Atwater THE CHAIRMAN OF THE REPUBLICAN NATIONAL COMMITTEE!!!" The audience went crazy. Sam Moore tugged on the president, got him up on the stage. "I taught Lee everything he knows about that kind of dancing," said George Bush. The crowd went crazier. "I know when to shut up and when to say something," continued Bush, "and this is a time to shut up." Though he didn't quite. He wanted to talk about how he'd thrown the White House—the "People's House" he insisted on calling it—open to the public that morning and how, even after these people had been waiting outside in the cold for what must have seemed like forever, they didn't complain. They looked around in awe "just like me and Barbara."

"We've got a little present for you," said Sam Moore.

"Dancing lessons, I hope," said the president half under his breath. And there was a smile of real pleasure when he saw the guitar. It almost looked as though "the prez" knew how to play it.

And when the music began again, something was shaking in the GOP. All across the auditorium thousands of honkies were coming out of their tuxedo jackets. The convention center was wall-to-wall in a pattern of jiggling suspenders over soaking-wet dress shirts, like a huge attack of extra Y chromosomes. Did they have rhythm? No. But this is America. You can achieve anything in America. Republicans might even achieve sympathy and a little soul.

We'd had eight years of talk about patriotism and family values from a man who saw less combat in the service than I saw as a hippie and whose children spent his whole administration exiled to the "Good Morning, America" gulag. Now there was an actual household in the White House, one where Dad really was a war hero (if not exactly an ace pilot).

Our country was all smiles and handshakes with the USSR. The first faint blush of political freedom was visible in Eastern Europe. Wars were petering out in Afghanistan and Angola. Central America was idling in neutral. The economy was OK. It seemed to be a genuinely promising moment in the history of the nation, a moment for—as Dr. Johnson said about second marriages—"the triumph of hope over experience."

THE THREE BRANCHES
OF GOVERNMENT:
MONEY, TELEVISION
AND BULLSHIT

Now and then an innocent man is sent to the legislature.
—Kin Hubbard

NATIONAL BUSYBODIES

Congress

Feeling good about government is like looking on the bright side of any catastrophe. When you quit looking on the bright side, the catastrophe is still there. The euphoria of the Bush inauguration wore off, and the government remained in its usual form—whatever that is—and persisted in its usual actions—whatever they may be.

The three branches of government number considerably more than three and are not, in any sense, "branches" since that would imply that there is something they are all attached to besides self-aggrandizement and our pocketbooks. I never determined how many sections there really are to the federal system. It probably can't be done. Government is not a machine with parts; it's an organism. When does an intestine quit being an intestine and start becoming an asshole? Nor did I ever determine any valuable rule for examining the branches of government, except one: If you want to know what an institution does, watch it when it's doing nothing.

On one of those warm and luminous spring days when the soul would fain soar free and the conscious mind wanders in reveries of—at my age—reseeding the lawn, I went to Capitol Hill and spent the day indoors watching the House of Representatives.

The House chamber—which, according to the Capitol building's tourist brochure, is "the largest national parliamentary room in the world"—isn't as big as an old-fashioned downtown movie theater nor as elaborately decorated, though the carpet is just as loud. The walls are covered in fussy Victorian paper on a background the color of fake Wedgwood china. There are lots of brass whim-whams and a remarkable number of doors (which do not, however, result in many quick exits from political life). Above the doors are medallions bearing bas-relief profiles of mankind's great and reasonably great lawgivers: Moses, Solomon, Alfonso X, Solon, Hammurabi, Pope Innocent III. No U.S. congressmen are included.

The only impressive part of the room is the three-tiered dais where the speaker of the House sits with his minders and butt boys. And this is only slightly more impressive than the set for the "Here Comes the Judge" skit on the old "Laugh-In" show. The speaker occupies a large chair in front of a large flag, and bracketing the flag are two huge gilded fasces. These pre-date Mussolini—at least I hope they do.

A visitor's gallery runs around three sides of the place, to let the public come hear the commonweal talked away. On the fourth side, above the speaker's dais, is a steep and narrow balcony, a pigeon's paradise for journalists. Electric tote boards hang below the gallery rails showing what is being voted on and giving a running tabulation of the yeas and nays so congressmen can tell which way their own wind is blowing. The ceiling is bordered with the seals of all the states—a plethora of sunrises, wheat sheaves, spear-carrying ladies in Liberty caps and tamed Indians.

The House convened at the gentlemanly hour of 11:00 A.M., and the session began, as sessions customarily do (unless something big like a war or a farm-price-support bill is afoot), with "One Minutes." These are speeches of said duration that any member may make on any subject. As a tool of political debate the One Minute cannot be very effective, at least not on the day I was there—only eighteen congressmen were in the place, and they were waiting to make One Minutes of their own.

The Democratic One Minute speechmakers had gotten together to exploit the approach of Earth Day. Each Democrat brought a poster to the microphone; each poster bore a quotation from George Bush on subjects ecological; and across each quotation was printed, in red stencilled lettering, "PROMISE BROKEN." The point was, I think, that President Bush had promised to clean up the environment, and now, a year and a half after his election, the environment was still not clean. The Democrats, with their posters propped on easels, looked like Amway salesmen touting pyramid franchising schemes. Although, in fact, more than half the members of Congress are lawyers, so that comparison is very unfair to Amway.

For the sake of political balance Republicans interpolated themselves among the Democrats. But the Republicans lacked an issue *du jour*. Thus ten Democrats fumbling with posters alternated with ten Republicans simply fumbling. Of the Republicans:

No. 1 was inaudible.
No. 2 wanted the Florida barge canal returned to Florida.
No. 3 was against international terrorism.
No. 4 was in favor of tiny, beleaguered Lithuania.
No. 5 had a new plan to end the budget deficit.
No. 6 was very much in favor of tiny, beleaguered Lithuania.
No. 7 was irked by tort law.
No. 8 eulogized a dead city councilman from Syracuse, New York.
No. 9 (I missed this one. I had to go to the bathroom.)
No. 10 was in favor of the census.

The members of the House are, to a man (and twenty-nine women), ridiculously bad at public speaking. Indeed, they don't speak at all; they read from prepared texts and are ridiculously bad at reading. Every clause is an exclamatory declaration. Every verb is in the present tense. Every subject is second person plural. You can tell, without watching, when a congressman has reached the bottom of a page—there will come a dramatic caesura, a full stop that lasts, no matter its violence to sense, until that page has been turned and the words at the top of the next page kenned.

> We are in a position! To mandate the expenditure! Of great amounts of money! By state and local governments! But we are not! [rustle of paper] Giving them financial aid!

said a Democrat from Massachusetts.

In every speech there is, however, one little section the congressman has managed to memorize. His head will come up from his typescript. He will boldly gaze at his (in this case nonexistent) audience. And, with only one or two deep breaths to buoy his confidence, he will recite his piece.

Our polluting ways! Are destroying our waterways!

said a Democrat from Mississippi.

The Democrats ended their "promise broken" presentation, but the One Minutes continued. Money laundering, Frank Lorenzo, U.S. trade policy, radioactivity, Stalin, Hitler and discrimination against people who have Hispanic surnames were denounced. Earth Day was praised. The navy was scolded for blaming a battleship gun-turret explosion on a person who lived in a member's district. Blue Cross was taken to task for something about bone marrow. It was questioned whether banning China from a conference on global warming was a fit punishment for the events of Tiananmen Square. It was noted that President Reagan had been a very popular president. A member stated that the number of homeless in America exceeds the population of Atlanta. (It doesn't.) A member from Kentucky announced the presentation of a Kentucky Earth Day Award, the recipient being himself. A dead senator was praised. So was an animated cartoon meant to combat drug abuse. An ecology-conscious Republican—in a very Republican piece of ecology consciousness—said he'd just come back from the Bahamas, and, boy, were the beaches littered. He proposed a tax on non-biodegradable items that litter beaches. Lax enforcement of the ivory trade ban was rebuked. And a parliamentary inquiry was made under the One Minute Rule about why there were so many One Minutes today.

A few more members of Congress had strolled in by now, for a total of twenty-five or thirty on the House floor. Two hundred regular citizens were in the visitors' galleries. And one member of the press—me—was in the press section. The congressmen stood in the aisles chatting. The public perched on their seats staring. And I just sat doing nothing. I was not even, to judge from my notes, taking notes.

Finally the One Minutes ended, and somebody moved that this be

National Crime Something-or-Other Week, which motion carried. After that a clerk read a bill called H.R. 644 to amend the Wild and Scenic Rivers Act by designating the east fork of the Jemez and Pecos rivers in New Mexico, read it so quickly that I could understand nothing about the bill except what its name stated. Then the speaker of the House recognized someone. (A telling concept, "recognized." The average representative has been in office for over nine years, so there aren't many strangers here.) This wasn't the real speaker speaking, however; this was the speaker pro tem, who is anybody the speaker wants it to be—usually someone who needs to have his picture taken in a large chair for campaign purposes. Another reporter came into the press section, peered down at the speaker pro tem, said, "Who the fuck is that?" and left.

The person whom the speaker pro tem recognized, a Democrat, extolled the Wild and Scenic Rivers Act, saying it was clearly an act that designated—as wild and scenic—rivers.

A Republican got up and said the Wild and Scenic Rivers Act was a swell bill and H.R. 644 was a heck of a fine amendment to it, or words to that effect, except many more of them. He finally sat down.

A Democrat who was actually from New Mexico said the same thing again and, in a fit of bipartisanism, thanked everybody there (although, as I pointed out, hardly anybody was) for supporting H.R. 644. "The Pecos River originates in the geologically significant Sangre de Cristo Mountains," said the Democrat, not wanting us to confuse these with any geologically insignificant mountains, which may be found elsewhere. "There was threat of development," he said. (That is, people making livings, building homes, staking out a future for themselves and their children—as a good environmentalist one shudders at the thought). And, said the Democrat, an amendment to the amendment was needed to ban the strip-mining of pumice stone within a quarter mile of these rivers. You would think that if a river was designated as wild and scenic, a ban on strip-mining within a quarter mile of it would go without saying, but apparently not.

A lone Republican objected to the amendment to the amendment, and someone objected to the objection. A dozen congressmen wandered away, and a desultory debate ensued among the remaining members. From this debate I learned that the mining of pumice stone along the Jemez and Pecos rivers always was and wasn't ever highly destructive to plant and animal life, that mine operators invariably did and obviously didn't restore the mined areas to their original condition and that mining claims in the area are adequately regulated and completely unsupervised by existing laws. The strip-mining ban passed by a voice vote of about fifteen yeas and one nay, after which one of the congressmen noted in passing that the House of Representatives had just legislated the stone-washed denim industry out of existence.

Meanwhile a number of children on a school tour or something had been led onto the floor and allowed to sit in some of the many empty congressmen seats. They fidgeted briefly and were led out. A vote on H.R. 644 itself was called. Voting in the House of Representatives is done by means of a little plastic card with a magnetic strip on the back—like a VISA card but with no, that is, absolutely *no*, spending limit. These cards are inserted into slots in boxes mounted on the back of the aisle seats—one box for yes, one box for no and one box (the one very few congressmen had any excuse for using) for present. The congressmen had fifteen minutes to vote. Pretty soon there were congressmen coming in through the doors in strings of ten or a dozen, like picnic ants, until 90 percent of the representatives we have had appeared on the floor. No opposition candidate back home was going to accuse them of letting rivers be nonwild or unscenic. H.R. 644 passed 391 to 1.

The clutter of members milled around clasping hands, gripping shoulders and patting arms as though there were campaigning for election by each other instead of by the somewhat mystified public in the balconies above. The leader of the Democrats in the House (and sometime presidential hopeful), Richard Gephardt, stepped to a microphone on the floor and announced that, it being almost three in the afternoon, legislative business was finished for the day—finished for the week, too, since this was a Thursday. Congressman Gephardt then listed some of the wonderful things Congress would do when it reconvened on Tuesday next. Newt Gingrich, the number-two man among Republicans in the House, went to another microphone on the floor and said to Congressman Gephardt (though they could easily have heard each other without amplification), "Since you did all those tough One Minutes, when will we see the clean-air bill out of committee?" This was apparently a very funny thing to say, because they both laughed for a long time. Then all the representatives who'd given those One Minutes pestered the speaker pro tem for permission to "revise and extend their remarks." That is, they wanted carefully typed versions of their speeches rather than verbatim transcripts to go on record so that they won't sound as stupid in history as I've made them sound in journalism.

The congressmen then drifted away, except for one or two who were going to speak to a completely empty chamber in what are called "Special Orders." These are speeches made only for the sake of the *Congressional Record* and the C-Span television coverage of Congress. As I left, a representative from Illinois was holding forth to the ether—with all the gestures, tropes and intonations appropriate to a demagogue swaying thousands—on the virtues of a high-school basketball team in his district, state champions with a record of 36 and 0.

Was this an average day in Congress? No. On an average day Congress isn't there at all. Congress only meets about 145 days a year.

This is not to say that congressmen are lazy. I followed one around for a day—a highly respected congressman from a fine political party representing an excellent district of a lovely state (and one who would just as soon not have his name in a book by me). The congressman had an 8:00 A.M. breakfast meeting in the Cannon Building (named, as all three House of Representatives office buildings are, after former speakers of no distinction) with an informal group of ideologically like-minded colleagues. They discussed ways to stifle that beggar's army of liberals that dominates the House, but I don't think they came up with anything surefire. At 8:30 there was a second breakfast meeting, in the Rayburn Building, this time for the executive committee of a private club on Capitol Hill where influence gets peddled, horses get traded, logs get rolled and metaphors get tired.

By 9:30 the congressman had to be down the hall at a Housing and Community Development Subcommittee hearing. Testimony was being given about the squalid living conditions in apartment complexes run by A. Bruce Rozet, one of the nation's largest developers of federally subsidized low-income housing. The Republicans on the subcommittee were furious at Rozet for renting apartments with "boarded windows . . . broken fire doors, crumbling walls and incredible filth." The Democrats on the subcommittee were furious at the Republicans for pointing out that Rozet was a major Democratic campaign contributor and served as a Jesse Jackson delegate at the 1988 Democratic convention. A former tenant of a Rozet development was just plain furious. And if the tenant's testimony about how the squalor in her apartment got so squalid is anything to go by, A. Bruce Rozet was probably furious at her:

> I am a recovering drug addict. I became addicted to crack-cocaine three years ago. I started using crack at Glenarden Apartments. . . . During the time using, I was going to school for data entry. I would come home and study but would become sleepy. So I thought that if I would smoke a little crack I could stay up and study longer. But there was not much success in that, then my addiction progressed more . . . and eventually I started running a crack house.
>
> I invited drug dealers in to sell drugs, store guns and money. In turn they would give me money and drugs. Then things became out of hand. . . . As a result of constant fighting and other distasteful conduct, my apartment became destroyed and unfit to live. (Examples of this would be: All of my doors were knocked off the hinges. My furniture became dirty and broken. . . . The commode was stopped up from human waste, which led them to use cups and other cooking utensils for the toilet. In general there was large holes knocked through the walls, light fixtures destroyed throughout. All of my clothing were scattered everywhere. I never used the closet.)

Amazing stuff. But the congressman didn't have time for amazement. He was due in the Longworth Building at 10:00 A.M. for a meeting of the Merchant Marine and Fisheries Committee. This committee intended to "mark up" (that is, fool around with) six different pieces of legislation that, if approved by a majority of the committee members, would be sent to the House of Representatives to be fooled around with some more.

One bill authorized spending half a billion dollars to keep America's practically nonexistent merchant fleet in tip-top shape. Another bill gave

$600 million to the National Oceanic and Atmospheric Administration for, I guess, Americans who find themselves up in the air or out to sea. A third bill "explicitly requires states to adopt or revise new coastal water quality standards based on EPA-promulgated water quality criteria." Which means, I think, that if you go to the beach this summer and the ocean is too cold for swimming, you can complain to the government. The fourth bill was a nonbinding resolution urging the president to work with Congress to "establish a comprehensive national oceans and Great Lakes policy." (Keep them filled with water would be my suggestion.) The fifth bill was exactly the same as the sixth bill except more carefully worded, to make sure that whatever the sixth bill did remained under the purview of the Merchant Marine and Fisheries Committee. And nobody knew what the sixth bill was supposed to do. It was called H.R. 4030, the reauthorization of the coastal-zone management act, and according to the summary handed out to committee members, its provisions all seemed to be obvious—"Defines 'coastal zone'"; weird—"recognizes sea level rise"; or weirdly obvious—"amends Coastal Zone Management Act findings and policies to indicate that development in the coastal zone must occur with environmental safeguards." The bill also "authorizes awards for excellence in coastal zone management" and, of especially vital importance to the nation, "changes the name of the National Estuarine Reserve Research System to National Estuarine Research Reserve System." Some nineteen amendments to this bill were also proposed, including one to name the award for excellence in coastal-zone management after the Merchant Marine and Fisheries Committee chairman.

This chairman was exceedingly old and supported on each side by members of the committee staff. These behaved toward the chairman like the "flappers" of Laputa in *Gulliver's Travels*, whom the abstracted Laputians employed to strike them now and then and remind them what they were doing.

A representative from Louisiana pointed out that under the terms of the technical language in H.R. 4030, 50 percent of his state was coastal wetland and thereby federally prohibited from any use by humans.

A representative from Alaska waved H.R. 4030 in the air and shouted, "Anybody who knows what's in this bill raise his hand."

Would half the population of Louisiana have to move to Arkansas? Would the committee ever figure out what it was voting on? Would the chairman stay awake? I'm sure the congressman would like to know, too. But we had to go. The House of Representatives was meeting at noon.

You already know what a meeting of the House of Representatives is like.

At 1:00 P.M. the Congressman went back to his office in the Longworth Building to meet volunteer firemen from his congressional district. They were shy and husky men in wool-blend sport coats that gaped at the back of the neck, and they gaped a bit themselves to be in the actual private office of a real congressman. (Members of the House have, on average, about six hundred thousand constituents and are thus governmentally no more important than a mayor of Indianapolis. But the Indianapolis Motor Speedway isn't on the back of a fifty-dollar bill.)

The congressman is genuinely likable—as most politicians are, whether they ought to be or not—and the firemen genuinely liked him. The congressman was interested in the volunteer firemen. Politicians *are* interested in people. Not that this is always a virtue. Fleas are interested in dogs. And—though the congressman had suffered a torch juggler's schedule all morning and was due across the street at the Rayburn Building in fifteen minutes—he treated the firemen to the same gracious and unhurried welcome that you or I would give to the Joint Chiefs of Staff if they happened to drop by our house.

The volunteer firemen were in Washington for a national convention. Besides sight-seeing and middle-aged, convention-style high jinks, they were pushing legislation in Congress. I believe they wanted everything in the country fireproofed. The congressman was frank with them. Politicians are not only likable and interested in people, they even tell the truth sometimes. (Though whether this says a lot for the politicians or very little for the truth depends.) The congressman told the firemen that he, too, thought everything should be fireproof. But before he decided how to vote, he would have to find out how much making America nonflammable would cost the public. The firemen gave him a fireman's hat.

At 1:15 the congressman went to be briefed on the European Bank for Reconstruction and Development. Why an American congressman needs a briefing on a bank for frog swallowers, bucket heads and various kinds of garlic nibblers who are already so reconstructed and developed that they're buying the United States in wholesale lots is a good question. If you find the answer, the congressman would like to hear it.

By 2:00 the congressman was back in his office, lunchless and working with his staff. When a congressman sits down with the people who work for him, the result is a sort of college-finals cram session. Congress meddles in every part of American life and then some. Congressional legislation reaches beyond the grave with estate taxes and back into those clouds of glory that Wordsworth says we trail when it touches upon abortion issues. A congressman needs to be informed about it all. During this particular week in the spring of 1990 the following bills, motions and resolutions were burrowing, meandering, sneaking, breezing, slipping or being pushed through the legislative process:

1. A five-year omnibus farm bill to pay the people who own the ground where we dig the hole that we pour our tax dollars down
2. A commodities futures trading commission reauthorization act to make sure the commodities market is as well regulated as, say, the savings and loan industry
3. A proposal to further complicate the above-mentioned commodities market complications
4. Consideration of who gets to be on the commission that will accomplish numbers 2 and 3 above
5. A food safety act to fund research into whether it's safe to eat food
6. Pesticide control to control the controlling of pests
7. Rural-development legislation to preserve rural life in the parts of America that remain rural because they're undeveloped
8. Supplemental appropriations for 180 miscellaneous items that Congress forgot to appropriate money for, including $1 million for family planning in Romania
9. Regular appropriations for everything else
10. A defense bill to defend us from the Soviet Union
11–14. Four treaties with the Soviet Union to do the reverse
15. A nonbinding *kvetch* about our allies not paying their fair share of number 10
16. A bill to sell fighter planes to Koreans (though whether these are

59

the Koreans in Korea or the Koreans who own grocery stores in Harlem, the bill does not say)

17. A bill to close unnecessary military bases unless those bases are overseas or in a congressman's district
18. A bill seeking "alternative nondefense uses for defense facilities"—aiming our ICBMs at Sally Jessy Raphael, for example
19. A housing bill to house people such as the young lady who testified at the Housing and Community Development Subcommittee hearing about not using her closets
20. A homeless housing bill to house people even worse than her

21–25. Four bills regulating U.S. exports, assuming we have any

And that, one would think, is about the limit of the human capacity for expertise. To be conversant with twenty-five disparate issues at once is as much as we can ask of a person. However, it is less than 10 percent of what we ask of a congressman. During this same week in 1990, 250 other items were also on the congressional calendar, including:

the federal budget
money laundering by organized crime
local bank check-cashing rules
whether the same truck can haul food and garbage, too
fish hatcheries
highway safety
outer space
children's television
airline ticket prices
phone service for the disabled
phone service for the rest of us
national forests
cable TV
whether Puerto Rico should be a state or a nation or what
indoor air quality
outdoor air quality
oil spills

oil shale
groundwater
coastal water
water resource development
tariffs
the economy of the Caribbean
tax-free retirement plans
Panama
Eastern Europe
El Salvador
South Africa
the Washington, DC, subway
civil service pay reform
whether federal employees can wear political campaign buttons to
    work
crime
price-fixing
immigration
the line-item veto
math and science education
vocational education (not to be confused with math and science
    education or job training)
job training (not to be confused with vocational education or
    getting a job)
public health
private health
family planning (other than that done in Romania)
child care for when the family planning doesn't work out
parental leave so that those parents who failed to practice family
    planning and now need child care can get some time off from
    work to screw the baby-sitter
nutritional labeling
guaranteed job security for federal employees who peach on their
    bosses
voter registration

veterans who were exposed to radiation

small businesses

whether presidential primaries should be held in groups, like AA
   meetings or something

how much free mail members of the Senate should be allowed to
   inflict upon the public

and, of all things,

   paperwork reduction

We expect our congressman to know more about each of these than
we know about any of them. We expect him to make wiser decisions than
we can about them all. And we expect that congressman to make those wise
and knowledgeable decisions without regard for his political or financial
self-interest. Then we wonder why it's hard to get first-rate people to run
for Congress.

So here was the congressman I was following, a good and conscientious
congressman desperately trying to master all 275 of these issues during the
approximately two hours a day when he didn't absolutely have to be
somewhere else. What could he do but cheat? Congressmen have crib
sheets. They're called voting cards. They are eight inches long and four
inches wide—just the right size to slip into a suit coat's inside pocket. They
look like this:

```
Bill Number: H.R. a billion-zillion

Title: Fiddlemeyer-O'Houligan Unbelievable
Grocery Bill

Info: Amends the federal anti-trust laws to make
the price of everything reasonable, like it used
to be, and includes provisions requiring kids
today to listen up when their dad talks to them

Committee Action: Passed by the House Means and
Ends Committee 3/17/90
```

Home: Constituents will murder you in November if
you oppose it.

Administration: President will kill you right now
if you support it.

Remarks: A toughie

Prior Votes: The 100th Congress was going to pass
it, but a lobbyist ate their copy of the
legislation.

Recommendation: Hide in the cloakroom during
floor vote.

After his staff work the congressman went into a brief flurry of signing
correspondence, well, not actually signing it—there's a machine that does
that—but a brief flurry of looking at correspondence to make sure the
machine hadn't signed anything horrifying. Then the congressman rushed
to the Cannon Building for a 4:00 P.M. meeting of his "class"—the congressmen of his own party who were first elected the same year he was. A
congressional class is one of the hundreds of groups and subgroups within
the Congress that constantly coalesce and disperse like the stuff inside a
lava lamp, and to about the same effect. At 5:00 P.M. the congressman
attended another political get-together, this one for important members of
his party from all walks of life (except, presumably—though I may be hasty
in this presumption—jail).

From 5:30 until 9:00 the congressman had to be at the National Fire
and Emergency Services Dinner at one hotel while, from 6:00 to 8:00 he
had to be with the governor of his state at another dinner in another hotel
on the other side of town. But a good politician can be two places at once
when it comes to public appearances, just as a good politician can be no
place at several different times when it comes to public issues.

Myself, I was completely exhausted by 7:00 and went home, leaving
the congressman, twenty years my senior, looking as animated and energetic as a full school bus—shaking hands and trading chat with governor,

firemen, ambulance drivers, other congressmen and even, at one point, his own wife.

This, according to the congressman's staff, was a "light day." The congressman normally spends three such days a week in Washington—Tuesday through Thursday—then flies halfway across the nation to his congressional district and spends Friday, Saturday and Monday doing more of the same at lectures, dinners, town-hall meetings and his two constituent service offices. He takes one week of vacation in August, one week at Christmas and one week at Easter. And he does all this for $125,100 per year, which, for all the public's caterwauling over the congressional pay raise, is less than what a shortstop hitting .197 makes.

The public—or things such as *Newsweek* that pass themselves off as the public—have also caterwauled about the size and cost of congressional staffs. This congressman has nine staff members: an administrative assistant, or AA, who is to the congressman as a master sergeant is to the lieutenant in an army platoon; three legislative assistants, or LAs, who hack through the legislative tangles and walk across the political mire of all the bills before Congress; two support staffers to man phones, word processors and signature-writing machines; two case workers in the district offices to cope with voters; and one field representative to visit shut-ins, plus a few unpaid interns and volunteers.

The inefficiency of government as compared with private enterprise is, everywhere, an item of faith. Even the most socialistic of pundits bothers us with this simile. But a company with six hundred thousand customers would have more than nine employees. And pay them more, too. A Congressman's allowance for hiring staff is $441,120. And the members of this staff, in return for salaries of between $20,000 and $80,000, have to do all the exhausting and exasperating things the congressman does without the gratifications of getting on the evening news.

Thus we Americans have struck a remarkable bargain. We pay $566,220 a year—less than a dollar apiece—for a congressman and his staff, and in return they listen to us carp and moan and fume and gripe and ask to be given things for free. Because this is, in the end, what legislators do. They listen to us. Not an enviable task.

* * *

The congressman whom I was shadowing, who is not the best-known member of the House and who does not represent a famously querulous district, gets thirty-eight thousand constituent inquiries a year, mostly letters, all of them answered within ten days. Some of this is crank mail, but not enough. Crank mail at least amuses the staff, and good crank letters go in the "Chuckles File." But these are answered, too. One constituent wrote every week for months saying that the CIA was using low-level pulsed microwave radiation to read his thoughts. Finally, the congressman suggested that he line his hat with tinfoil, and the fellow has not been heard from since.

Most of the inquiries, however, involve real things—all the things already mentioned that Congress is considering and all the things it has or will or might consider and all the world's other things besides. There are protests; appeals; calls for legislation to be passed, revoked and amended; letters on behalf of cousins who want to immigrate, sons who want to go to West Point and daughters who want civil service jobs; and problems with Medicare, the Veterans Administration, the IRS, the FHA, DOT, OSHA, AFDC, ABCDEFGHIJKLMNOP. There's something that must be done about each of these, say we voters; what's more, our Social Security check was late again last month. And out to every inquiry goes a respectful, responsible, dutiful reply, a reply that is as helpful as possible.

I read a week of the congressman's mail, more than seven hundred letters. There were exactly two thank-you notes in the pile.

ONLY HUMAN, IN HIS OWN
IMMORTAL WAY

The President

The members of Congress are busier going to and fro in the earth than I had expected. But the president, on close inspection, seems slightly unemployed. For nearly two generations, since the middle of the Great Depression, we've been hearing that to be president of the United States is almost more of a job than one man can handle. Yet consider some of the men who've held this job, and tell me how true this can be.

What does the president do? He provides leadership, but I don't know what that means. There was always a lot of talk about leadership in the Boy Scouts. So maybe the president is the first person in the nation to learn how to tie twenty-five different knots and the last person to admit that he'd rather be necking with girls than building an Indian wigwam. With this president it's possible. Also, leadership presupposes that we, as a nation, are all going someplace together. I haven't noticed that we're going anywhere lately. And this is a free country, anyway—each of us should choose his own destination. In a truly American kind of leadership the president would be a person headed in two hundred fifty million different directions at once. With this president that's also possible.

So the president provides leadership. The president also makes decisions. The president has, as head of the executive branch of the federal government and commander in chief of the armed forces, enormous power to make decisions for the rest of us. And he makes these decisions by carefully minding public opinion so that what he decides we will do is whatever we've decided he should decide. Thus the president is a national toddler, with the same kind of enormous power to make decisions that a two-year-old has: "Do we want to lower the capital-gains tax? No-no-no. Put that down. Naughty old tax breaks. What a good president we are! Do we want to send troops to the Middle East? Ooooooo! Let's send those troopie-whoopies riiiiiight over to the Middle East. What a big President!"

Like any toddler the president often gets it wrong and eats out of the ashtray or sticks our dress shoes in the toilet. In which case we give him a good one right on the opinion poll.

But at least the president can blow up the world. He has that briefcase that goes everywhere with him, the "football." And in that briefcase is . . . Let's think about this for a minute. Do you suppose the president understands how the computer codes that activate our nuclear arsenal work? When he opens the "football," will he be able to tell whether the stuff in there is real or whether it's just some readouts and LED displays slapped together by the Pentagon Art Department to look cool? And if you were the person who *did* know how our nuclear arsenal is activated, would you design the "football" so that anyone except you could activate it? Say you are this very smart but jerkish MIT computer genius who works in an extremely secret part of the Defense Department and gets picked on by beefy military types. And they come to you and say, "Hey, Numbers-Butt— you with your glasses taped together—rig something so the president can blow up the world." Would you do it? Besides, how often does anybody look inside the "football"? Do you suppose George Bush kicks back after a long day muddling sound bites and says, "Gosh, let's open the blow-up thing and, hey, take a gander"? Nixon, maybe, but not Bush. There's probably nothing inside but a copy of *Penthouse* and a pint bottle of Hiram Walker—a *Penthouse* from back in the seventies when *Penthouse* was really dirty, I'll bet.

* * *

What the president really does is get watched. We, and the journalists who do our bidding, watch his every move. His slightest comment is analyzed and puzzled over. Even his tone of voice is dissected and assayed. There are three hundred or so members of the White House Press Corps who do nothing but this. Sometimes they all watch the president at once, such as when he gives a press conference or attends a public event. Sometimes they watch him in shifts, or "pools." For instance, if there is a "photo opportunity" in the Oval Office, one White House Press Corps print reporter, selected on a rotating basis, will accompany the photographers and write a "pool report." Here—in an example from July 24, 1990, by a Ms. or Mr. Seib of the *Wall Street Journal*—is the kind of vital news data such reports contain:

> Someone attempted to ask whether Bush was pleased with the initial reaction to the Souter nomination. "Don't even try," the president said. "I'm in a bad mood." Someone then tried to ask about progress on the budget and Bush replied, "Don't even try." This was said with a small smile and produced chuckling all around, so it isn't clear whether the bad mood was legitimate or simply the latest excuse to avoid photo op questions.

Of course, every time the president does anything in particular the White House sends out its own press release, a document at least as momentous as a pool report:

> The President today announced the appointment of Richard W. Porter to be Special Assistant to the President and Executive Secretary for the Domestic Policy Council.

And there are also scores of television camera crews on hand at all times, with videotape constantly running, waiting for the president to say "fuck" or get shot.

Try this scrutiny on yourself:

> Someone attempted to ask the reader if he was going to sit around on his duff all day watching football or was he finally going to paint the

downstairs bathroom? "Don't start," the reader said. "I'm in a bad mood." Someone then asked if he could have a new skateboard and a haircut with stripes on the side of his head and the reader replied, "I'll give you stripes on the side of your head all right." This was said with a dull stare and prolonged kneading of the temples so it isn't clear whether the bad mood was legitimate or simply a result of the latest hangover.

What if every time you went to get into your car there were three hundred members of the media between you and the garage, and if your fly's unzipped, it's on the front page of every newspaper in the country? What about that joke you told at work the other day? "How many mayors of Washington, DC, does it take to . . ." That would result in Al Sharpton and hundreds of his friends with bullhorns marching around the receptionist's desk at your office, and what would the boss say? And imagine having to stand up in your rec room every couple of weeks to justify everything you've done and then getting questioned about it?

Mr. Reader, *why* didn't you separate the different kinds of plastic in your garbage? Aren't you setting a bad example for the nation?

The White House is very grand, with its pillars and gates, its Blue Room, Green Room, Room in a Color Only Visible to Bees, etc. But the business end of the White House, the West Wing, looks like the administration building at a small midwestern college. There are some nice paintings and old pieces of furniture out in the halls, but the offices themselves— except for that oval one—are cramped and the carpeting is the same mediocre wall-to-wall stuff we all have at home. Desks, chairs, file cabinets and so forth are of a standard-issue institutional kind, no better than what a state parole board gets. The computer gear is less up-to-date than a Dayton travel agent's. And the dining hall, the "White House mess," is a window-less couple of rooms decorated in bogus colonial furniture with food served by the navy.

The space given over to the White House Press Corps is worse, verging on squalid. Representatives of the most prestigious newspapers and wire services work in cubicles like high-school students in detention study hall. The most powerful television networks have offices the size of airplane toilets. The main room of the press center, where the president gives his press conferences and the president's press secretary gives his briefings, is built over the top of Franklin D. Roosevelt's indoor swimming pool. It is therefore possible that somewhere in the West Wing is a button that can open the floor and dump the entire White House Press Corps into the deep end—but probably not, because it would have been used by now.

It is here, in this briefing room, that the most fervid and passionate watching of the president transpires. The place is wallpapered in a casualty-ward green fake grass cloth, has a low ceiling and a trampled blue carpet with a greasy synthetic shine. The reporters sit in hardwood lecture-hall seats, and that is mostly just what they do—sit, waiting for the president to appear or for someone to appear who is going in to see the president or for someone to appear coming out from having seen him.

Rows of aluminum stepladders lean against one wall of the briefing room. Are all the reporters going to get together and do something about that wallpaper? But these belong to the photographers, so that they may photograph, in excelsis, the president. Every now and then someone from the White House Press Office staff announces a "photo op," and the photographers grab those stepladders and troop out. Then, the service conducted, they troop back in.

Once a day there's a briefing by the president's press secretary in which the press secretary describes what the president has been doing, this to a group of people who've spent all day watching the president do it. Then the reporters ask the press secretary questions ranging from the unanswerable to the pointless.

"Does anyone in the administration know anything about Souter's views other than what they've found out by asking him?" asked one reporter in reference to the Supreme Court nominee whose appointment was then under consideration by the Senate.

A blond woman who works for one of the television networks and is proverbial for her idiocy asked, "Is the Soviet Union still the enemy we arm against?"

And a French wire service reporter whose accent was as piquant as his question was bland, wanted to know if an upcoming speech by the president would be on matters "intern-nashun-all or dumb-mistake?"

The press secretary's responses are Delphic:

> The President has his own words and those would be the ones he would choose to use.

> There's a good deal of space between a litmus test and a question, and I don't intend to fill it.

There is rapid scribbling down of these utterances. Then there are long debates between the reporters and the press secretary about whether what the press secretary just said was "on the record" or "off the record." Thus, it is decided which dicta constitute secret prophecies and which may be made known to the laity.

Being in the White House Press Corps is essentially ceremonial. It entails—as all ceremonial roles do—ceaseless repetition, stultifying dullness and swollen self-regard.

That goes double for being the president. Here is a typical presidential schedule, this one from July 25, 1990:

> 7:55 A.M. Drop by at fund raiser for [Rhode Island Republican senatorial candidate] Claudine Schneider at the Mayflower Hotel.

The president has to do nothing here. His wondrous presence is all that matters.

> 8:35 A.M. The president receives intelligence briefing, Oval Office.

Again the president has to do nothing. Acolytes do the talking.

> 8:45 A.M. The president receives national security briefing, Oval Office.

This time the president really has nothing to do, because he just got an intelligence briefing, and if an intelligence briefing isn't about national security, what is it about?

> 9:00 A.M. The president participates in budget meeting, Oval Office.

Of course the president doesn't really participate. What does any person without a PhD in economics know about the budget? (And we have copious evidence that persons with those PhDs don't know anything about it either.) Here the president acts as a human augury, smiling upon certain incantations spoken by math wizards from the administration or the Congress and giving unpropitious signs—being a sheep with two livers or whatever—to others.

> 10:15 A.M. The president participates in Congressional Leadership Meeting, Cabinet Room.

The last thing the leaders of a Democratic Congress want is any help leading from a Republican president. Whatever goes on in this conclave is pointless ritual, like the Blessing of the Animals or, these days, a wedding.

> 1:30 P.M. The president participates in ceremony honoring Captive Nations Week, Rose Garden.

Which does exactly the same amount of good for Latvia, Lithuania and Estonia as burying a black cat in a graveyard at midnight does for warts.

The next day the president healed the sick.

There was an enormous ceremony on the South Lawn of the White House, where the president signed the Americans with Disabilities Act. Two thousand of the disabled and their family members were invited to attend in the broiling summer heat. People in wheelchairs were yelling at the deaf to sit down and the blind were bumping the palsied with their dogs. In a crueler age some onlookers might have laughed, but we never laugh at misfortune today. In fact, we're all trying to get in on it. A White House press release claimed that forty-three million Americans "have some form of disability." That is one out of five people, and it can't be true unless disability to balance checkbooks is being counted. A number of other things about this legislation can't be true either. Under the new law, "public accommodations are prohibited from discrimination on the basis of disability in the full and equal enjoyment of goods, services, facilities, privileges, advantages or accommodations." But people with disabilities, by definition, do not have full and equal enjoyment of goods, services, facilities and so forth. Otherwise, what disability do they have? And the bill also guarantees that there will be no discrimination in employment. Does this mean one-legged firemen? Don't worry, the question will be equitably settled in the courts. Meanwhile, ill health and bad luck have been made against the law.

The president, surrounded by very big and undisabled men from the Secret Service, came out of the White House and up onto a stage where various disabled dignitaries were waiting—Senator Bob Dole with his war injuries, industrialist Justin Dart in a wheelchair, the Reverend Harold Wilke, who has no arms—dignitaries who were there as examples of why the Americans with Disabilities Act was so needed though they hadn't needed it. The president shook hands with everyone and was halfway to offering his hand to Reverend Wilke but managed to stop himself. Then the president gave a speech as sweet and silly and utterly affectless as any childhood bedtime prayer:

> Our problems are large but our unified heart is larger. Our challenges are great, but our will is greater. And in our America, the most generous, optimistic nation on the face of the earth, we must not and will not rest until every man and woman with a dream has the means to achieve it.

We treat the president of the United States with awe. We impute to him remarkable powers. We divine things by his smallest gestures. We believe he has the capacity to destroy the very earth, and—by vigorous perusal of sound economic policy—to make the land fruitful and all our endeavors prosperous. We beseech him for aid and comfort in our every distress and believe him capable of granting any boon or favor.

The type is recognizable to even a casual student of mythology. The president is not an ordinary politician trying to conduct the affairs of state as best he can. He is a divine priest-king. And we Americans worship our state avatar devoutly. That is, we do until he shows any sign of weakness, any disability, as it were. Sir James Frazer, in *The Golden Bough,* said:

> Primitive peoples . . . believe that their safety and even that of the world is bound up with the life of one of these god-men. . . . Naturally, therefore, they take the utmost care of his life. . . . But no amount of care and precaution will prevent the man-god from growing old and feeble. . . . There is only one way of averting these dangers. The man-god must be killed.

Thus in our brief national history we have shot four of our presidents, worried five of them to death, impeached one and hounded another out of office. And when all else fails, we hold an election and assassinate their character.

DOING THE MOST IMPORTANT KIND OF NOTHING

The Supreme Court

Even more august and dignified than the divine priest-king—and a lot more secure in their jobs—are the members of the Supreme Court. The duties of the Supreme Court are the simplest and best defined of any part of government. The Supreme Court justices have to do nothing but sit and let others make ugly fools of themselves in front of the Supreme Court bench.

You would have to go miles down under the ocean in a bathysphere to find anything as ugly as the plaintiffs in the 1990 Supreme Court flag-desecration case, though their wacky old left-wing lawyer, William Kunstler, was also quite a sight. But Kunstler—with eyebrows the size of squirrels and mouth, mind and long, gray tresses going every which direction and who was wearing a hobo literature-professor-type suit no doubt carefully pre-rumpled at the special Pinko Dry Cleaner and Valet that they have in New York ("Be a Liberal or Just Look Like One"), where you can also get your hair uncut and your shoes scuffed—was the kind of ugly that begs to be played by Paul Newman. Kunstler's clients were the genuine item: screaming, nose-ringed fat girls with hair by Mop & Glo and slug-colored boys in fake motorcycle jackets who had had their faces tattooed.

These appalling young people thrust their fists into the air and did other things from before they were born, such as shout, "Power to the People!" Then they "made statements to the press":

> Confiscated from me on October 30 was a red, white and blue maternity bra which I intended to burn in protest while standing on a flag.
>
> I burned the U.S. flag because of the 50 million Blacks who were murdered by this state during the times of slavery. For the fact that 1 in 4 women is raped in this country and that every 15 seconds a woman is beaten. . . . Yes, I burned the flag. Someone had to do it.

They weren't well washed. Some of them had trouble reading their statements. One pallid, snub-nosed youth with a crest of purple hair on an otherwise shaven skull stepped to the fore and announced, "I am a Mohawk," getting himself confused with his haircut.

The flag desecraters and their lawyer were standing in front of the Supreme Court of the United States, on the wide marble steps below the graceful stand of Corinthian pillars, flanked by sculptures in heroic scale representing contemplation of justice and authority of law.

A ring of journalists, including twenty-eight television camera crews, surrounded the desecraters. The journalists were dressed in Banana Republic safari clothes and so festooned with cables, lights, video- and still cameras, microphones and tape recorders that they looked like offspring of a mating between a human game-park attendant and a Radio Shack catalog.

The journalists were, in turn, encased by demonstrators. Some resembled the grubby, addled flag plaintiffs. Others were dressed in clean polyester and carried signs indicating they approved of God.

And around the demonstrators was a belt of Washington summertime tourists looking as only Washington summertime tourists can—mature adults visiting their nation's most solemn monuments and greatest institutions in cartoon-character T-shirts and candy-colored running shoes the size of teddy bears, with porky desk-job thighs sticking out of tiny iridescent gym shorts and wearing fanny packs like phylacteries for the worship of fat.

Concentric circles of fools, each more ridiculously clad than the next, spread across Capitol Hill from the Supreme Court's grand portico. What America needed was not a flag-desecration law but a dress code.

It got neither. And, in the end, the most interesting thing about the great flag-burning debate of the late 1980s would be how quickly that debate evaporated.

As I write, it has been less than seven months since the mob scene in front of the Supreme Court and less than six months since that Court ruled unconstitutional the federal law making it a crime to burn, deface, tease, annoy or horse around with the American flag. This decree came after two years of nonstop flag noise and a presidential campaign where, at times, the most important issue seemed to be which candidate thought the flag most swell. There was also remarkable public concord on the subject. According to a *New York Times*/CBS-TV news poll taken in June 1990, 83 percent of Americans thought burning the flag should be illegal. Besides, burning almost anything—the tobacco in a cigarette, for example—was getting to be against the law in the U.S. New Hampshire congressman Chuck Douglas, defending a proposed anti-flag-burning amendment to the Constitution, said, "My constituents can't even burn *leaves.*"

But today in newspapers and magazines and on the TV news and public affairs shows, flag burning is no more likely to be mentioned than whether women should bob their hair. Another fashionable principle has gone out of style.

For the time being, flag burning joins fluoridated water, the ERA, states' rights, welfare reform, free coinage of silver, the debate over letting high-school students read *Lord of the Flies* and all those other life-and-death matters that have slipped the public mind. I can't even remember what my own opinion was on the flag issue, though I remember I had a strong one.

We Americans are an unprincipled nation, when you come down to it. Not that we're bad or anything. It's just that it's hard for us to pay attention to abstract matters when we have so many concrete matters—cellular phones, ski boats, salad shooters, trail bikes, StairMasters, snow boards, pasta-making machines, four-door sport utility vehicles, palmcorders, rollerblade skates and CD players for our cars—to occupy us. No wonder all the great intellectual concepts such as monotheism and using the zero in arithmetic come from pastoral societies where herdsmen sit around all night with nothing to do except think things up. (Though it *is* a wonder more cosmologies aren't founded on screwing sheep.)

Flag burning was, however, vitally important to everybody right up until the moment we all forgot about it. And on May 14, 1990, when the flag case was being argued, the Supreme Court was flush with spectators, lawyers and press. We less prominent journalists had to be squeezed in on folding chairs behind a screen to one side of the bench, like poor female cousins at a Hasidic wedding. We couldn't even see the justices. A guard had to stand at the edge of the screen and tell us who was speaking.

There were some pounding noises, and we were told to stand up. The marshal of the Court hollered, "The Honorable the Chief Justice and the Associate Justices of the Supreme Court of the United States. Oyez! Oyez! Oyez! [Law French for "Yo"] All persons having business before the Honorable, the Supreme Court of the United States are admonished to draw near and give their attention, for the Court is now sitting. God save the United States and this Honorable Court." (This last phrase being a clear violation of the First Amendment separation of church and state, by the way.)

A fifteen-minute flutter of court business followed, and two rulings were meted out—*United Steel Workers v. Somebody* and *Atlantic Richfield Corporation v. Somebody Else.* Jobs, lives, millions in profits and lofty precepts of moral law were no doubt at stake here, but the judgments were delivered with the bland finality of a blackjack deal. Then the marshal hollered, "We will now hear argument."

Contra (as a lawyer would say) the incessant and interminable nature of lower-court litigation, each party in a Supreme Court case gets thirty minutes to say his piece, and that's that. The Supreme Court is one of the few departments of government to do its job with dispatch, just as the Supreme Court building is one of the few government structures to cost less than what was authorized for its construction. When the handsome Parthenon-with-family-room-wing-and-attached-garage design was completed in 1935, $94,000 was returned to the U.S. Treasury.

Kenneth W. Starr, the solicitor general of the United States (a title that makes Mr. Starr sound like a military man intent on sleeping with everyone in the country), said that the question before the Court was whether the First Amendment to the Constitution prohibits us from prosecuting people for burning the flag. A voice from the most primitive, the medulla oblongata, section of my brain (we all have a little lawyer inside us) said, "It doesn't prohibit you from prosecuting people for burning a house. Hang them." But the solicitor general said there were four far more sophisticated reasons why it is all right to hang—jail, anyway—people who burn the flag. He said that in writing this new flag-desecration law:

1. Congress had "acted carefully." (By which he meant who knows what plus I doubt it.)

2. Congress had "acted narrowly." (That is, the law is very specific, and you can't be arrested for having a smart look on your face near the flag or anything like that—which is good because being specific is the essence of lawmaking and the whole difference between having a Congress and having a mom.)

3. "Flag burning leaves a major message gap." (You can't call this free speech. They didn't say anything. They just set something on fire and smelled up the place.)

4. Some other reason that had to do with national intangibles but was too nationally intangible for me to grasp.

Associate Justice Antonin Scalia said, "I don't understand this line of reasoning." And he pointed out that burning the U.S. flag didn't leave much of a gap in the message that you hated the U.S.

"With all due respect," said the solicitor general, "there's no mention of hating the U.S. in the record."

"What else could burning the flag mean?" asked Justice Scalia, sounding peeved.

Associate Justice John Paul Stevens said that if hating the U.S. wasn't the message, "maybe we should prosecute these people on the basis of misleading speech."

The solicitor general tried another tack, using argument number five on his list of four. He said nothing prevented legislatures from extending physical protection to symbols such as churches and bald eagles.

Justice Scalia wanted to know if Bible burning could be banned.

The solicitor general wasn't going to wait for the justices to shoot him down this time. "The government cannot protect symbols to the detriment of other sections of the Constitution," he said and shot himself down first.

The justices kept bugging the solicitor general. Associate Justice Anthony Kennedy pointed out that by saying the flag was a national symbol, the solicitor general was calling the message of flag burning narrow, whereas he had, in the message-gap argument, called the message of flag burning too broad.

Chief Justice William Rehnquist wanted to know who owned the burned flags in question. The solicitor general said that in one of the cases the desecraters had come flag-equipped, but in the other case the flag belonged to the Park Service.

"Were they indicted for destruction of government property?" asked the chief justice in the tone teachers use to ask why you don't take care of your hair grooming at home.

Justice Scalia said, "If I get a spot on my tie, I don't say, 'Gee, I've defiled my tie,' or if I tear my jacket, I don't say, 'My, I've mutilated my jacket.'"

The solicitor general began to sound confused. "An individual may deface the flag by sewing the letters 'I Love the Supreme Court' on it," he said.

Associate Justice Byron White asked if the solicitor general was saying that burning a flag was just "like burning anything else at a demonstration, like an overloud loudspeaker?" And the solicitor general said yes, even though that wasn't what he was saying at all.

Finally, the solicitor general retreated into the It's-my-ball/I'm-going-home school of argument, saying, "If Congress had the power to create this flag, it has the power to protect it."

"Did Congress identify their source of constitutional authority for this law?" asked Justice Kennedy, getting in one last dig.

Next William Kunstler addressed the court. I sneaked a look at him from our press seraglio. He was staring around in space as if he were searching for his glasses, which were on top of his head. Kunstler cited a number of legal precedents as reasons for letting his clients burn flags, including *Marbury v. Madison*, which doesn't have anything to do with flags but is the case that established the Supreme Court's review powers, thus making the Supreme Court supreme. I think you more or less have to cite it when you're arguing before the Supreme Court. It's like telling your wife her dress looks pretty before you go to a party.

Kunstler, who sounds more or less reasonable as long as you can't see his clients—or him—then said that the new federal law against defacing the flag is not content neutral. It singles out one political symbol for protection. It is viewpoint-based, proscribing conduct that shows disrespect for the flag but allowing ceremonial burning of same and permitting conduct that is dangerous to the flag, such as flying it in a hurricane (or near his clients).

Justice Scalia said, "Would the statute be OK if a bunch of frat kids burned the flag for kicks?"

Kunstler mumbled.

The justice went on to say that if the law is invalid because it permits some kinds of flag destruction but prohibits other kinds, the law is not "facially invalid" (a legal phrase similar in etymology, I think, to "my face and your ass").

Kunstler mumbled some more.

Justice Stevens (taking up, just for fun, the solicitor general's "message gap" argument) asked how he could tell what message was being conveyed by burning a flag. "Call this telephone number, and we'll tell you why we burned this flag?" he suggested.

But, complained Kunstler, arguing against vagueness would eliminate all nonverbal speech.

Justice Kennedy wanted to know if flag desecraters who violated some other law—by destroying government property, for example—could be given harsher sentences for causing public outrage.

Kunstler said adamantly, "No."

"According to your rule, then," said Justice Kennedy, with a twinkle in his voice, "you get the same sentence for spray-painting the alley wall of a government building as you get for spray-painting the Washington Monument."

There was a very small "yes" from Kunstler.

"Fighting words," said Justice Scalia, sounding like a man who'd just gotten an idea. Why couldn't burning the flag be banned on the basis of being, in a symbolic sense, fighting words. "You have no right to engage in conduct that's likely to incite a riot," said the justice. (Why hadn't the solicitor general thought of this?)

Kunstler maintained that burning the flag did not constitute fighting words—proof, if proof were needed, that he's from the planet Manhattan. Then he mumbled yet again and cited additional legal precedents. He seemed at a loss. Perhaps his famous eloquence was called for.

"Respect for the flag must be voluntary," said Kunstler, his voice swelling to fill the occasion. "Once people are compelled to respect a political symbol, they are no longer free. . . . It is as if Congress had ordered us to fall down and worship a golden image—" But before we got to hear what we golden-image-hating Americans would have done about such an atrocity as this, Chief Justice Rehnquist said, "Thank you, Mr. Kunstler. Your time has expired."

Four weeks later the Supreme Court returned its decision that, no, you can't just outlaw flag burning and let every other form of obnoxious symbolic speech run around loose bothering the public like a William Kunstler client. American citizens should have the same opportunity to punch flag burners as they have to throw urine-filled balloons at David Duke or swat airport Hare Krishnas with carry-on luggage. Though that is not, of course, how the Supreme Court put it. The majority opinion read, "Applying our recent decision in *Texas v. Johnson* (1989) [a case involving a state law against flag desecration] the District Courts [lower federal courts] held that the Act cannot constitutionally be applied to the appellees [fat girls with nose rings, etc.]. We affirm."

And how did the Supreme Court come to this decision?

We don't know. Nobody knows. Back in 1979 *Washington Post* reporter Scott Armstrong and Watergate tattletale Bob Woodward (who later wrote a book about how nobody knows why John Belushi did what he did) wrote a whole book about how nobody knows. In this book, *The Brethren*, it was revealed that members of the Supreme Court get together and talk the cases over, then vote. But that may not be true. Journalists are notoriously easy to kid. All you have to do is speak to a journalist in a very serious tone of voice, and he will be certain that you are either telling the truth or a big, important lie. It has never occurred to any journalist that he was having his leg pulled. For all we know, the Supreme Court decides cases by playing nude games of Johnny-on-a-pony. This would be a more interesting theory if the members of the Supreme Court were younger and better looking. Let's say they toss darts. Anyway, nobody has the slightest idea. The Supreme Court is a secret and autocratic institution. What it says, goes, and if you don't like it, you can go live in Colombia and buy your own Supreme Court at the annual Medellín Cartel Justice Auction.

That all our public freedoms and democratic rights depend on a secret and autocratic institution is an irony, if you're stupid enough to think so. Life is full of ironies for the stupid. And you'd have to be fairly stupid to believe democracy could be preserved by democratic means: "In the final D-day invasion results, Normandy was a decisive winner, with 54 percent of the votes, while 43 percent of American soldiers thought we should re-invade North Africa and only 4 percent favored a massive land, sea and air attack on the folks back home." There wouldn't even be any democracy to defend if our every national whim were put into law. We'd sacrifice the whole Constitution for those lost kids on milk cartons one week, and the next week we'd toss the Rights of Man out the window to help victims of date rape. That's why we—and the solicitor general and William Kunstler—have to take this guff from the Supreme Court.

And so we were left with the flag burners. How to dispose of these creatures? The Supreme Court had thrown us back on our own resources. Do we do as one southern state did and pass a statute fining people $25 for assaulting a desecrater of the flag? But that's pinning a "kick me" sign on the backside of the majesty of the law. Do we pass a constitutional amendment? It wouldn't be the silliest amendment in the Constitution, but it would be using a four-by-eight sheet of plywood to swat flies.

What we should do is what we did do, by default. Free societies often do do what they should, usually by default. Freedom is, after all, a matter of letting other people alone, and that's best done by default. So we forgot about flag burning and the flag burners, who were—for all their astonishing ugliness—a thoroughly forgettable bunch. We let them and their ilk and their lawyer go back to doing what they wanted to do and being who they wanted to be. The Supreme Court knew best after all. Freedom is its own punishment.

PROTECTORS OF A BLAMELESS CITIZENRY

The Bureaucracy

The actual work of government is too unglamorous for the people who govern us to do. Important elected office-holders and high appointed officials create bureaucratic departments to perform the humdrum tasks of national supervision. Government proposes, bureaucracy disposes. And the bureaucracy must dispose of government proposals by dumping them on us.

An example of these dreary labors can be picked at random from any part of the federal system covered by the Civil Service code. Because I am sometimes an automotive journalist, I chose a subsection of the Department of Transportation that was dealing with a specific technical problem having to do with cars. Watching any particular agency do any particular thing would teach the same lesson, however. Which lesson being that there's not much to be learned from bureaucracy.

For twenty years the National Highway Traffic Safety Administration has been getting complaints about "unintended acceleration," or "runaway car syndrome." People claim that their automobiles take off at high speed for no reason. Usually this happens while the gear-shift selector is being moved from P to D or R. The drivers swear that they didn't have their feet

on the gas and often swear that they were pressing on the brake as hard as they could.

These alarming episodes of mechanical self-will are officially known as sudden-acceleration incidents. By 1987 six thousand SAIs had been reported, and cars leaving without permission had supposedly caused three thousand accidents, two thousand injuries and fifty-six deaths. There was a great outcry in consumerism circles. Demands were made for the government to put a stop, as it were, to this.

The term *consumerism* has been current since the middle 1960s, about the same length of time as the Department of Transportation itself. Literally interpreted, the word means "an ideology based on the opposite of being productive." This ideology has caused enormous changes in the American economy. At one time complaining was a cottage industry. The typical maker of complaints gave them to (or traded them with) friends and family members. Sometimes the complaints were sent to newspapers or included in prayers. Friends, family, the press and God then ignored the complaints. In the sixties, however, various consumer advocates began to help complainers find a market for their wares. There is only one organization that is required to take everyone—and their complaints—seriously. So the government became the foremost grumble customer. And it is, of course, the government's bureaucratic agencies who have to do the buying. Congress caused the Department of Transportation to establish the National Highway Traffic Safety Administration (NHTSA) for just this purpose in 1970.

For a long time complaints to NHTSA about sudden-acceleration incidents had nothing in common as to type of automobile, except that SAI's occurred in cars with automatic transmissions. But in 1986 sudden acceleration became associated in the public mind almost exclusively with the Audi 5000 sedan. No one is sure exactly why. The Audi 5000 was introduced in 1978 and, aside from styling, remained unchanged thereafter. In the first four years that the 5000 was sold in the United States, only thirteen Audi SAI incidents were reported. Then, in February 1986, an article on sudden acceleration appeared in the *New York Times.* The article focused on SAI accusations against General Motors, American Motors, Ford, Nissan and

Toyota. Audi was mentioned only in passing. But a certain Mrs. X of Long Island read the article. Mrs. X had had two accidents in her Audi 5000, both, she claimed, results of SAIs. Mrs. X contacted the Center for Automotive Safety, a group founded by Ralph Nader, which called the New York Public Interest Research Group, another consumerist organization. NYPIRG put the arm on New York State attorney general Robert Abrams, who held a press conference and denounced the Audi 5000 as an unsafe car. Mrs. X founded a support group made up of some forty people who claimed their Audis had gotten away from them. In November 1986 the CBS "60 Minutes" television news show picked up the story:

> ED BRADLEY: When an automobile malfunctions, causing several deaths, hundreds of injuries and thousands in property damage, you would think the National Highway Traffic Safety Administration could do something about it. The fact is, they don't even know what's causing it. What we're talking about is the sudden rocketing of a car out of control after the driver switches gears. . . . Over the last several years there've been reports of all makes of cars doing this, including some made by GM. Now the car motorists point to most is the Audi 5000, years 1979 to 1986. Audi says it happens when a driver steps on the gas pedal when he means to step on the brake.

> MRS. X: If we mistook the brake pedal and the gas pedal, wouldn't the wall of your garage stop you? Why are people landing on diving boards? Why are they leaping over marina walls? Why are they going down elevator shafts? Why are they driving through people's houses and landing on their beds? Each day the stories become more and more bizarre.

In the month following the "60 Minutes" broadcast, fourteen hundred people claimed that their Audis suddenly accelerated.

A mysterious phenomenon in which silly people with lawyers get into an Audi 5000 and—all of a sudden, for no apparent reason—go through the back wall of their garage and onto the CBS "60 Minutes" television program is obviously a threat to the commonweal. Therefore, in accordance with a recent modification of the U.S. Constitution ("The powers not delegated to the United States by the Constitution, nor prohibited by it to the States, are reserved for network television"), the federal government swung into action. The Department of Transportation gave the go-ahead to the National Highway Traffic Safety Administration to tell its Office of Defects Investigation to have the Department of Transportation's Transportation Systems Center convene a panel of experts at the Transportation Systems Center's Operator Performance and Safety Analysis Division's Vehicle Research and Testing Center and look into this.

In the twinkling of an eye (by the standards of bureaucratic time, which is slower than geologic time but more expensive than time spent with Madame Claude's girls in Paris) the thing was done. On March 7, 1989, the DOT-NHTSA-ODI-TSC-OPSAD-VRTC (you'd think the initials alone would be enough to slow down any runaway cars) effort produced an eighty-one-page report written by an eight-man group of engineering savants with more than fifty years of college among them. This document presented evidence from exhaustive experiment and analysis that proved what everybody who understands how to open the hood of a car had known all along about SAIs: "Pedal misapplications are the likely cause of these incidents."

Yes, the dumb buggers stepped on the gas instead of the brake. Thus sudden-acceleration incidents, or SAIs, closely resemble those sudden-unintelligence incidents, or SUIs, that many of us have experienced with our automobiles, especially when we were in our teens and early twenties. We'd be driving down a country road at a reasonable and prudent 115 miles per hour and—all of a sudden, for no apparent reason—the car would suffer an SUI and roll over five times in a cornfield. I seem to remember that sudden-unintelligence incidents were often associated with sudden-regurgitation incidents (SRIs), where my friends and I would—all of a sudden, for no apparent reason—drink four six-packs of warm Pabst. No doubt the DOT-NHTSA-VRTC will be investigating these mysterious phenomena ASAP-PDQ-BYOB.

Anyway, the truth was out at last. The government had released a huge report showing that there was no such thing as unintended acceleration in automobiles. Stand by for huge government reports on fairies stealing children and poker wealth gained by drawing to inside straights. Meanwhile cars did not fly away of their own accord. They could be safely left unattended. You can fold up the camp cot and quit spending nights in the garage keeping an eye on the family minivan.

The NHTSA report also cast some dim light on how the admirable Audi 5000 sedan came to be the favored bait in the Sudden-Acceleration Media Hack and Liability Lawyer Bottom-Feeder Tournament. Audi had the bad luck to be the lowest-priced German luxury car during the great German-luxury-car fad. And Audi had the worse luck to be designed with its brake and accelerator pedals close together (where, for the sake of quick stopping, they belong) instead of in separate counties, as they are on typical American luxury cars. Thus Audi got a large number of plush-bottom yoohoos suffering from daytime-television brain buying the 5000. These people had never driven a European car before and were too busy attaching Garfield the cat suction-cup toys to the rear window to watch what their feet were doing.

It's worth noting (and the NHTSA report did note it) that the Honda Civic's pedal placement is nearly identical with the Audi 5000's, yet the Civic got few SAI complaints. On the other hand, the Mercury Marquis—where, on a clear day, you can almost see the accelerator from the brake—was in the SAI top ten. We don't need a "60 Minutes" investigative team to tell us what kind of person buys a little Honda rice rocket and what kind of person buys a huge Mercury Medicare sled.

So the truth was out, and we people who like automobiles and can tell our right foot from our elbow should have been glad. But there was, in fact, no reason to celebrate. This message from the federal bowl of Alpha-Bits had cost us taxpayers millions of dollars and came too late to save Audi from the ignorance, credulity, opportunism and sheer Luddite malice directed toward that corporation and its products. Furthermore, the Department of Transportation press release introducing the SAI report absolved the paddle-shoed, dink-wit perpetrators of sudden acceleration. It just let Betty Dumb-Toes and Joe Boat-Foot right off the hook:

> NHTSA declined to characterize the cause of sudden acceleration as driver error. Driver error may imply carelessness or willfulness in failing to operate a car properly. Pedal misapplication is more descrip-

tive of what occurs. It could happen to even the most attentive driver who inadvertently selects the wrong pedal and continues to do so unwittingly.

The next time I get pulled over by the state highway patrol, I'm telling the officer, "You probably intend to ticket me for speeding, which would be driver error. But pedal misapplication is more descriptive of what occurred. It could happen to even the most attentive driver who inadvertently selects the wrong pedal and continues to do so unwittingly."

And, if "pedal misapplication" weren't enough, there was also this statement in the same DOT press release:

NHTSA currently has research underway to determine the relationship between pedal placement and driver pedal misapplication, and to analyze potential improvements in pedal design.

So the government was working on another huge report showing that it's dangerous to have the thing that makes a car go next to the thing that makes a car stop. Let's move the accelerator to a safer location—outside the car, for example. Maybe we should mount it on a pole beside the highway.

It is not, however, doing the job of journalism to just make fun of the Department of Transportation. A real reporter must go there, interview people, collect facts, balance opinions, weigh allegations and then make fun of the Department of Transportation. So I phoned the department and made an appointment.

Most of Washington's government buildings are not modern in style, but when they are, they're doozies. The stark, haute sixties headquarters of DOT is the kind of thing that's called cracker box and lifeless. But a cracker box is admirably suited to its purpose of being full of crackers. The DOT building isn't suited to anything but getting lost in its fluorescent-lit corridors longer than Madonna concert-ticket lines. Nor can a design be said to lack life when it exhibits such animated hatred of beauty. And comfort. In Washington, Jimmy Carter's moral-equivalent-of-war energy-saving rules are—sixteen years later—still in force (this is getting to be the moral equivalent of the War of the Roses), so it's always a little too hot or a little too cold in a government building. But in the DOT building, with the benefit of modern central climate control and hermetically sealed windows, it's both.

I'm not sure what I expected at the Department of Transportation, maybe wire-rimmed young women earnestly bicycling up and down the halls and sitting cross-legged on the floors of offices decorated with SAVE THE ROAD KILLS posters. Or maybe I expected sweaty fanatics throwing child-restraint seats with live children in them against walls to see if the kids get hurt. I didn't expect ordinary, friendly men about my own age. And they were car buffs. Almost everyone who works for NHTSA owns a sports car or a motorcycle or a hot rod or a dragster. They spend their spare time rebuilding and tuning and fiddling with them and riding around in and on them. I felt as if I'd gone to the DEA and found the staff making hash pipes.

These men read the automotive press, too—including an article I'd written about NHTSA's sudden-acceleration report in *Automobile* magazine, where I'd suggested that the National Highway Traffic Safety Administration be buried at a cloverleaf interchange with a DEAF CHILD sign driven through its heart. I think their feelings were hurt. So were mine, in a way. It's embarrassing to discover that bureaucrats are not only human but the same type of human as you are.

An interview with a NHTSA administrator was arranged, an interview "on background," which in Washington means not just "don't quote me" but "you didn't come here and I didn't say this." One of the craft mysteries of Washington journalism is how so many reporters generate so many stories by not meeting with people who say nothing.

The titleless, nameless but—as reporters always say—"highly placed" NHTSA functionary explained to me that all his car-safety experts were trained as automotive engineers. They came to work for DOT because they could get better jobs and more responsibility taking mechanical and electronic structures to pieces at NHTSA than they could get by spending fifteen years as the third assistant headlight bezel engineer at GM's panel-truck division.

This was the most disheartening thing I ever heard in Washington. This was much worse than hearing about government malfeasance, incompetence and corruption. When it's better for enthusiastic and ambitious professionals to go to work for a country's government than it is for them to go to work, the country is in trouble. Indian babus, British civil servants and eunuchs at the court of the emperor of China traveled this career path. In Japan and Singapore they probably make government jobs awful on purpose.

Then the NHTSA functionary gave me an explanation—the second most disheartening thing I ever heard in Washington—of why the DOT had to commission a multimillion-dollar study to prove that there is no such thing as sudden acceleration even though he and everyone else at DOT knew sudden-acceleration incidents didn't exist: SAIs would be reported to NHTSA. NHTSA would investigate them thoroughly. NHTSA would say they were caused by human error. And no one believed NHTSA.

The public would say, "Who, *me?* Make a mistake? Me, the *voter?*"

In a democracy we regular citizens don't make mistakes. We never get in a car and step on the wrong pedal and run people over. Somebody does these things to us. The Trilateral Commission or the Freemasons. Maybe it's part of the Iran-contra conspiracy or a big foreign corporation's fault. You can't blame us.

And, indeed, the DOT couldn't blame us. Even after completing its massive study of SAIs and showing that SAIs were all our own fault, the DOT couldn't quite bring itself to blame us.

Still, the study had to be done. Before the SAI study, blame evasion was getting out of hand. Newspapers were saying that sudden acceleration was caused by malfunctioning cruise-control mechanisms. The Center for Automotive Safety was claiming that radio waves made the computers in cars act up. Other ignorati pointed fingers at arcane goings-on within transmission housings and fuel-injection systems. Then, when "60 Minutes" did its piece on SAIs, Audis began jumping and leaping and cavorting in suburban driveways like killer whales at Sea World, and the sky turned legal-pad yellow with law suits.

The people at DOT had to make their investigation of sudden acceleration not because they're fools, but because we are. They have the job of making all known forms of conveyances as safe and harmless as Whiffle Balls, so that none of us will ever get hurt again by any bad old technology that we don't understand. But while they were engaged in that large task, they also had the impertinence to try to slip some sense of reason, scientific method and individual responsibility into the public consciousness.

WOULD YOU KILL YOUR MOTHER TO PAVE I-95?

The Federal Budget

Congresses, presidencies, Supreme Courts, the Department of This, the Department of That, the Department of All Get-Out—where does the money come from?

Federal spending is determined by a simple mathematical formula: $X - Y = $ A Huge Stink. X is what we want from the government, which is everything in the world. Y is how much we're willing to pay for this in taxes, which is not very much, and we're going to cheat on that. In 1990 the smell was particularly ripe. So much so that George Bush went, in a matter of weeks, from being the most popular unassassinated president in American history to somebody who might be dropped from the 1992 Quayle ticket.

To give the briefest version of an uninteresting quarrel, Bush was elected because he promised Y would not get bigger. Congress was elected because it promised X would grow. Congress also promised that Y would get bigger only for people who voted against the growth of X. After much empty posturing and other posturing that was full of it, X won. Congress passed a federal budget for fiscal 1991. That is, the country's purse was snatched by 282 yea-saying ballot leeches in the Senate and House, all of them pimping for reelection and eager to mortgage the nation's future so that they could slop the electorate at that hog trough called a voting booth.

And this with the permission, nay, the connivance of President George "You Doormat, You" Bush, the Carter of the nineties, a man with the same grasp of economic principles and knack for public relations as Imelda Marcos except, by the time George got through, *nobody* would be able to afford shoes.

The final budget compromise (which was a compromise in the sense that being bitten in half by a shark is a compromise with being swallowed whole) was "hammered out" (the Washington press corps uses the phrase "hammered out" as though sitting in chairs spending other people's money were a form of physical labor) at 6:58 A.M. on Saturday, October 27, 1990. The result of this congressional sleep-over was more than one thousand pages of legislation—a pile of paper ten inches thick, weighing twenty-four pounds and containing . . . Here's an interesting point: Nobody knew what it contained. No one, not one single person in the entire United States had read this document.

In the first place, it's impossible to read the federal budget. Richard Darman, the director of the Office of Management and Budget, actually said so in his introduction to the president's original 1991 budget proposal:

> It contains almost 190,000 accounts. At the rate of one per minute,
> eight hours per day, it would take over a year to reflect upon these!

In the second place, it was, no kidding, really impossible to read the federal budget because during the congressional debate on the final budget proposal there was only one copy in the House of Representatives (and, at twenty-four pounds, it wasn't being passed around very quickly).

On the Monday after the budget vote I called a congressional staff member friend of mine and asked for the new budget's final revenue and outlay figures.

"We don't know," he said. "We've been trying to find out all morning." He called me back a few hours later. "I just got a memo from the Budget Committee. It says tax revenues will be $20 billion more."

"More than what?" I said.

"It doesn't say."

* * *

95

There's only one thing we know for certain about the 1991 federal budget. It is bigger than the 1990 federal budget. And the 1992 budget will be bigger than 1991's. And so on ad infinitum.

You may be under the impression that the Gramm-Rudman-Hollings balanced-budget act of 1985 cut the federal budget in a noble attempt to save the American commonweal from bankruptcy.

Or you may be under the impression that the Reagan administration slashed the federal budget in a rascally attack upon the poor and disadvantaged.

But spending on social programs and income entitlements grew from $313 billion to $533 billion per year under Reagan—twice the increase of the Carter administration. And the total budget has gone from $946 billion to more than $1.23 trillion since Gramm-Rudman-Hollings was passed.

This is only what the government admits to. These are the figures we get after Congress and the president have performed all sorts of math-defying budget stunts. One trick is just to leave large chunks of spending off the budget. That's not much of a trick—no smoke or mirrors required—but you have to admire the brazenness of the thing.

Brazenly enough, it's called "off-budget spending." We taxpayers will spend about $2 billion next year giving credit subsidies to "government-sponsored enterprises"—the Federal Home Loan Mortgage Corporation, Farm Credit Banks, the Student Loan Marketing Association, etc.—but never mind; that $2 billion is off-budget. The Post Office was moved off-budget in 1990, allowing us to pretend that we didn't spend $2.3 billion on annoying, desultory mail service. And at least $10 billion of the savings-and-loan mess is not present, much less accounted for, in the 1991 budget.

Various government receipts are also put off-budget, including $314.5 billion in Social Security tax payments, which are so treated in hopes that we citizens won't notice how our retirement contributions are being poured down the same rathole as the rest of the federal revenues.

Other budget tricks are even dumber. In the 1990 budget the government moved one military payday back from a Monday to a Friday so that it fell in fiscal year 1989. Thus $2.9 billion was "saved" in 1990 and the Gramm-Rudman-Hollings deficit target was met because there's no G-R-H penalty for increasing the budget of a *previous* year. The 1990 budget bill also delayed certain Medicare payments to doctors and hospitals until fiscal 1991, "saving" another half a billion.

But even when we believe the lies and accept the legerdemain, the budget continues to grow. The official budget has, with one brief $1-billion pause in 1965, grown lustily for thirty-six years. It has grown much faster than inflation. In constant dollar terms, the budget has tripled since 1955. Meanwhile, population has increased only 65 percent. And disposable income has doubled, so you'd think people would need less from government. Yet federal spending, which was 10.6 percent of the gross national product at the height of the pinko New Deal, reached 23.7 percent of the GNP during the capitalist Reagan administration.

The budget grows because, like zygotes and suburban lawns, it was designed to do nothing else. Essential to the budget-making process is a concept called the baseline. If you or I were drawing up a budget, we would start with the sensible and traditional number zero. Not Congress. They start with the "current services baseline," which is an estimate of what it's going to cost the government to do what the government does when it does it again next year. Baselines for any given government program are generated by taking this year's costs and adding money for inflation, population growth, number of moron nephews that congressmen intend to appoint to jobs in that program and so forth. It is thus assumed that all government programs will grow.

Say the federal government has a program to teach self-esteem, motivation and marketable job skills to debutantes. Call it DebSelf. And say that Congress has authorized $100 million in 1990 DebSelf funding. 1991 budgeteers would then factor in 5 percent inflation, note a 10-percent increase in the population of girls who had coming-out parties in the Standard Metropolitan Statistical Areas' civilian labor force, assume a 10-percent increase in DebSelf program utilization based on Census Bureau surveys of cotillion-ball activity and give DebSelf a $125 million baseline. (Note that using the current services baseline reasoning, DebSelf grows to be a $10 billion program in twenty years.)

This is how a president can—using last year's actual budget figures—claim that he plans to increase spending on some piece of federal tomfoolery while congressmen in the opposing party can—using current services baseline budget figures—claim that the president plans to drastically cut the same identical folly. And they can both be telling the truth—or, to put it in layman's terms, lying. During the Reagan administration, Medicare spending increased by $48 billion, although there was a $49-billion cut in Medicare spending according to the current services baseline budget. And it's no use asking old people which figure is right—they're too busy bitching about Medicare to notice.

The federal budget also blimps up because of "mandatory program spending" on such things as farm price supports, Social Security payments, Aid to Families with Dependent Children, veterans benefits and the like. Mandatory programs normally have a current services baseline built into them in the form of cost-of-living adjustments (COLAs), and they are open by law to everyone who qualifies. Mandatory programs always grow larger than planned. If the government promises one can of cat food per week to every cat owned by an American or resident alien no matter what the price of cat food or how many cats are signed up, it breeds kittens. Mandatory programs account for more than 45 percent of all federal spending, twice what's spent on national defense.

One more cause of outlay tumescence is "unspent budget authority"—money that previous budgets promised would be spent in the future, and—uh-oh—the future is now. Usually this is money for enormous government projects that take years to build and then explode on the launch pad or are eight lanes wide and go right through the middle of a national scenic treasure.

If you combine mandatory program spending with unspent budget authority and interest on the national debt, you get a horrifying and truly gigantic thing that the government comes right out and calls "relatively uncontrollable spending." This is money disbursed by the U.S. Treasury automatically from now until the entire nation is reduced to washing windshields at stoplights. Of the $1.2 trillion in the 1990 budget, $903 billion was classified as relatively uncontrollable.

Of course, relatively uncontrollable spending is not uncontrollable, not even relatively. The president could introduce, and Congress could pass, legislation that would stop it all. But this would leave recipients of government booty—many of whom vote on a regular basis—grouchy. And we don't want that.

Where did the Gramm-Rudman-Hollings act stand in all this? No-where. G-R-H had nothing to do with government spending, only with the relationship between spending and revenue—it said there has to be some. And even if the government was naughty and spent more than G-R-H said it could, thereby setting off "across-the-board" spending cuts, whole vast areas of spending were immune: Indian tribal trust funds, the president's salary, Food Stamps, the Panama Canal Commission, Social Security, the Synthetic Fuels Corporation and more than 120 other programs ranging from FDIC to wool price supports. Congress could overrule the other cuts anyway. Gramm-Rudman-Hollings was like trying to stop smoking by hiding cigarettes from yourself and then leaving a note in your pocket telling you where they are.

The good news is I balanced the budget. It took me all morning but I did it. You're probably wondering how a middle-aged amateur—who is under the impression that double-entry bookkeeping is what you do when you have to explain that you spent the taxpayers' money on obscene performance art and who can't count three without removing a mitten—did this. It helps that I am not up for reelection to the position of being me. I also tried to avoid looking for ridiculous examples of government waste. This is the first mistake made by most budget critics. They page through the minutiae in the "Notes and Appendices to the U.S. Budget," sifting the "Detailed Budget Estimates by Agency" section until they come up with something like the Department of the Interior's Helium Fund. Which really exists:

> The Helium Act Amendments of 1960, Public Law 86-777 (50 U.S.C. 167), authorized activities necessary to provide sufficient helium to meet the current and foreseeable future needs of essential government activities.

Then the budget critics grow very indignant or start making dull, budget-critic-type helium jokes.

The Helium Fund is amazingly stupid, even by government standards, but it only costs around $19 million—.0015 percent of 1991 federal spending. This chapter would be as large as the budget itself if I tried to balance that budget by eliminating Helium Funds. And, if you think about it, running a Helium Fund is just the kind of thing our politicians *should* be doing. It's much less expensive and harmful to the nation than most of what they do, plus, with any luck, they'll float away.

The other secret to balancing the budget is to remember that all tax revenue is the result of holding a gun to somebody's head. Not paying taxes is against the law. If you don't pay your taxes, you'll be fined. If you don't pay the fine, you'll be jailed. If you try to escape from jail, you'll be shot. Thus, I—in my role as citizen and voter—am going to shoot you—in your role as taxpayer and ripe suck—if you don't pay your share of the national tab. Therefore, every time the government spends money on anything, you have to ask yourself, "Would I kill my kindly, gray-haired mother for this?" In the case of defense spending, the argument is simple: "Come on, Ma, everybody's in this together. If those Canadian hordes come down over the border, we'll all be dead meat. Pony up." In the case of helping cripples, orphans and blind people, the argument is almost as persuasive: "Mother, I know you don't know these people from Adam, but we've got five thousand years of Judeo-Christian-Muslim-Buddhist-Hindu-Confucian-animist-jungle-God morality going here. Fork over the dough." But day care doesn't fly: "You're paying for the next-door neighbor's baby-sitter, or it's curtains for you, Mom."

Armed with these tools of logic and ethics, I went to work. I took the original 1991 Bush budget because, as I mentioned, it was the only budget available in detailed form and, also, because—for all the budget-crisis noise—the Bush budget was not very different from the final budget approved by Congress. I turned to the "Federal Programs by Function" section, being careful to work in the "outlays" column, which shows what we really spend, rather than the "budget authority" column, which shows what we say we're spending. I ignored all appropriations of less than half a billion dollars—even NEA grants—as chump change. And I used the "unified budget" figures to avoid most off-budget spending dodges.

Then I cut all *international security assistance* (it hasn't generated any international security that I've noticed), all *foreign information and exchange activities* (if foreigners want information, they can subscribe to *Time*) and all *international-development* and *international financial program* funds (let

them spend their own money for a change). In fact, I cut the entire *international affairs* "budget function," as they call it, except for *food aid, refugee assistance* and *conduct of foreign affairs* (because the State Department gives us a way to ship Ivy League nitwits overseas). Total savings: $13.6 billion.

In the interest of the free-market ideology, for which America is a symbol worldwide, I cut the whole *energy* budget (leaving only the *Nuclear Regulatory Commission,* because it upsets tree huggers). Total savings: $2.7 billion.

In the *natural resources and environment* budget function I cut all spending for *water resources* (if they want water out West, they can go to the supermarket and get little bottles of it the way the rest of us do) and *recreational resources* (people who can afford Winnebagos can afford national park entrance fees). Total savings: $6.1 billion.

I cut all *farm income stabilization:* $12.7 billion. And I made the *Postal Service* pay for itself or sell out to Federal Express: $2.1 billion. I dumped savings-and-loan bailout costs (which are seriously underestimated in the Bush budget, by the way) back on the savings-and-loan industry, where they belong, and cleaned out the rest of the government's involvement in *mortgage credit and deposit insurance:* $13 billion. And I ditched *other advancement of commerce* (if it advances commerce so much, why isn't it paying for itself?): $2.1 billion.

I got rid of all *transportation* spending. Let 'em walk: $29.8 billion.

You may have noticed how well *community and regional development* has worked. Examine Detroit or downtown Newark. This is also the part of the budget where the government recently found $500,000 to restore Lawrence Welk's birthplace and make Strasburg, North Dakota, a tourist attraction. I eighty-sixed all of this except for disaster relief: $6.6 billion.

Per-pupil spending on public school education has increased by an inflation-adjusted 150 percent since 1970, while reading, science and math scores have continued to fall. The hell with the little bastards: $21.7 billion.

Training and employment is properly the concern of trainees and employers: $5.7 billion.

Insurance companies should gladly pay for *consumer and occupational health and safety:* $1.5 billion.

If I outlaw rent control and discriminatory zoning and give landlords

the right to evict criminals and deadbeats, I should be able to cut *housing assistance* in half: $8.8 billion.

And I just lowered food prices by eliminating farm subsidies, so I can also cut *food and nutrition assistance* by 50 percent: $11.7 billion.

If unemployment insurance is really insurance, it ought to at least break even: $18.6 billion.

So-called *other income security,* except what goes to refugees or the handicapped, probably does not meet the gun-to-mom's-head test: $19.9 billion.

And *federal litigative and judicial activities* should turn a profit in these days of white-collar crime and RICO seizures: $4.3 billion.

That's $180.9 billion cut from the budget already, and I haven't even touched defense or the larger entitlement programs. Next let me "means test"—that is throw the rich people out of—Social Security, federal and railroad employee pensions, Medicare and veterans' benefits. The government figures it loses $19.8 billion per year by making only half of Social Security benefits liable to income tax. That $19.8 billion is 8.25 percent of Social Security spending. I'll take that 8.25 percent plus another 8.25 percent from well-off geezers, and I'll bounce the richest 3.5 percent of the old farts from the system entirely. Thus, I can cut Social Security—and analogous programs—by 20 percent, for a savings of $71.9 billion.

National defense is tough. I like having lots of guns and bombs. Besides, you can always turn an aircraft carrier into a community center (plenty of space for basketball courts), but just try throwing a rehabilitated drug addict at a battalion of Iraqi tanks. Nonetheless, something has to go. I had friends at Kent State, so screw the National Guard: $8.4 billion. And I cut air force missile procurement by half since, for the moment, we don't have anyone to point those missiles at: $3.6 billion. I also cut military research and development by 25 percent and sent the weapons wonks back to playing Dungeons & Dragons on college computer systems: $9.2 billion. Military construction can stop (if they need money for paint or something, they can sell a few bases to the idiots at the savings-and-loan bailout's Resolution Trust Corporation, who'll buy anything): $5.5 billion. And I turned the Corps of Engineers over to private enterprise. Just let the Mississippi wash the Midwest away if people won't

pay their flood-control bills: $3.3 billion. This gives me $30 billion in military cuts.[1]

Add it all together, and I've cut $282.8 billion, leaving a federal budget of $950.5 billion, to which I apply O'Rourke's Circumcision Precept: You can take 10 percent off the top of *anything*. This gives me another $95 billion in cuts for a grand total of $337.8 billion in budget liposuction.

Now for revenues. I'm a real Republican (unlike some current presidents of the United States I could name), so I won't raise taxes; but since I'm temporarily in charge of the federal budget, I don't mind squeezing the bejabbers out of the people who pay them. There's an appendix to the federal budget called "Tax Expenditures." These are revenues that the government loses because of things you can deduct when you figure your income taxes. It takes fourteen pages just to list them all. Tax expenditures used to be called loopholes when they were mostly for rich people. And some tax expenditures still mainly benefit the rich: Keogh plans and deductions for mutual-fund-management expenses, for instance. These cost the government $2.1 billion. But most TEs are middle-class subsidies of one kind or another. The revenue lost to home-mortgage-interest deductions alone is $46.6 billion. Taxes not paid on employer-provided pension-plan contributions, insurance premiums and health benefits equal $89.8 billion. Deductions of state and local taxes cost another $34.3 billion. Combine these with untaxed interest on life-insurance savings, home-sale capital-gains exemptions, tax deferrals on savings-bond interest, employee stock plans, IRA contributions, child- and dependent-care expense deductions and earned income credit, and the middle-class take from tax expenditures is $209.9 billion.

Various businesses get another $6.9 billion in egregious tax expenditures—oil- and mineral-depletion allowances, indulgent accounting rules for corporations with branches overseas, special treatment for credit unions and timber companies and tax credits for investing in Puerto Rico and

---

[1]This paragraph was written before the commencement of Operation Desert Storm. Therefore, all these military spending cuts should be restored. Then let's hold the Saudi Arabians, Kuwaitis and whatever Iraqis remain alive at gunpoint and make them pay the costs.

Guam. And tax-free state and municipal bonds cost the federal government $21.6 billion. All told, at least $240.5 billion worth of tax expenditures should be just plain taxes.

Let us now compare the Bush budget with the PJ budget:

	BUSH BUDGET (in billions)	PJ BUDGET (in billions)
Outlays	$ 1,233.3	$ 855.5
Receipts	1,170.2	1,410.7
Surplus/(Deficit)	$ (63.1)	$ 555.2

Not only is the PJ budget balanced, but every taxpayer will get a $5,000 rebate check from the government this year, and next year there will be a 39-percent cut in all personal and corporate income tax rates. This ought to set the economic Waring blender on puree and make up for whatever minor inconveniences I've caused with lowered government spending and elimination of tax deductions. Was that so hard?

My budget cuts are (what fun) ham-fisted. But smarter, fairer people who know what they're talking about could cut this much and more. Why don't they? They don't because they don't quite have to yet. Despite the alleged panic over the budget of '91, the deficit and the national debt aren't big enough to wreck America. In the 1980s the annual budget deficit averaged 4.1 percent of the gross national product. This isn't so bad compared with the average deficit of 22.8 percent of GNP during World War II. And our total national debt now stands at 56 percent of the gross national product, not much worse than the 53 percent of GNP national debt we had at the end of the Great Depression. The problem is we aren't in a world war or a great depression (although both those options are being explored). In a relatively peaceful, relatively prosperous era, there's no excuse for these budget trends. There's also no likelihood that they'll change. The problem isn't a Congress that won't cut spending or a president who won't raise taxes. The problem is an American public with a bottomless sense of entitlement to federal money.

If just two of our federal programs—Social Security and Medicare—continue to expand at their present rate, they will cost the nation $1.4 trillion in 2010, more than the whole current budget.

Maybe our future economy will survive this expense. But is it wise in any case to put the awesome power of such spending in the hands of our silly government? This is not a matter of being conservative or liberal. Do you want Teddy Kennedy *or* Newt Gingrich to run your life? Yet everybody is asking for a federally mandated comprehensive national-health-care program.

Selfishness consumes our body politic. The eighteenth-century Scottish historian Alexander Tytler said:

> A democracy cannot exist as a permanent form of government. It can only exist until a majority of voters discover that they can vote themselves largess out of the public treasury.

Our modern federal government is spending $4,900 a year on every person in America. The average American household of 2.64 people receives almost $13,000 worth of federal benefits, services and protection per annum. These people would have to have a family income of $53,700 to pay as much in taxes as they get in goodies. Only 18.5 percent of the population has that kind of money. And only 4.8 percent of the population—12,228,000 people—file income tax returns showing more than $50,000 in adjusted gross income. Ninety-five percent of Americans are on the mooch.

OUR GOVERNMENT: WHAT THE FUCK DO THEY DO ALL DAY AND WHY DOES IT COST SO GODDAMNED MUCH MONEY?

The whole aim of practical politics is to keep the populace alarmed (and hence clamorous to be led to safety) by menacing it with an endless series of hobgoblins, all of them imaginary.

—H. L. Mencken

DRUG POLICY

The Whiffle Life

Our government needs to be reduced in size and scope. But we are not a nation of anarchists or even libertarians. There are some things the government should do—no matter what the cost or bother. The government should do something about drugs, shouldn't it? We all say so. Drugs are terrible, and the government should do something about them. We, as a nation, agree on this. So, what is our government doing?

One thing our government is doing is vigorously agreeing with us that it should be doing something. Among President Bush's first acts in office was to create a drug czar, whatever that was supposed to be. A couple of months later the president went on television and gave a drug-policy speech to the nation. In the middle of this speech President Bush reached under his desk and pulled out a Baggie with a lump of crack in it the size of a cellular phone and waved this cheerfully at the camera. It was the same kind of thing Captain Kangaroo always did on his Saturday morning show, and everybody in the television audience under the age of forty-five expected the president to say, "Bunny Rabbit, you leave those carrots alone." Instead, the president described his administration's new drug policy. The new drug policy was to hire more police officers and send them to prison in Bolivia, or something like that. (I must admit I wasn't listening too carefully.)

The Democrats vigorously agreed that the government should be doing something about drugs, too, and only disagreed with the president by reason of being more vigorous in their agreement. "A lot more of whatever needs doing needs to be done—let's spend, spend, spend," said Senator Joe Biden in a prime-time response to the Bush drug-policy speech. (I'm not using Senator Biden's own words here, but that's OK, because if you remember the 1988 presidential campaign, Joe doesn't use his own words either.) The Democrats were in favor of increased funding for treatment, though no very effective treatment for crack addiction exists. And they wanted more educaton. More education about what? Consumer economics? Maybe government experts could fan out across the ghettos and try to convince crack dealers that Mercedes 190s are overpriced; they'd get more for their money if they bought Saab 9000s.

This kind of energetic concurrence that the government should do something about drugs is part of a time-honored American tradition of getting hysterical over dope.

I can remember the antediluvian age of dope hysteria, when the occasional bebop musician's ownership of a Mary Jane cigarette threatened to turn every middle-class American teenager into a sex-crazed car thief. (This particular hysteria proved well-founded. Every middle-class American teenager did try marijuana and did become sex crazed—although no more car-thievish than usual.)

Then there was LSD, which was supposed to make you think you could fly. I remember it made you think you couldn't stand up, and mostly it was right. The much-predicted heavy precipitation of wingless adolescents—which caused people to move their cars out from under trees near hippie pads—failed to materialize.

The early-seventies heroin craze likewise petered out before emptying the nation's scout camps and Hi-Y chapters. And by the time PCP came along to make kids psychotic, kids were acting so psychotic anyway that who could tell the difference? The only unifying theme in these drug scares seemed to be an American public with a strong subconscious wish to be rid of its young people.

Crack is a drug for those who are already fucked up. In fact, getting fucked up is for those who are already fucked up. Nationwide, drug use is down 37 percent since 1985, according to the alarmist-in-chief George Bush's own figures. Crack use has shown few signs of infecting this nation's well blessed. County fairs will not be filled with holsteins that are bruised and bleeding because 4-H members went into milking frenzies while smoking rock. There isn't going to be a sudden dearth of nuclear physicists because Asian kids are selling their homework to buy vials.

Nor is crack some uniquely horrible concoction where one whiff turns you into a human drive-by shooting with a daily habit that costs as much as the Valdez oil spill. It's just cocaine. I've smoked free base, which is the couture version of crack. It felt great. Actually, it felt too great. It reminded me of that experiment you read about in college psychology textbooks, where a rat has an electrode inserted directly into the pleasure center of its brain, and then it pushes the little lever that activates the electrode and keeps pushing it and pushing it and pushing it until you have to read about the rat in a college psychology textbook.

Crack is, of course, pretty bad stuff. It's as though, after years of trying, we finally come up with a kind of dope that's as evil as the government (and our parents) said dope was. Most other drugs are self-limiting. If you drink, you act like hell. But if you keep drinking, you pass out. Then your battered wife sets fire to your bed, and Farrah Fawcett stars in a TV movie about your brief, sorry life.

Marijuana also has a built-in payback. Marijuana makes you acutely sensitive, and in this world, what worse punishment could there be?

Heroin turns people into amoral scuzz balls. But a heroin addict who gets his fix is well behaved, or dead (and you can't get any better behaved than that).

Cocaine is worse than heroin, but it's expensive, and—overexcited anti-drug TV commercials to the contrary—it's subtle. Cocaine is a long run for a short slide.

But crack has it all. It's cheap, addictive, makes you feel like Arnold Schwarzenegger and act like Abu Nidal, and it keeps you awake to take more. Maybe we *should* get hysterical about crack. Experiencing emotional excitability, excessive or uncontrolled feelings and motor disturbances is not, however, a very effective anti-drug strategy (although it did get rid of XTC).

If hysteria is no good, how about racism? Read the following sentences:

Crack is ruining America's inner cities.

Crack is killing policemen, overburdening courts and filling jails beyond capacity.

Crack is devastating thousands of families.

Crack is putting the lives and well-being of our children at risk.

Now delete the words "crack is" and insert the words "niggers are." Isn't this the secret message of the drug-free America campaign?

Hysteria is stupid, racism is wrong and both are useless. But if gross panic and finding a scapegoat—two of the most common political reactions to an intractable social problem—don't work, what *can* the government do?

One thing the government can do is get some information on the subject. I went to talk to Dr. Marc Galanter, professor of psychiatry and director of the Division of Alcoholism and Drug Abuse at the New York University–Bellevue Medical Center. Dr. Galanter assured me that the crack problem was legitimate, not just something New York City mayors, *Washington Post* reporters and screaming, abandoned, underweight babies born addicted to cocaine were making up. "From this vantage point it's a disaster," he said. "It's overwhelming the hospital. . . . Thirty percent of Bellevue psychiatric patients have cocaine problems. . . . Cocaine makes people paranoid, makes people kill each other—pharmacologically."

Dr. Galanter explained that there is no methadone for cocaine, no Antabuse. He said there were a few drugs—desipramine, amantadine, bromocriptine and an anticonvulsant called Tegretol—"which cut back on cocaine cravings in certain controlled settings."

"But will they work in the inner city?" Dr. Galanter asked with a shrug. "Drug-free therapeutic communities are effective for a certain number of patients. . . ." Dr. Galanter shrugged again.

Putting large numbers of semicriminal ghetto residents into drug-free therapeutic communities would be as expensive as sending them on a carnival cruise to Bermuda and about as politically popular. "We're opening a treatment program for crack at Bellevue," Dr. Galanter said. "We'll help a number of people, but the number of people who need to be helped . . ."

Dr. Galanter's thoughts wandered, I imagine, to that land where there's infinite funding and an infinite number of properly trained professionals to spend it and patients with the infinite wisdom to give a shit.

"Realistically," I said, "what can be done about drugs?"

"Realistically?" said Dr. Galanter, "we're going to end up doing what we're doing. Nobody has done much except follow the guy ahead of him. The point is making sure you don't look bad."

"What would you do if you were given the drug-czar job?" I asked. "I mean, besides not take it?"

"I'd make a big splash about something that was basically a side issue, such as assault rifles" (which is exactly what the first drug czar, William Bennett, did), "then wait for things to get better on their own and take credit for it" (which is exactly what the first drug czar did).

Things do get better on their own. Nothing, not even government, keeps getting worse forever. Dr. Galanter estimated that the crack problem would burn out after about ten years. "Because the people who take crack will be," he explained, "dead."

While the government is waiting for everyone to die, it can create government agencies and organizations, such as the drug czar's office, to combat the sale and use of illegal drugs. There are now a total of forty-one federal government organizations and agencies combating the sale and use of illegal drugs. The drug czar's Office of National Drug Control Policy is typical. The drug czar was given the responsibility for curing the entire nation's drug ills and was also given the same approximate civil authority as Ann Landers.

The drug czar is a general without soldiers. But the hell with metaphors, in the war against drugs we've got real generals without soldiers. We could send the marines to Latin America and put some holes in the blow lords. But we won't. It would upset our foreign policy. You know how it is when you've got a well-thought-out and carefully crafted foreign policy that consists of cuddling up to Pol Pot, apologizing for everything Israel does, abandoning the democratic opposition in China and congratulating Hafez Assad on his human rights record—you don't want to do anything to upset that.

Former Customs Commissioner William Von Raab calls the State Department "conscientious objectors in the war against drugs." Von Raab instituted the "zero tolerance" customs policy, which means you can kiss your yacht good-bye if customs agents find so much as a roach clip in your scuppers. He advocated shooting down drug-smuggling planes on sight and putting a price on the heads of drug traffickers. Von Raab is serious about drugs. He's also looking for work.

What the federal government really ends up doing about drugs is palming the problem off on local police departments. I went cruising for drug dealers with the District of Columbia police.

Past a certain hour of the night, when all the good people have gone—or been chased—indoors, the nation's capital turns into a life-style septic tank. It's strange to look at a well-populated street and know that everybody you see is doing something wrong. It's strange, in the first place, when a street is well populated at two in the morning. It's like ordinary life with the clock on backward, except nighttime people don't move the same way daytime people do. Nighttime people go in circles. The whores parade in wide rotations. The pipe-heads spin in tight loops. The drunks describe ellipses and figure eights. Or nighttime people don't go anywhere at all. The little kid lookouts sit stock still. There's a distinct walk to nowhere the dealers have—the self-enforced confidence of the pimp roll combined with leery, hinky, darting turns of the head that set a couple of pounds of gold "dope rope" swaying until you wonder if the fellow's neck vertebrae will hold. Then there's the dumb strut of the buyers—the asshole college kids, the stoner white trash from the trailer suburbs and the local jerks with the Third World briefcases blaring stuff they'd get arrested for saying if they said it without a beat. What you never see at night is any useful movement, such as somebody going to work or going to school or going home.

I was with the cops in squad cars, on stakeouts and at surveillance posts as they made their endless harvest of dope users and sellers, the perpetrators or perps. I saw the cops busting perps, chasing perps, wrestling perps to the ground. I watched perps being cuffed, perps being transported and perps being herded by the dozens into the precinct house.

The squad room looked like someplace you'd hold a grade-school class, except all the desks were teachers' desks. Each had a chain bolted to the front with a manacle on the end of the chain. And that's how the perps were fastened, like cockatoos to a perch, but with less amusing chatter. The only thing that resembled the world of TV cops was the typing—painful, cop-style typing with one thumb and two forefingers,

A modern arrest requires—thanks to the Supreme Court, which is *not* one of the forty-one federal government agencies and organizations combating the sale and use of illegal drugs—a stack of forms as thick as a Sunday *New York Times* "Arts and Leisure" section. And filling them out is as complicated as buying something at Bloomingdale's with an out-of-state check. A modern conviction requires just as much effort and tedium in court. The average DC cop spends twenty days of his month testifying or waiting to do so. The end result of the dangers, annoyances, delays, boredom and paper shuffling that go into a bust is . . . nothing. The perp is turned loose. Mostly the perp is turned loose right there in the precinct house. Mere possession of cocaine usually gets you a citation, a ticket, like you'd turned left on red with your nose. Get caught selling to the UCs, the undercover policemen, and you might have to stay in jail until tomorrow morning, which it practically is already by the time you're arrested. What you have to do to actually get put in jail and be kept in jail I didn't have the heart to ask.

I watched all this, and then I sat in an unmarked car and watched it begin all over with a fresh crop of perps rooster-walking around on the streets. I asked the officer behind the wheel if there wasn't maybe some wasted effort here. Wouldn't it be a lot less bothersome, hazardous and expensive to just legalize drugs? The policeman pointed to the crowd on the other side of the windshield. "We're talking scum here," he said. "Air should be illegal if they breathe it."

Several hours earlier I'd gone with the police to raid a crack house. They were using leased sedans and their private cars to keep from being "made" too quickly on the street. But every head turned as we drove through. You don't see brand-new cars like these in this neighborhood. That is, you don't see brand-new *cheap* cars. We should have come in BMWs.

It was a poor neighborhood, of course, a street of little houses, each with a double-bed-sized lawn. The houses mostly looked like hell, and there was trash spread all over the place. But a color-TV glow flickered through the window of every front room, and not a kid in sight was more than one degree behind the fashion curve. It's hard to get too wet and sentimental about poverty that wears hundred-dollar gym shoes.

In fact, this *wasn't* a poor neighborhood, not by the standards of history and the rest of the world. What it was, was a lousy neighborhood—littered, dilapidated and dangerous. There's been too much barbering about poverty and drugs, as though some pure, hopeless cause-and-effect relationship existed. As though if you fired Thurgood Marshall and took his bank account, he'd be cracking down in the Port Authority men's room tomorrow.

Yes, there were poor people who lived on this street, people working desperately to keep themselves fed and housed, people working long hours for low pay at lousy jobs—jobs such as being a District of Columbia police officer. But these weren't the people we'd come to see.

The crack house was not a sinister crib. Cabbages and turnips were being grown in the little front yard. The house was owned by a man and wife, the police said, whose grandson was using it as a base for takeout and consumption-on-the-premises. They'd busted the guy a couple of times already.

Twenty cops jumped out of the cars and went at the front and back doors with shoulders, shoes and battering rams, though I don't think either door was locked. Pistols were drawn, shotguns were waved and there was a great deal of yelling, "the police!" by the police. So many officers ran into the house that there was hardly room left for criminals. No criminals were home anyway, only the grandparents and a couple of large, nondescript nieces. The grandparents were not the gray, venerable type, but fairly young and very fat and dirty, though not so dirty as their house. Whatever criminal atmosphere the place had was overpowered by just atmosphere—a thick, low stink of old, permanent dirt.

The grandparents and nieces sat impassively on a busted couch in the grease-frescoed kitchen, not looking when a detective showed them the

search warrant and not listening when he read it aloud. The rest of the cops pulled the house apart. The floors were so covered with muss that you couldn't tell where the horrible linoleum ended and the loathsome rugs began. The walls were the hue of spoiled meat, and even the ceilings had turned that handled, scabby color of old schoolbook pages. The furniture was too bad to throw away. You wouldn't put it outside your house, not if you ever wanted to face your garbagemen again. Mattresses stained with Rorschach patterns of dried body fluids were flopped in each room, dirty clothing was piled everywhere and more dirty clothing was stuffed into plastic trash bags.

Every movement in the house opened a wellspring of cockroaches. Lifting one of the awful mattresses unleashed a plague of Egypt. I watched a policewoman who didn't look scared of much shrieking in the upstairs hall, jumping in panic, trying to knock the roaches out of her pants leg. Of course, once the policewoman had put the idea in their heads, all the officers began to feel "Brooklyn butterflies" headed north up their socks, and nobody could take three steps without stopping to shake a leg, until it looked like the police had given up their criminal investigation to dance the hokey-pokey.

The grandson's room was dirty, too, but it had decor—a Pier 1–type wicker and macrame wall hanging and a framed "BACKFIELD IN MOTION" poster of football-cheerleader behinds. There was too much stereo equipment in the room. Much more, the cops were quick to point out, than any of them owned. And there was even less fresh air here than in the rest of the house. It was midsummer and ninety degrees outside, but the room's one window had been carefully sealed with layers of dry-cleaning-bag plastic.

Unmarked cars were spread around the street in front of the house, parked the way cops park cars, which is any way they want. Some black-and-whites and a paddy wagon had pulled up, too. The neighbors were watching through their screen doors with the enthusiasm that all neighbors show for neighborhood trouble other than their own. Cops in uniform and cops in blue nylon raid jackets with "POLICE" stenciled big across the shoulders were milling among the cabbage heads in the front yard, cradling guns, smoking cigarettes and making P-U gestures at the house.

Down this law-clogged street comes a big, good-looking kid about

eighteen years old wearing a high-top fade haircut with four lines razored into the side. He's walking "the walk" and carrying a new stone-washed denim outfit under his arm. He makes right for the knot of policemen in the yard, and their heads pop around. This is the guy they came looking to get—the grandson for whom they have a warrant in their hands. But the cops can't get a word out before the kid says, "I lives here. Can I go in?"

Wham, and the grandson is against the side of the house, getting a pat-down that's just short of a beating while somebody reads, or rather hollers, his Miranda rights.

I'm an upright citizen, this week, anyway, and there's nothing and nobody in my home that's of interest to the law-enforcement profession. But I'll tell you, if I turned the corner into my street and saw two dozen cops with guns in front of my house, I'd be back around that corner very smartly and ambling away in a casual but highly rapid fashion and I would not stop ambling until I got to, say, Chicago.

The policeman next to me shook his head at the grandson. " 'I lives here,' " he mimicked. " 'Can I go in?' This boy's got something worse wrong than drugs."

You bet he does. This whole country's got something worse wrong than drugs. We are the richest nation in the world—richest in our weight class, anyway (get out of here, Brunei)—and you can't walk one block in any city in the United States without being accosted by wackos and soaks and insistent practitioners of that most rapidly expanding sector of the American service economy, beggary. One out of five American children is growing up needy, and 53 percent of needy kids have nothing for a father except a blind, microscopic, wiggle-tailed gamete that hasn't held a job since it got to the womb.

Drugs are an improvement on some of these problems. Who wouldn't rather have a couple of plump, flaky lines on a mirror and half a disco biscuit than lead the lives these people are leading? I, for one, couldn't go back in that crack house without taking some kind of drug. Dramamine, anyway. Drugs are the answer, after all, if the question is, "How can I get high as a kite?" or, "How can I make money without working?"

*   *   *

What this country has wrong that's worse than drugs is that we're not serious. We're not serious about the drug problems, we're not serious about the problems causing the drug problem and we're not serious about anything else either. We have a child welfare system that pays women to have illegitimate children. We have big city property laws where if you buy a piece of rental property, you're penalized with a price freeze, but if you wreck a piece of rental property, no force on earth can evict you. When somebody screams obscenities at the corner lamppost and relieves himself on your front steps, you can't get that person committed to a mental hospital. But if you walk through the park after 8:00 P.M., all your friends call you crazy. We are not a serious nation.

Personally, I don't think all drugs-of-pleasure should be illegal. I'm not even sure if it's much use making any of them against the law. But it is one more measure of our lack of seriousness that we won't dispassionately investigate or rationally debate which drugs do what damage and whether or how much of that damage is the result of criminalization. We'd rather work ourselves into a screaming fit of puritanism and then go home and take a pill.

If a drug-free America is such a good idea, why aren't members of the House of Representatives taking drug tests? Why isn't the U.S. Senate pissing into jars on C-Span? "Get serious" is the phrase I heard a hundred times from cops, DEA men, customs agents and people living in drug-soaked neighborhoods. I'd be talking to them and they'd just start yelling, not at me, but just yelling.

Even the receptionist in a Washington city councilman's office yelled—this in a town whose very mayor was arrested for taking drugs. I told her I wanted to interview somebody in the District of Columbia government about the federal government's drug policy, and she exploded. "Those *doughboys* need to talk to the regular people," she said, "the minimum-wage people who have to be up at 5:00 A.M., who don't get home until 1:00 A.M., who are living in deteriorating neighborhoods, who've been forced out of gentrifying neighborhoods."

Mario Perez, the public information officer in the DEA's Washington field office, did the same thing, suddenly boiling over in the middle of some boring recitation of statistics: "The U.S. public and government are not getting serious about drugs—no user accountability, no hitting anybody in the pocketbook, and the ACLU's fighting drug-user evictions from public housing."

Dick Weart, acting director of Public Affairs at Customs, yelled about the drug destruction of families and social fabric: "This is the way ancient Rome went down the tubes." He said the Customs Service did not want more money or manpower—an amazing, unheard-of thing for a person in government to say. "We just want people to get serious," he said.

I asked Mike Mullin, deputy chief of the DEA's Cocaine Desk, "Do you want more agents? More judges? A bigger budget?"

"Not necessarily," he said.

So that was twice I'd heard a federal bureaucrat not ask for money. This *is* serious. "What we want from the taxpayers is *continual* cooperation!" said Mullin.

"Everybody wants to go to heaven," said the DEA's Perez, "But nobody wants to die."

I would have liked to say something comforting to these very furious people, but who am I to talk? The only time I've ever been serious about drugs was back in college, when I seriously took a whole bunch of them. And I still take drugs now and then. Like most Americans I'm perfectly willing to tell the government where to go and then stand out in the road to keep it from getting there.

While I was engaged in this guilty meditation and, at the same time, was trying to make sense out of my notes and interviews about government drug policy, I got a phone call from a friend. He said, right on cue, "My kid got busted for selling heroin."

"Oh, Christ," I said, because my friend's kid is a good kid—a spoiled and self-destructive brat, maybe, but a *good* spoiled and self-destructive brat, not mean or anything. "Is he OK?" I said. "Did you get him out on bail all right?"

"Yeah, yeah, yeah," said my friend. "He's staying with his mother."

"Well, what's the prognosis?"

"I've got about five lawyers and three psychiatrists on it," said my friend, "and what we're trying to do is, you know, get him off the 'punishment track' and onto the 'treatment track.' They figure if he pleads down to simple possession, they can get him into a halfway house or maybe probation, but he's got a couple of priors." (Interesting how twenty-five years of hipness in America has taught ordinary middle-class parents like my friend a vocabulary once known only to cops, criminals and criminal lawyers.)

My friend and I talked for a while about drug therapy and whether it was better to send the kid off to East Butthole, Minnesota, to dry out or put him on methadone or cut his allowance or what. And it wasn't until I'd hung up that I realized what we'd been saying. My friend's kid didn't need to suffer any consequences, not serious consequences, anyway. After all, addiction is a sickness and he needs treatment. Besides, he's got personal problems and comes from a broken home. It's not like he's a criminal or anything. If he were a criminal, he'd be poorer and darker skinned.

My friend's kid lives in a well-padded little universe, a world with no sharp edges or hard surfaces. It's the Whiffle Ball again. The kid leads a Whiffle Life, and so does my friend and so do I.

We're Americans. These are modern times. Nothing bad is going to happen to us. If we get fired, it's not failure; it's a midlife vocational reassessment. If we screw up a marriage, we can get another one. There's no shame in divorce. Day care will take the kids, and the ex-wife can go back to the career she was bitching about leaving. If we get convicted of a crime, we'll go to tennis prison and probably not even that. We'll just have to putz around doing community service for a while. Or maybe we can tearfully confess everything, join a support group and get off the hook by listening to shrinks tell us we don't like ourselves enough. Hell, play our cards right, and we can get a book contract out of it. We don't have to be serious about the drug problem—or anything else.

And what about the kid at the crack house? The kid who walked right up to the police and said, "I lives here. Can I go in?" It's the same for him. Except in his case, instead of nothing bad happening, no matter what he does, it's nothing good. Why should he care if he gets arrested? Is it going to go on his record so he won't get into med school? You think he's worried about going to jail? I was in his home—jail is cleaner. He can see all his friends in jail. And he's going to be in jail for about ten minutes anyway.

As soon as he gets out, he can tell everybody how cool it was that he walked right up to the police and said, "I lives here. Can I go in?"

Maybe the drug laws should be changed. But drug laws aren't immoral laws the way the laws of segregation were. They aren't the laws of an unjust system the way the laws of East Germany were. Drug laws don't cry out for acts of civil disobedience. Read Thoreau, Gandhi and Martin Luther King, and you won't find any of them going to jail or fasting or getting smacked on the head so mankind can do tootski.

This is a democracy. We're free to change what our government does any time we want. All we have to do is vote on it. In the meantime, if people like me—rich, white, privileged, happy—cannot even bother to abide by the legal standards of their freely constituted society, of a society that has provided them with everything a civilization can be expected to provide, then those people deserve their drug problems and everybody else's drug problems, too. They deserve—*I* deserve—to have every crack addict in the country knocking on the front door saying, "I lives here. Can I go in?"

POVERTY POLICY

How to Endow Privation

OK, the federal government can't do anything about drugs. But it really should do something about poverty. Or has it already?

I went to a federal low-income housing project in Newark, New Jersey, and just going inside and climbing the stairs was more exposure to questions of poverty policy than most people can stand and not pass out. The stairwell was a cascade of filth, a spillway of human urine and unidentifiable putrefying matter. There was nothing on these steps wholesome enough to call trash. It would have cheered me up to see anything as vibrant as a rat. The housing project was one of those War on Poverty, a-Hand-Not-a-Handout, Great Society, Give-a-Damn edifices that they tore down a perfectly good slum to build in the 1960s. The stairwell was lighted by dim, bagel-shaped, twenty-two-watt fluorescent tubes—"landlord halos"—each protected by a steel cage lag-bolted to the reinforced-concrete ceiling. Only the strongest and most purposeful vandals could destroy light fixtures like these, but that's the kind of vandals this housing project has, and dangling electric wires and foot-wide craters in the cement marked the former location of each lamp. There was some illumination, however, from a large puddle of lighter fluid blazing away on the third-story landing, and phlegm-colored sun shone through a befouled skylight seven stories above.

I don't know what, or if, the stairwell walls had once been painted. I couldn't even tell what they were made of. Smoke, dirt, spray paint and marker-pen scribbling were caked on every surface in a cover-all hue of defeat and exasperation, the same shade small children achieve with their first set of watercolors. Graffitied names and signs overlapped, layered in a density of senselessness to do a Yale semiotics professor proud. The only scrap of writing I could make out was in the lobby by the front door: "THE FUCK-UP POSSIE," spelled thus, with one more fuck-up.

It should have been thought provoking to climb those stairs, but it wasn't. People often say a place is "too noisy to think." This place was too smelly. What I thought later, however, was that I have been to some dirty, hapless, hungry, out-of-luck spots in twenty years of journalism. I've been to Beirut, where people were living in holes scooped out of rubble. I've been to the Manila city dump, where people were living in holes scooped out of garbage. And I've been to villages in El Salvador where people weren't living at all anymore because they'd been shot. I've been to rioting Soweto shantytowns and besieged Gaza Strip refugee camps and half-starved *contra* outposts in the jungles of Honduras, and I've never been to a place I would less rather live than this housing project in New Jersey.

I had other, more airy, thoughts, too—about the symbolism of climbing stairs, about "Up on the Roof" by the Drifters and *Fiddler on the Roof* with Tevye singing about his dream house in "If I Were a Rich Man":

> *There would be one long staircase just going up,*
> *And one even longer coming down*
> *And one more leading nowhere just for show.*

And I was thinking about the books I'd been buying lately in secondhand bookstores, books from thirty years ago, when poverty as we know it was just being invented. I've got Michael Harrington's *The Other America*, which explained that the United States had a special, "hidden," kind of poverty that nobody had noticed. And I've got *The Negro in the City* from the Washington Square Press "Problems of American Society" series, the very title of which oozes condescension. And I've got a pamphlet by one Maxwell Stewart called *The Poor among Us—Challenge and Opportunity,* as though poverty were some kind of marketing strategy. Many of these books are inscribed on the flyleaves with the earnestly penciled names of college students. My copy of future senator Moynihan's famous tract, *The Negro Family: The Case for National Action,* says,

> *Pat O'Rourke*
> *321 McBride Hall*

And all these books are now for sale in secondhand bookstores—very cheap.

There is no poverty in America. I can prove it mathematically. According to Census Bureau statistics collected in a government publication called *Poverty in the United States*—which comes with a depressing set of three-ring-binder holes already punched in its cover and ready for use by the kind of people who fill three-ring binders with statistics about poverty—there are about 32.5 million poor people in the U.S. Some 25.7 million of these poor people live in some 7.1 million poor families, and the remaining 6.8 million ask me for fifty cents every day on my way to work.

Poor families have an average income deficit of $4,600. In other words, their annual household income is, on average, $4,600 below the official government poverty line. The average income deficit of poor people who live alone is $2,600. Income being counted here includes all the cash making its way to the person or persons in question: paychecks, welfare payments, veterans' benefits, Social Security, etc. Now if we multiply 7,100,000 by $4,600 and add 6,800,000 times $2,600, we will . . . make our pocket calculators flash in that irksome way they do when we calculate figures too grand for cheap Taiwanese circuitry. One problem with delving into government-sized numbers is that, unless you go out and buy a science-geek calculator with logarithmic cube-root functions and so forth, you end up with paper and pencil doing those giant, wedding-cake-shaped arithmetic problems that you thought you'd never see again when you left fifth grade.

After a lot of scribbling and erasing and memory lapses about the part of the multiplication table beyond seven sevens, we see that the national income deficit is about $50.3 billion. This is the amount of money it would take to make all the poor people in the country unpoor. In that great poker game that is America, the pot is fifty big ones light.

Or so says *Poverty in the United States.* Yet if we look in another government publication, *Budget of the United States Government, Fiscal Year 1991,* we see that some very large amounts of money have been spent on the poor: $15.7 billion for Food Stamps; $2.1 billion for the Special Supplementary Food Program for Women, Infants and Children; $1.9 billion for Head Start. None of this counts as income in the Census Bureau poverty statistics, because it isn't cash. But there it is: $1.4 billion for Low Income Home Energy Assistance, $3.2 billion for community Planning and Development, $6.9 billion for something called Human Development Services, $7.3 billion for subsidized housing like that project in Newark and a whopping $40.2 billion for Medicaid. You could argue about the value of this or that part of the package, but if any of us got these things from our employers, the IRS would tax us.

And I have by no means listed all the charity in the federal budget. I haven't mentioned Rural Electrification, the Legal Services Corporation, the Appalachian Regional Commission or the Alcohol, Drug Abuse and Mental Health Administration.

The Heritage Foundation, a conservative policy institute in Washington, argues that there is $98 billion in government spending on low income and elderly persons that is not counted as income in Census Bureau poverty statistics. Thus, $50.3 billion minus $98 billion equals no poverty in America, QED.

There also can't be poverty in America because, according to the government's own Congressional Research Service, combined federal, state and local antipoverty spending is $126 billion per year. This amounts to $3,876.92 per poor person. Thus the average poor family, with its mean size of 3.54 people, gets $13,724.31 worth of government help, which puts those poor people above the official poverty line ($12,092 for a family of four). And if there's one minimum-wage earner in that ménage—bringing home, say, $8,500 per annum (little enough to leave all poverty benefits available)—the theoretical compensation that our theoretical poor family is theoretically getting comes within one good stereo system of the after-tax income for an average American family.

(As for poor people who live alone, if they wish to make up the difference between $3,876.92 in government aid and the $5,068 government poverty line for single-person households, they need only find twelve returnable beverage cans per hour—assuming a forty-hour work week and allowing for two weeks of vacation in the summer.)

There's certainly no poverty in America, historically speaking. According to social scientist Charles Murray, poor families in the United States now have a median cash income (using constant 1987 dollars and the Census Bureau income definition) equal to 124 percent of what a middle-class American family had in 1900. And in the high-rolling 1920s, almost two thirds of U.S. households had incomes that would be considered below poverty level today. I'm not saying it's easy to support a family of four on $12,092 a year. And $5,068 will not make you the guy Marla Maples bats her eyes at in the bar. But the biblical injunction is to clothe the naked, not style them.

In comparative terms, there's no poverty in America by a long shot. Heritage Foundation political scientist Robert Rector has worked up figures showing that when the official U.S. measure of poverty was developed in 1963, a poor American family had an income twenty-nine times greater than the average per capita income in the rest of the world. An individual American could make more money than 93 percent of the other people on the planet and still be considered poor. Economist George Gilder has pointed out that 40 percent of the poor people in America own their own homes, more than 80 percent possess telephones and color televisions (not to mention large, amazingly loud portable tape players), the majority have cars and an American poor person has twice as much housing space as an average Japanese. In fact, some 22,000 "poor" American households have a heated swimming pool or a Jacuzzi. And I've got a big, technical, chart-and-graph-laden academic paper by Harvard Center for Population Studies researcher Nick Eberstadt to prove that America's poor feed themselves on 19 percent of their cash income—as compared with 18 percent for all Americans and over 30 percent for people living in Italy or Japan.

OK, so there's no poverty in America. Then what was that back in Newark? I don't know.

And not only don't I know, there's an entire cabinet-level department of the federal government—Health and Human Services—that's clueless. And another—Housing and Urban Development—that's baffled, too. Not to mention Congress, which doesn't have the slightest. And the president— it beats his pair of jacks. The experts who wrote those 1960s books on poverty and told people what to do about it—they don't know. The people who read those books and did those things—they don't know either. Nobody knows why places like the Newark housing project continue to exist in America.

Charles Murray, in his 1984 book on the failure of poverty programs, *Losing Ground,* tried to calculate the grand total of all types of government spending intended to relieve and/or eliminate poverty. Murray added together Social Security, Supplemental Security Income, Aid to Families with Dependent Children, Unemployment Insurance, Medicaid, Medicare, Food Stamps and the principal low-income housing programs and said that total expenditures have amounted to (in 1980 dollars) over $100 billion a year from the late sixties until the middle seventies and more than $200 billion a year since. That's $3,800,000,000,000—enough to give every poor person in America $117,000 to start his own war on poverty. And the spending of this truly vast amount of money—an amount equal to the nation's gross national product in 1987—has left everybody just sitting around slack jawed and dumbstruck, staring into the maw of that most extraordinary paradox: *You can't get rid of poverty by giving people money.*

I wanted a good look at this poverty we don't have and can't cure, so I called Curtis Sliwa, founder of the Guardian Angels. The Guardian Angels are, like Batman, Miss Marple and the Baker Street Irregulars, unarmed amateur fighters of crime. Such groups are ubiquitous in popular fiction but never exist in real life. Unarmed amateur crime fighting would be useless in a lawful society and suicidal in a lawless one. In America, however, we have managed to produce a combination of vandalized wealth and spoiled want, police legalism and ACLU firepower that makes something as fundamentally absurd as the Guardian Angels not only possible but a godsend.

And it says a lot about the nature of American poverty that I went to see it with a group of young men trained in the martial arts and operating under military-style discipline instead of with a social worker.

Correct choice, incidentally. We got out of the subway in the Mott Haven section of New York's South Bronx just as some fellow down the block was shot stepping into his Cadillac. He was carrying a gun. Obviously his assailant was, too. And so were all the witnesses on the street. *"Everybody* had a gun," a cop said later, stringing yellow "crime scene" tape around the Coup de Ville.

Mott Haven was once a district of substantial apartment houses, comfortable if not luxurious, the tract homes of their day. These sheltered the Jewish middle classes on their way from the Lower East Side to White Plains. Now the buildings are in various stages of decomposition, ranging from neglected paint to flattened rubble. Abandoned buildings are office space for the local criminals, who deal almost entirely in drugs. (There's not much felonious creativity in a modern slum.) Scattered among the remaining turn-of-the-century structures and the empty lots piled with trash are various housing projects with large, ill-lighted areas of "public" space, dead to all traffic and commercial activity. Squalor and overcrowding are often spoken of as almost a single phenomenon, but in New York's poor neighborhoods the lower the population density, the greater the filth and crime.

The Guardian Angels walked through this neighborhood in single file looking for muggers and drug users. The Angels got handshakes, thumbs-up signals and loud shouts of encouragement from the old people. Women flirted with them. Little kids wanted to know how old they had to be to join. But the young men looked away or yelled—from a distance—*"maricon"* or "Charlie's Angels." It was interesting, the percentage of these young men who were visibly drunk at nine in the evening—100. But it was also interesting to look through lighted windows here, in the streets Tom Wolfe picked to terrify his Mercedes-driving anti-hero in *The Bonfire of the Vanities,* and see freshly painted walls and bright curtains, pictures of Christ and the Madonna (the one who *didn't* get her video banned from MTV), cooing women with crying babies, families clearing away supper plates and kids eating ice cream in front of the TV—interesting to see how much tame and ordinary life goes on in the notorious South Bronx.

We walked on through the odd landscape, with its equal parts of the depraved, the deserted and the normal, down to one more decayed apartment house with the Bruckner Elevated Expressway nearly running through its back hall. The Guardian Angels had helped squatters here resist an eviction order. The building was clean but an utter wreck, and the squatters' small-time attempts at big-time repairs hadn't helped. The people in the building to whom I talked—an earnest sculptor, a couple belonging to some Muslim-type religious group and a neo-hippie—had a complicated tale of woe.

The building's landlord had offered tenants cheap apartments in return for help repairing the building, a so-called sweat-equity deal. But the leases the tenants signed weren't legally binding because the corporation that actually owned the building hadn't paid property taxes in ten years. Then the city took over. New York has so many laws about rent control, occupancy permits, real estate transfers, co-op conversions and so forth that a special housing court is needed to sort it all out. A housing-court judge appointed an administrator to run the building. The tenants went to another city agency, the Department of Housing, Preservation and Development, which promised them that in return for an enormous amount of bureaucratic frog-walking, they'd be able to buy the building themselves. But while the tenants tried to repair the building they thought they were buying, the court-appointed administrator went into cahoots with a real estate speculator who obtained the building's mortgage, paid off the back taxes and got the tenants (now squatters) evicted by the same housing-court judge who'd appointed the administrator.

If you've ever been to New York and wondered how a city where a decent apartment is almost impossible to find got mile after mile of abandoned, semi-abandoned and eminently abandonable apartment buildings, this is one of the ways it's done.

Mott Haven is by no means the worst section of the South Bronx. That's probably Hunt's Point, where we went next.

Riding with the DC police, I'd been in neighborhoods where there was a lot of drug use and even in neighborhoods where drug use was the dominant factor, more important in shaping the environment than weather or wealth. But there are parts of Hunt's Point where the actual numerical majority of the residents are drugged to the eyes. Hunt's Point doesn't look much worse than other lousy neighborhoods, but the people do—dirty, skinny, disordered base-heads yelling at each other and us and people who aren't there. American slums are usually stylish places, their residents far up the fashion scale of evolution from the sack-assed, Brooks Brothered princes of Wall Street. But in the crack neighborhoods people are still wearing whatever they happened to have on at the moment the crack craze hit.

Here the women, too, jeered the Guardian Angels, and when our group had passed one gaggle of druggies on the corner of Hunt's Point Avenue and Lafayette, bottles and brick-halves were thrown at our backs. The Guardian Angels held their pace and disdained to duck or look over their shoulders as stuff smashed onto the sidewalk around them.

Farther down Hunt's Point Avenue the Angels' patrol leader, José Miller ("GI Joe"), went up to an old car hood leaning against a burned-out building and pulled it away to reveal a scarecrow-shaped addict piping down. José smashed the pipe. On the next block the Angels took drugs away from several large guys in an alley. The largest of the guys feigned a threatening gesture at the Angels, then rounded on his fellows shouting, "Just walk away! Just walk away! They got . . ." He pointed at the Guardian Angels. "They got . . . They got . . ." He couldn't seem to think what it was the Angels had that justified his backing down. "Just walk away!" he yelled and walked away.

Around the corner on Casanova Street, near the Spofford Juvenile Detention Center, a woman on a porch stoop said crack addicts were smoking in the empty building next door. The Guardian Angels ran into the building with no caution and not enough flashlights, leaping across abysmal pits left by missing steps in the stairwells and pounding down wrecked hallways through smashed doorframes into black, stinking rooms full of burned mattresses and human shit. But the addicts had fled.

The building hadn't been derelict long. You could tell because only half the copper plumbing had been ripped out to sell for scrap. I found someone's photo album lying in the muddy courtyard. Snapshots of weddings and christenings and first communions had been carefully arranged beneath sheets of clear plastic and then just left in the dirt. It was the kind of orphaned possession you might find in the wake of a tornado or after a war.

José wanted to show me a couple of wood-frame houses on Casanova that the Angels had raided repeatedly. But when we got there, the houses were gone. The night-shift workers at a freight depot across the street said somebody had taken a bulldozer from a road repair site last weekend and crushed the homes. "We're beginning to have an effect," said José. Maybe. Or maybe not. In the gutter in front of the razed crack houses was a brand-new Porsche 928 flipped on its back and wadded like Kleenex.

The next afternoon I went with Curtis Sliwa to the Emil Gelber public housing project in Perth Amboy, New Jersey. The project rose, like a nine-story beige brick growth, from the middle of a blue-collar neighborhood of small frame houses with donkey planters and plaster elves in the yards. It was one of those neighborhoods built in the 1920s for that 60 percent of the population that would be considered poor today, a neighborhood like my father grew up in, except this neighborhood didn't have the political clout or requisite number of deer rifles and duck guns to keep a housing project from being built in the middle of it.

The Guardian Angels had been asked by the Gelber project's residents and by the Perth Amboy Housing Authority to come do something about the druggies and thugs who'd overrun the place. Four Guardian Angels were now living full-time in one of the project's apartments.

Curtis Sliwa explained to me why housing projects offer such powerful attractions to crime. A large percentage of public-housing tenants are, he said, welfare mothers—women with little money, lots of kids, no husband, not much future and minimum opportunities for leisure-time fun. Housing projects are girlfriend farms for drug dealers. The women living there on Aid to Families with Dependent Children, Food Stamps and daytime television are ready recipients of sweet talk, not to mention cash. The drug dealer comes in and Romeos around in his gold knuckle-rings and moon-boot basketball shoes. He tells the lady of the house that he'll give her three or four hundred dollars a month if she and the kids will just make themselves scarce every so often so he can do a little business. "The woman gets the money—once," said Sliwa. "After a month she finds herself addicted, intimidated, a prisoner in her own home, if she's got any home left. Then there are the kids in the projects, hundreds of kids all over the place, the Huckleberrys. The dealers recruit them as lookouts and runners and whatnot."

The Guardian Angels, however, had so far been unable to recruit anyone from the Gelber project.

The project's stairwells (if you've spent any time in public housing, you don't even bother to check whether the elevators are working) were better than that stairwell in Newark. These were just covered with graffiti and stank of piss, and nothing was the matter with the light fixtures except all the bulbs were broken.

The upstairs hallways were dirty and lined neck-high in Double-Bubble pink ceramic tile beneath paint in that special shade of psychiatric-ward green that appears everywhere in the lives of poor people. I think even the rainbows over the ghetto include only the portion of the light spectrum that falls between blue and yellow.

But the apartment the Angels were living in was clean and white and not bad-sized—three bedrooms, a bath and a living-dining-kitchen area reminiscent, more or less, of a small SoHo loft. Even if you filled the apartment with Mom, Grandma and three or four kids, there would still be freshly graduated MBAs living in Manhattan with less space and air. Nonetheless, there was something subtly horrible, a rarefied awfulness, about the place. True ugliness, like true beauty, is all in the details—details such as the gooseneck grease trap from the bathtub in the apartment upstairs, which protruded in a chrome dip through this apartment's low ceiling, a hemorrhoid of plumbing overhead. The apartment walls were all cast concrete—cold as a brass truss in the winter and sweating like a pitcher of iced tea on this particular hot spring day. The speckled brown linoleum was intended, I'm sure, to not show dirt, and it accomplished this by looking exactly like something very dirty. The windows were the steel casement type, into which it's almost impossible to fit an air conditioner, and the windowpanes had been replaced with Plexiglas to thwart the rock-throwing pleasures of the local little ones. The Plexiglas was fogged and scratched and lent a raw-clam color to the light in the apartment.

The place was immune to personalization. Linoleum over cement is difficult to carpet. Ordinary paint won't hold on concrete walls, and even hanging a picture on them requires power tools and molly bolts. Such walls, of course, cannot be moved, and, anyway, the government owns the rooms, and you aren't allowed to change them. The apartment was an aesthetic version of the Elizabethan torture device, the cell of little ease, where the occupant could neither stand nor sit nor lie down. Here the occupant could neither remodel nor redecorate nor—given the cost of housing in the New York area—move.

We went, next, from the depressing Perth Amboy housing project to the loathsome and terrifying project in Newark. The Newark tenants were a cheerful and welcoming bunch, however, all standing around having a few beers in the relatively fresh air next to a gigantic garbage dumpster.

Like the squatters in Mott Haven, the residents of the Newark project were full of complaints against various government agencies, which seem simultaneously to control every aspect of poor people's lives and to pay no attention whatsoever to poor people. The Newark tenants beefed about the police department, the housing authority, the welfare office—about the "thems" in general. Hell is other people, as Jean-Paul Sartre pointed out (especially true, by the way, for someone with Simone de Beauvoir around the house), and other people—strangers; officials; tired, irritable bureau-crats—loom large in the lives of the poor.

The Newark gripes were simpler, though, than the lawyer-boggling Mott Haven bellyaches. "The housing authority, they treat us like a dog," as one woman who'd lived in the Newark project for thirteen years put it. This was an untruth. There are laws about keeping dogs in places like these. And she described to me how, whenever someone was evicted, the housing authority would weld the door of that apartment shut, leaving whatever food and garbage was inside to rot until the project was a vertical Hamelin-town of rats and a brood lodge for bugs that could play defense for the Giants. From what I gathered, the Newark Housing Authority is trying to empty this project. Although what they intend to empty it into I don't know, since most of Newark's inexpensive housing was obliterated to make room for projects like these.

On the other hand, nobody at the project was rushing to take any blame for its condition. In the other awful places I've been to in the world, people were making the best of their destitution, sticking a brightly painted statue of Jesus in front of their hovel if they could or tacking a handsome photograph of the ayatollah to their bullet-riddled wall. Not here. Visiting the Newark housing project was like going into a warring Beirut neighborhood and finding the residents firing artillery shells straight up into the air to land back on their own heads.

I tried the conservative current wisdom, the Jack Kemp-style privatization and empowerment ideas on the woman who'd lived here for thirteen years.

"What if," I said, "you and the other tenants had a chance to buy your apartments, no down payment, with mortgage and maintenance no higher than the rent you're paying now. Then you could control the building, get rid of muggers and drug addicts and order repairs and renovations yourself."

"I'm not going for any of that," said the woman.

"But you'd own something," I said, "You'd be building equity. You could sell it later and make a profit."

"I'm not going for any of that," said the woman.

"But you wouldn't be at the mercy of the housing authority, the city council, all those people. You'd be a property owner. You could tell *them* what to do." And I told her about various other advantages that would accrue to her and her family through privatization—all very good arguments for the case, I'm sure.

The woman looked up at this seven-story sewer in the sky that she lived in and looked back at me like I was a big idiot and said, "I'm not going for any of that."

My own family was poor when I was a kid, though I didn't know it; I just thought we were broke. My father died, and my mother married a drunken bum who shortly thereafter died himself. Then my mother got cancer. But I honestly didn't know we were poor until just now, when I was researching poverty levels. I was looking through some family records, trying to figure out—for comparison's sake—how much money my family had when I was growing up in the sixties, and I came across the student-loan application that my mother had filled out for me. My mother's total income in 1966 was $4,220, minus uninsured medical costs of $1,213. This put us under the then-current $3,300 poverty line for a family of four.

How my mom managed, between hospital stays, to help put me through college and keep my Clairol-brained teenage sisters in penny loafers and madras Bermuda shorts I cannot imagine. It had nothing to do with our being too proud for welfare. Mom probably would have jumped on a loose Food Stamp with both her feet. But it never occurred to us that a family who owned a power mower, lived in a four-bedroom house and had an (albeit aging) Buick in the garage could qualify for any entitlement more valuable than Sis being elected homecoming queen. Nor did we have "positive self-esteem" or "traditional family values." That is, Mom must have had some, but my sisters placed no value on anything beyond dating and the Dave Clark Five, and I was majoring in street pharmacology at school. What's more, we were in a female-headed household with bad role models present—my mother married another drunken bum in 1970. Nonetheless, we didn't wind up on that staircase in the Newark housing project. I had to work for years at being a hippie before I saw anything remotely resembling that kind of squalor.

Most people without much money are as hard working and respectable as my mother and probably have better sense about conducting their love life and letting their children run wild. But my mother had the luck to live in a world where society as a whole came first and the *welfare,* as it were, of any given individual was a secondary concern.

This didn't seem like luck at the time. It was a narrow, stuffy, priggish world and deaf to excuses:

> *If "ifs" and "buts"*
> *Were fruits and nuts,*
> *We'd have Christmas every day*

And it was a world that punished not only antisocial behavior but any deviation from the norm. My mom was not guaranteed housing by being a single mother; it almost lost her the house. A live-in boyfriend would have been out of the question for a woman who worked as a secretary at the board of education and was a member of the Monroe Street Methodist Church. Mom had to go out and find another husband even though no very good ones seemed to have been available. I wasn't given counseling for my drug use or put in a therapy program filled with sympathetic peers. I was threatened with loss of my scholarship, expulsion from college, arrest and maybe even having to find a job. My sisters wouldn't have earned any increase in status by getting pregnant out of wedlock. They would have been drummed right off the pep squad, and—as for gaining the unconditional love of another creature—they already had stuffed animals. Where I grew up, you didn't get a chance to live in poverty; you couldn't afford it.

There were plenty of families around us who were as strapped for cash as we were. My friend's father across the street was out of work for a year, and my friend's mother took in sewing. The man next door had emphysema and was dying on a small pension. Social Security benefits were paltry in those days, and there were old people on the block who weren't tending their vegetable gardens for the sake of aerobic exercise. Still, we didn't riot. I would have liked to myself, because in those days I hated this *petit bourgeois* life and all its sanctimonious hypocrisies and prejudices. I would have gladly put a torch to the rec room. But this was a neighborhood where you didn't even let your lawn go for two weeks.

What we managed to escape in 1966, in Squaresville, Ohio, was not poverty. We had that. What we managed to escape was help.

That night the Guardian Angels invited me to come with them back to Hunt's Point. Michael Dixon ("Recon"), an Angel who specializes in dirtying himself like a dope user and scouting vile locales, had discovered a gruesome nest of drug behavior—a crack house, shooting gallery, dope bazaar and place to get a cheap blowjob all in one. And the Angels were going to raid it.

At first I assumed this would be a privatized version of the police raid I'd gone on in Washington. But the Guardian Angels said no, that wasn't the point. The Angels weren't going to arrest anyone, because a citizen's arrest means—just as a cop's arrest does—days spent in court, only to see some scumbag released on probation. And the Angels weren't trying to convince any individual person to stop taking drugs. "There's plenty of education—everybody knows drugs are bad," one of the Angels said. What Sliwa and his men intended to do was wreck this crack house—break everything breakable, rough up the patrons and take their drugs and money away. The Guardian Angels call it slamming and jamming. The purpose is to show the flag of decency, to destroy the permissive atmosphere of the inner city and to provide, by main strength of hand, the social opprobrium missing in the slums. The Guardian Angels are trying to enforce the kind of propriety, the mores, that were usual in American society, at every income level, twenty-five years ago. They're trying to make the South Bronx as dull and bland and conventional as my mother's old neighborhood. But modern society has become so lawless and screwy that the Guardian Angels have had to start a street gang to teach people decorum.

Twenty-seven Guardian Angels went on the raid, most of them in a U-Haul-style moving truck and the rest in a van and a car. The Angels arrived in the Bronx about sunset and gathered in an Amtrak rail yard, where Curtis Sliwa scratched battle plans on the pavement with a rock. The crack den was in the basement of a large, empty building on the block where we'd had bottles and bricks thrown at us. The only way inside was across a board over a four-foot ditch and through a hole in the basement wall.

The Guardian Angels were divided into three squads. The first squad was to rush through the hole and grab all the dopies and immobilize them, that is, throw them against walls. The second squad was to come in behind the first, pass through the melee in the basement and fan out through the upper floors to clear the rest of the building. The third squad would secure a defense perimeter.

Speed was important. Crack houses are defended by armed enforcers, but the enforcers, to avoid being caught by police, stay several blocks away. Lookouts with walkie-talkies would send the alarm, and the enforcers would get there, the Angels told me, in about ten minutes. "I want this operation completed in six to eight minutes," Sliwa told the Angels.

I went into the building between the first and second squads. Electricity had been pirated from somewhere for a couple of bulbs, and a sofa, half-burned and half-moldering, had been dragged off the street. On one damp-stained, scaly wall a skull and crossbones had been spray-painted above the words NO CREDIT. There were humps of garbage and rags, piles of busted cement and broken pipes and earth and muck everywhere in a retching funk of shit and drug-addict body odor. About a dozen crack-heads were down there, the men shrieking for mercy and the women just shrieking while they tried to pull their clothes back on over skaggy, mottled flanks. "My shoes! Let me get my shoes!" one woman yelled, and I thought this was an odd, feminine-vanity sort of concern to be having at the moment until I looked at the basement floor. There were hypodermic needles lying like spilled pretzel sticks all around the thin rubber soles of my Topsiders.

The Guardian Angels were shoving drug addicts and hollering horrible imprecations at them, then dragging them outside and making them kneel on the sidewalk. There the crack-heads had their pockets emptied; their drugs, pipes, needles and paraphernalia given the bootheel and their money torn up in front of their faces.

I was down in the terrible basement taking notes. The raid seemed to be a success as far as I could tell. But outside things were going awry.

When the second squad came through the basement, they found the stairs to the rest of the building had been blocked with rubble. They ran back out, hoisted themselves past the bricked-up first floor and went in the second-story windows. Meanwhile, the perimeter squad had, as Sliwa described it later, "gotten greedy." Seeing how some of the bystanders were obvious druggies, the Angels began grabbing people out of the gathering crowd and tossing them in with the kneeling crack-heads. The crowd grew and turned uglier, throwing things and pushing its way in on the defense perimeter.

After the second squad finished its sweep through the upper floors of the crack house—which were empty—they found themselves cut off from their fellows. They jumped down into the angry crowd, and putting their backs together, began to fight.

Sliwa gave the signal for retreat—a long blast on a whistle. When the remaining Angels in the basement and I ran out through the hole in the wall, all hell had broken loose. Bottles and beer cans and chunks of masonry were coming down like animated polka dots out of the pink evening sky. The enforcers had arrived from their outposts and were firing shots from a nearby roof. The fuddled crack addicts were tossed aside, and the first squad sprinted for the Guardian Angel vehicles while the perimeter squad fell in behind them. I had just dived into the van when something huge and heavy hit its roof. The van, truck and car took off with the street crowd running down on us. The three Guardian Angel drivers, winching on the steering-wheel rims as hard as they could, squealed around the block and into the backside of this same crowd, where the second squad of Angels was surrounded.

We were in the lead in the van and came through the drug mob at about twenty-five miles an hour, grazing several people and sending dozens leaping out of the way. In front of us two guys with complicated haircuts were pulling open their sports-team jackets and reaching into their waistbands, but the van's driver chased them up on the sidewalk before they could get their pistols free. The moving truck was right behind us, and as it came through, the members of the second squad jumped into the back. Just as the last Guardian Angel was being pulled onboard, his legs still dangling over the tailgate, some lunatic ran out of the crowd swinging an ax. The lunatic took aim at the Angel's foot but hooked his swing and only connected with the flat of the ax head. The two Guardian Angels bringing up the rear in the car smashed the lunatic's knees between their bumper and the back of the truck. Then we got the hell out of there.

The Guardian Angels were lucky. Only four of them were injured and only one seriously—John Rodrigues ("Hot Rod"), a young Angel on his first patrol. John's face was badly cut by somebody using a gin bottle as a shillelagh, but what was bothering John most was what his mother was going to say. The mob of drug lovers was not so lucky. I looked out the van's back window and saw a score of people staggering around in the middle of Hunt's Point Avenue holding parts of their bodies, such as groins and faces.

The Guardian Angels went back to the relative calm and safety of Mott Haven to get some sodas and first aid. At 138th Street and Cypress Avenue the block association was holding a street festival with a salsa band, and all the respectable citizens were out on the sidewalks with their children, eating cuchifritos and doing dance steps.

"This neighborhood used to be just like Hunt's Point," an Angel who'd grown up in Mott Haven told me.

"Before you guys started patrolling it?" I said.

"It's not because of us," said the Guardian Angel with remarkable modesty, considering the amount of adrenaline still in the air. "It's because of the support that the people here give to getting the scum out of their neighborhood."

And when the officers of the block association saw Curtis Sliwa, they insisted he come up to the bandstand and give a speech. Curtis tried to demur. He doesn't speak Spanish, and most of these people don't speak English. But that didn't matter to the crowd. The Guardian Angels had a real poverty program, one that could actually mitigate some of the horrible effects of privation. The people of Mott Haven didn't need to understand Curtis Sliwa's exact words, any more than they needed to understand every aspect of federal social legislation. They could see the results of government policy, and they could see the results of the Guardian Angels. They could tell what works.

AGRICULTURAL POLICY

How to Tell Your Ass from This Particular Hole in the Ground

There is one kind of interfering in private life that the federal government has been doing for much longer than it has been proscribing narcotics or hectoring poor people, and this is messing around with agriculture. The government began formulating agricultural policy in 1794, when the residents of western Pennsylvania started the Whiskey Rebellion in response to an excise tax on corn liquor. The agricultural policy formulated in 1794 was to shoot farmers. In this case, the federal government may have had it right the first time.

Like that of most Americans of the present generation, my experience with agriculture is pretty much limited to one three-week experiment raising dead marijuana plants under a grow light in the closet of my off-campus apartment. I did, however, once help artificially inseminate a cow. And you can keep your comments to yourself—I was up at the front, holding the thing's head.

This was a dozen years ago. My old friend George, who'd done all sorts of madcap stuff such as join the marines, go to Vietnam, learn to fly a stunt plane and get married, decided to raise cattle. To that end George bought a farm in New Hampshire, along with some cows (the technical term for female cattle), and now it was time for the cattle to fructify.

Getting a cow in a family way is not accomplished, as I would have thought, with a bull and some Barry White tapes in a heart-shaped stall. It's like teenage pregnancy, only more so. The bull isn't even around to get the cow knocked-up. Instead, there's a liquid-nitrogen Thermos bottle full of frozen bull sperm (let's not even think about how they get that) and a device resembling a cross between a gigantic hypodermic needle and the douche nozzle of the gods.

George got a real farmer to come by and actually do the honors. So while I held the cow's head and George held the cow's middle, the real farmer, Pete, took the bovine marital aid and inserted it into a very personal and private place of the cow's. Then Pete squirted liquid dish soap on himself and inserted his right arm into an even more personal and private place of the cow's, all the way up to the elbow. Pete did this not in order to have Robert Mapplethorpe take his photograph, but in order to grasp the inseminator tube through the intestine wall and guide the tube into the mouth of the uterus. It's an alarming thing to watch, and I'm glad to say I didn't watch it because I was at the cow's other end. But I'll tell you this, I will *never* forget the look on that cow's face.

The same look—and for the same reason—appeared on my own face when I began reading the 1990 omnibus farm bill. Every five years or so the U.S. Congress votes on a package of agricultural legislation that does to the taxpayer what Pete and George and I did to the cow.

The last farm bill cost American taxpayers over $100 billion in direct out-of-our-paycheck-into-the-feed-bag costs and another $50 billion in higher prices we paid at the supermarket. This was the Food Security Act of 1985, which got its name from the fact that it left America's food supply about this secure: "Yes, officer, the stereo, the TV and the coin collection are gone but, thank god, the refrigerator wasn't raided."

The new farm bill will only cost about $50 billion, although there's no telling what any farm bill is really going to cost. The 1981 farm bill was budgeted at $12 billion and ended up costing $60 billion, and the 1985 bill was supposed to represent a substantial cut of 1981 allocations. You see, if the weather's bad and we have lots of droughts and freezes, we'll have to give disaster aid and crop-insurance payments to farmers, and the farm bill will end up costing us more. On the other hand, if the weather's good and we have plentiful harvests, we'll have to buy up surplus commodities and pay farmers to cut down on planting, and the farm bill will end up costing us more yet. And if—God forbid—the weather is good some of the time and bad some of the time—if, in other words, the weather is *normal*—then we can all just start backing toward the barn door and mooing for frozen bull sperm.

But all this money goes to poor farmers laboring from sunup to sundown on millions and millions of farms across the nation, doesn't it? No.

In the first place, there aren't millions and millions of farms in America. There are about two million if you use the very inclusive Bureau of Census definition of a farm as any place with $1,000 or more annual gross sales of farm products. My off-campus apartment closet would have qualified if the grow lights hadn't blown the fuse box off the wall. There are, in fact, only about 314,000 full-time commercial farms in the U.S. These are farms that have gross annual sales of over $100,000. These are also the only farms where farm income exceeds income from nonfarm sources, such as factory jobs, retirement benefits, or sticking up 7-Eleven stores.

Nor are farmers, in general, poor. Farm-family income has exceeded average family income in America for more than twenty-five years. And federal farm spending doesn't go to poor farmers, anyway. The largest farms in America, those with gross receipts of more than $500,000, receive 60 percent of all price-support money.

So what are our Department of Agriculture tax dollars buying for us? A Department of Agriculture. The USDA has 106,000 employees, one for every three full-time farms in the country.

These 106,000 people would be more useful to the farm economy if we sent them out to hoe weeds. But they can't go; they're too busy doing things like administering the Federal Wool and Mohair Program. According to the U.S. General Accounting Office report to Congress on the 1990 farm bill, "The government established a wool and mohair price-support program in 1954 . . . to encourage domestic wool production in the interest of national security." Really, it says that. I guess back in the fifties there was this military school of thought that held that in the event of a Soviet attack we could confuse and disorient the enemy by throwing blankets over their heads. Then, while they were punching each other in the dark and trying to figure out who turned the lights off, we'd have time to run into our missile silos and destroy Russia with ICBMs. From 1955 to 1980, $1.1 billion was spent on wool and mohair price supports, with 80 percent of that money going to a mere six thousand shepherds and (I guess) moherds. This is $146,400 per Bo Peep. And, let me tell you, she didn't lose those sheep. They're off at boarding school in Switzerland.

Then there's the U.S. Honey Program, instituted in 1952 to stabilize honey prices (you remember how the American economy was almost brought to its knees by wild swings in the price of honey) and to "maintain sufficient bee populations for pollinating food and fiber crops." The honey program spends $100 million a year on about twenty-one hundred beekeepers—more than $47,000 each. For that kind of money, hell, *I'll* go sit in the flowers and wiggle around and get pollen all over my butt.

James Bovard, policy analyst at the libertarian Cato Institute and author of the book *The Farm Fiasco*, notes that between 1985 and 1989 government spending on rice farms was equal to $1 million for every full-time rice farmer in America and that the annual subsidy for each American dairy cow is between $600 and $700—greater than the per capita income of half the world's population.

Walter Williams, an economics professor at George Mason University, points out that since 1985 federally mandated attempts to boost citrus prices have resulted in the destruction (or use as cattle feed) of three billion oranges and two billion lemons (which explains why we so rarely hear about a cow with scurvy).

And Congressman Dick Armey, in an article for *Policy Review* entitled "Moscow on the Mississippi: America's Soviet-Style Farm Policy," says the 1985 farm bill paid farmers *not* to farm sixty-one million acres—an area equal to Ohio, Indiana and half of Illinois—and that the amount we've spent on farm subsidies in the past ten years is enough to have bought all the farms in thirty-three states.

"Moscow on the Mississippi" is an apt phrase. U.S. farm policy is coercive, collectivist and centrally planned and has been since 1929, when that wild radical Herbert Hoover created the Federal Farm Board in an attempt to corner the commodities market and control farm prices.

The New Deal successor to the Federal Farm Board was the Commodity Credit Corporation, or CCC, one of the Roosevelt era's Goldilocks programs, so-called because it barged in on the taxpayer fifty years ago, and *it's still there.* The CCC is empowered by its 1933 charter to ". . . undertake activities for the purpose of increasing production, stabilizing prices, and insuring adequate supplies; and to facilitate the efficient distribution of agricultural commodities." A more Brezhnevian set of instructions to a government agency is hard to imagine.

U.S. farm policy is, along with North Korea and the Stanford liberal arts faculty, one of the world's last outposts of anti-free-market dogmatism. Congressman Kika de La Garza, who is the exasperatingly powerful chairman of the House Agriculture Committee, wrote in the Capitol Hill newsletter, *Roll Call,* that, "most Americans believe the unique nature of agriculture—the lengthy production cycle, dependency on the weather, susceptibility to price swings, etc.—justifies a certain level of government involvement." But you can say the same thing about the unique nature of selling Mazda Miatas. Why isn't the government giving $50 billion to car dealerships?

A GAO report on federal dairy policies contains this sentence: "The federal government first developed dairy policies when low milk prices appeared to threaten the adequacy of the nation's milk supply." Which is insane. Everybody from wife-bartering savages to Michael Milken knows that low prices mean surplus, not shortage. Yet this statement appeared in a GAO report criticizing the federal dairy programs for *not* being "market oriented." Meanwhile, the dairy farmers themselves, through their lobbying organization, Dairymen, Inc., issue position papers that sound like extracts from Albanian newspaper editorials: "Dairymen enthusiastically supports a strong and flexible federal milk marketing order program. Such a program is essential for the maintenance of orderly marketing of milk in fluid and manufactured dairy product markets."

Thus, while America was fighting Commies all over the world, Communism grew apace in our own back forty. American farm policy is exactly what, during the McCarthy era, people were jailed, fired and blacklisted for advocating in this country—unless, of course, they were American farmers.

This being America, we haven't pursued Marxist goals with tanks, secret police and gulag camps; we've used money. And the result has been a uniquely American totalitarian screw-up. Instead of terrible shortages, we've created gross overproduction. Instead of making people dirt poor, we've made them filthy rich.

As with anything that's had too much attention from the government, farm policy is a mess and a tangle, an immense dog's breakfast of programs, laws and regulations. The farm policy briefing package prepared by the Library of Congress for U.S. senators and representatives begins with a "Glossary of Agricultural Terms" forty pages long.

But farm policy, although it's complex, can be explained. What it can't be is believed. No cheating spouse, no teen with a wrecked family car, no mayor of Washington, DC, videotaped in flagrante delicto has ever come up with anything as farfetched as U.S. farm policy.

To begin with, there is the concept of parity—the deep thought behind all of the USDA's price- and income-support measures. Parity is the idea that the price farm goods bring ought to be the same, now and forever, in inflation-adjusted dollars, as the price farm goods brought in the years 1910 through 1914. Parity was conceived in the twenties, when increased mechanization and better seeds and fertilizers were causing agricultural prices to fall. Farmers liked the fact that they could grow more stuff. But they didn't like the fact that other farmers could grow more stuff, too, and that all the stuff being grown was therefore less rare and valuable. The farmers wanted the calendar turned back to those golden pre-World War days, when—as they remembered it—a peck of wheat sold for a bushel of money, and every load of manure was pitched by a hayseed Vanderbilt.

The U.S. government is a sort of permanent frat pledge to every special interest in the nation—willing to undertake any task no matter how absurd or useless. So our government obliged the farmers, or tried to, and parity was born.

If we applied the logic of parity to automobiles instead of feed and grain, a typical economy car would cost forty grand. $43,987.50 is what a 1910 Nash Rambler cost in 1990 dollars. And for that you got a car with thirty-four horsepower, no heat, no A/C, no tape deck or radio and no windows around the front seat. If farm parity were a guiding principle of human existence, we'd not only have lousy, high-priced economy cars, we'd have a total lack of civilization. Cheap, plentiful food is the precondition for human advancement. When there isn't enough food, everybody has to spend all his time getting fed and nobody has a minute to invent law, architecture or big clubs to hit cave bears on the head with. Agriculture prices have been falling, relative to the prices of other goods and services, not since the 1920s, but since the Paleolithic age. And it's a good thing. Otherwise we wouldn't grow food, we'd *be* food.

The government has any number of ways of inflicting parity on taxpayers and food shoppers. For example, there's the "nonrecourse loan." This is a loan farmers can get from the government using their crop as collateral. But the government sets the value of that collateral not by the crop's price but by what the crop's price *ought to be* in a dream world full of parity and happy farmers. Say wheat is selling for $3.50 a bushel, but the USDA thinks farm life would be a more fulfilling experience if the price were $4. So the USDA sets the "nonrecourse loan rate" at four bucks, and farmers can get a loan of $4 for every bushel of wheat they've got lying around. Then if America happens to suffer a terrible outbreak of toast weevils and the price of wheat goes up to $10 a bushel, farmers can pay back their $4 loans, sell the wheat for $10 and bank the profits.

But if everybody in the United States suddenly goes on an all-meat diet and the price of wheat drops to fifteen cents, the farmers can blow off the loans, make the government eat the wheat and not even get an ink smudge in their credit histories. It's an absolutely no-risk business transaction, like doing real estate deals with your dog. "Beach front? You don't want beach front, Fido. I've got some prime dumpside acreage, chicken bones and dead rats all over the place. I'll trade you straight up."

Or if a nonrecourse loan is too complicated for the farmer, the government has another program, called "loan-deficiency payments." In this program the government pays the farmer *not* to take a nonrecourse loan.

The "conservation reserve program" is almost as simple. The government gives annual payments to the farmer in return for the farmer removing highly erodible land from production—as if erosion weren't doing that already. A farmer on the conservation reserve program will doubtless want to be on the "acreage conservation program," too. That way the government will pay him up to $3,500 a year to practice soil conservation in general. This is like going into a Dairy Queen and giving the owner money to keep his ice cream freezers plugged in.

"Marketing orders" are used to keep farm prices high at the retail level. The growers of various commodities are encouraged to get together and fix the price for which their commodities will sell. In other industries there's a name for people who do this: felons. Some marketing orders are enforced by "marketing quotas." Growers decide how much growing each grower can do. If shoeshine boys tried this, you'd only get one loafer polished during shine-business slumps.

During the mid-1980s the dairy industry had its own plan to limit production, the "whole herd buyout." Dairy farmers decided there was too much cheap milk at the supermarket. Hell, even homeless welfare babies were drinking moo juice. So the government bought and slaughtered 1.6 million dairy cows. How come the government never does anything like this with lawyers?

Farm-product bargains are also eliminated by means of the "commodity import program." Our government gives foreign governments grants and loans to buy stuff grown in the U.S., stuff that would otherwise be a glut on the domestic market. I guess we should be thankful that similar programs have not been undertaken by the governments of Colombia, Bolivia and Peru.

While some government programs are making farm products more expensive to buy, other programs are making farm products cheaper to produce. For example, farmers get cut-rate credit to the extent that the federal government now controls half of all farm debt. Farmers also get subsidized crop insurance. And, for those farmers who didn't feel like buying subsidized crop insurance but had a crop failure anyway, there are free disaster benefits.

This conflict between policies that send prices up and policies that drive prices down results in the need for a third category of policies that do nothing at all. These are the famous programs that give farmers money for not farming. In the "payment-in-kind program" the farmer is given the excess farm products that other farmers grew in return for not growing any of his own. In the "paid acreage diversion program" the more farming the farmer doesn't do, the more the government pays him. And in the best program of all, "0/92," the farmer does absolutely nothing and gets 92 percent of all the payments and benefits he could have possibly gotten from the largest crop he could have possibly grown. A USDA scheme like this gives every government agency something to shoot for. With 0/92 as an inspiration, Health and Human Services will probably dream up a way for us taxpayers to catch clap from whores without getting laid.

Just when you think the farm issue can't get sillier, here comes Willie Nelson pounding on the gut-fiddle and adenoidaling away at Farm Aid. Yes, Willie and such thoroughly improbable acts as L. L. Cool J, Guns n' Roses, Iggy Pop and Lou Reed (hey, there's a bunch of sheep in fishnet stockings out here, they've got drugs, and they say they're with the band) have raised a few more bucks for the farmers who just euchred Congress out of $50 billion.

There are farm families in need of charity, of course. But singling out farmers and getting all soggy-nosed and soak-eyed over their plight has less to do with facts than with romantic nostalgia for a pastoral ideal that never existed. Throughout history farm life has been brutish, dirty and mostly stupid. Not that any of us would know. This country is so urbanized we think low-fat milk comes from cows on Nutri/System weight-loss plans.

According to the *Statistical Abstract of the United States*, about 1.3 million people in America define themselves as farmers. But there are 4.1 million secretaries. These secretaries are poorly paid, hold jobs that provide little satisfaction or chance for advancement, are frequently working mothers and often the sole support of their families. Where's the "Lend a Short Hand" concert for them? Where are the famous ode-yodelers singing "Momma Was a Hard-Typing Gal"? Why'd farmers get cinematic encomiums like *The River, Country* and *Places in the Heart* while secretaries got nothing but *Nine to Five*?

Farming has always carried emotional freight. Thomas Jefferson, caught in a moment of rare idiocy arguing against the industrialization of the United States, said, "Those who labor in the earth are the chosen people of God . . . whose breasts He has made a peculiar deposit for substantial and genuine virtue." This, by the way, from a gentleman farmer who owned two hundred slaves and kept at least one of them as his mistress.

The farm lobby makes good use of such lofty forms of nonsense and, also, of less lofty forms of nonsense, such as congressmen. For instance, sugar growers donate about half a million dollars a year to congressional election campaigns, and the dairy industry donates $2 million. Even though only 46 out of 435 congressional districts are controlled by farm votes, farmers have gained heavy leverage on Capitol Hill by combining rhetoric, ready money and a talent for political logrolling that dates back to the Constitutional Convention, when southern farmers managed to get slaves counted as three fifths of a voter without letting any slaves do three fifths of the voting. As a result of this disproportionate influence, 25 percent of the net income U.S. farmers receive is in the form of direct cash payments from the government. The only other businessmen who put this kind of lip clamp on the public teat are defense contractors. And at least when we give billions to defense contractors, we get something back for it, Star Wars or something. Maybe we don't need Star Wars, maybe it doesn't work, but at least the defense contractors were thinking of us. They made, you know, a gesture. But we give billions to farmers and don't even get a basket of zucchini on the front porch.

Our that-ain't-hay farm policy is useless. Even Willie Nelson acknowledges that four hundred thousand small farms have gone out of business since he began giving his Farm Aid concerts, and I don't think we can blame all four hundred thousand on Willie's awful music. A 1988 Government Accounting Office report concluded that one quarter of the bankruptcies among Farmers Home Administration borrowers were the result not of any credit crunch, but of an excess of cheap, subsidized loans.

Agricultural economist Clifton B. Luttrel estimates than an old-fashioned money-vomiting Great Society-style welfare system to keep needy farmers in business would cost only $4 billion a year, less than half what current programs cost.

I went to see Pete, the dairy farmer who'd helped my friend George get his cow pregnant. Pete's family has been dairy farming in New England all this century, and dairy farmers, as a group, have been on the receiving end of great federal largess—on the order of $6 to $7 billion a year. Pete, however, had just sold his cows and was subdividing his land to build vacation homes. I had a very short interview with Pete.

Me: As the result of price supports, product purchases, marketing orders and other federal dairy programs, how much better off are local dairy farmers?

Pete: There are only two local dairy farmers left.

Me: Are they better off?

Pete: Nope.

U.S. farm policy, besides not doing what it's supposed to, does do what it isn't supposed to, and lots of it—the law of unintended consequences being one piece of legislation Congress always passes.

Many farm-program payments are doled out according to an "acreage base." This is the amount of land on a farm that's planted in a particular crop. In order to protect their acreage base and continue getting government payoffs, farmers are forced to practice "monocropping"—planting the same thing every year instead of rotating crops to replenish soil nutrients. Monocropping requires more chemical fertilizers, which pollute ground water, and more pesticides and weed killers, which cause severe side effects, such as Meryl Streep appearing in front of congressional committees to complain about what's in her food.

The acreage-base system also discourages experimentation with new crops, such as canola (vegetable oil) and kenafe (paper pulp), both of which show enormous potential as dinnertime child disciplinary threats. ("No TV until you finish your canola.")

Other farm-program benefits, such as "deficiency payments," are paid on the basis of yield rather than acreage. The more you grow, the more you get paid. Yield-based deficiency payments for feed corn, combined with disaster payments based on yield projections, encourage farmers in drought areas to plant the highest yielding varieties of corn rather than the varieties that are most drought resistant. Meanwhile, wind erosion blows the top three inches of North Dakota into downtown Duluth.

Farm programs even make American foreign policy more screwed up than it is already—not an easy thing to do. The USDA sugar program spends a quarter of a million dollars per year per American sugar grower. This to keep the sugar industry healthy in a climate phenomenally unsuited to producing sugar. These subsidies and the sugar-import quota that goes with them cost sugar-cane-growing U.S. allies such as the Philippines more than $800 million a year in lost revenues. That's $319 million more than we pay the Philippines to rent our military bases there.

And while the USDA is spending $10 billion a year to increase farm income, the same government agency is spending $20 billion to make food affordable to poor people through the Food Stamp program. A moron, an imbecile, an American high-school student can see there's something wrong with this equation. Just give the $10 billion to the poor people, and let them buy their own damn food from the farmers.

I spent two and a half years examining the American political process. All that time I was looking for a straightforward issue. But everything I investigated—election campaigns, the budget, lawmaking, the court system, bureaucracy, social policy—turned out to be more complicated than I had thought. There were always angles I hadn't considered, aspects I hadn't weighed, complexities I'd never dreamed of. Until I got to agriculture. Here at last is a simple problem with a simple solution. Drag the omnibus farm bill behind the barn, and kill it with an ax.

VERY FOREIGN POLICY

Whatever it is that the government does, sensible Americans would prefer that the government do it to somebody else. This is the idea behind foreign policy.

Foreign policy seems as though it should be a large part of government. Conducting foreign policy is, after all, a perfect example of something an individual can't do for himself (though I'd love to—especially if it involved sanctions against France). And yet, though common sense—and the president and the network TV news—tells us that foreign policy is a vital aspect of government, you'd be hard put to prove this by examining American history. Notice the elegant diplomatic poise with which, in 1812, we maintained neutrality in the Napoleonic Wars. Then, after the British had fought us to a standstill in that pointless fray, we boldly proclaimed the Monroe Doctrine, holding that no European power should ever meddle in the Western Hemisphere . . . unless it wanted to or something. When Mexican sovereignty and U.S. Manifest Destiny collided in the 1840s, America's crafty statesmen, whoops, blew it again, and we had a big war. We couldn't even manage to exercise diplomacy on our own selves. The Compromise of 1850, proposed "to settle and adjust amicably all existing questions of controversy . . . arising out of the institution of slavery," led directly to the War between the States. We used eloquent persuasion to peacefully assist the Cubans in the struggle for independence from Spain. We gave the world a generation of peace and political justice by refusing to be lured into the Great War in Europe. We conducted brilliant negotiations with Japan in 1941, made a swell deal with Stalin at Yalta and so forth.

Maybe it's understandable what a history of failures America's foreign policy has been. We are, after all, a country full of people who came to America to get away from foreigners. Any prolonged examination of the U.S. government reveals foreign policy to be America's miniature schnauzer—a noisy but small and useless part of the national household.

Any prolonged examination of the U.S. government also reveals foreign policy to be remarkably elusive. I was under the mistaken impression that I could learn something about American foreign policy simply by going to a foreign place where some foreign thing was happening and watching how Americans made policy about it.

The war in Afghanistan seemed like a good place to start. Here U.S. diplomacy had actually worked for a change. Our guys had gotten the better of the entire International Communist Conspiracy (which only had another nine months to live, but, come on, a win's a win) without a single American having fired a shot. This was the Great Game as it was meant to be played. Kabul was ours. Well, not ours exactly, but not theirs anymore either. The U.S. State Department had achieved a master stroke of realpolitik. Our diplomats had gained their ends by means of determination, persistence, savvy and just a little help from six million dead, maimed and displaced Afghans.

February 15, 1989, was the deadline for the last Soviet troops to be withdrawn from Afghanistan. I went to Peshawar in Pakistan's North-West Frontier Province to see what would happen in the wake of this U.S. foreign policy triumph. Peshawar was the principal Afghan War "listening post," which is journalese for "place that's close, but not too close, to the action and has bottled water."

Not that there wasn't action in Pakistan. There was plenty of shooting and killing. It just didn't have anything to do with the collapse of the

Brezhnev Doctrine or freedom and self-determination for the peoples of Central Asia. It was literary criticism. The locals were busy debating the merits of Salman Rushdie's novel *The Satanic Verses.* And their arguments were more spirited than those in the *New York Review of Books.* On February 12, 7 people were killed and 127 injured in a riot in front of the American Cultural Center in Islamabad. (Rushdie is a native of India with British citizenship whose book was published by an English corporation, so naturally the demonstrations were directed at the U.S.)

On February 15 Peshawar's English-language newspaper, the *Frontier Post,* carried 142 column inches of Rushdie argle-bargle and one five-line paragraph about the Soviet last post in Kabul. A couple of days later Edward Girardet, correspondent for the *Christian Science Monitor,* came out of Afghanistan after spending a week with the *mujahideen* guerrillas. He'd been walking for hours, and when he finally got across the border into the relative safety of the North-West Frontier tribal areas, he sat down to write a few notes. Moments later he was being held at gunpoint, surrounded by Pathan tribesmen who were convinced he was Salman Rushdie and were ready to collect the $3-million price on his head. The thing was clear enough to the Pathans. Salman Rushdie is a foreigner. Salman Rushdie is a writer. And here was a foreigner writing.

Sneer at the mysteries of the East if you will. Not I. I was covering a war that we won without being in it from a war zone where the principal danger to life and limb was from the use of magical realism in modern fiction.

Whatever setback American foreign policy may have been receiving on the literary front, it was moving full speed ahead in the much more important endeavor of abetting political muddles. All the leaders of the anti-Soviet Afghan Alliance—the seven officially recognized *mujahideen* political parties that, despite being called the Alliance, hate each other— were gathered in the Pakistani capital of Islamabad. There the *"muj"* were declaring themselves winners of the war and electing themselves to a provisional government. Note that this declaration of a victory in Afghanistan and election of a government for Afghanistan was taking place in Pakistan. That way, the totally defeated forces of the Soviet-backed Najibullah regime wouldn't be able to blast the completely victorious forces of the American-backed *mujahideen* to pieces with air strikes and artillery.

The Alliance get-together took the form of a tribal conference, or *shura*, an ancient tradition of the Pathan peoples, who make up the majority of the population in Afghanistan. To judge from the amount of double-crossing, backstairs deal cutting and making of windy pronouncements, a *shura* is an ancient tradition the Pathans inherited from the John Tower confirmation hearings in the U.S. Senate.

And in matters of media strategy, the *muj* are ready for Roger Ailes. They held a press conference where absolutely no information was divulged, especially not to the press, and it turned out the purpose of the press conference was to bawl out reporters for reporting the amount of double-crossing, backstairs deal cutting and making of windy pronouncements at the *shura*.

"You've set the world to worrying," scolded *shura* spokes*muj* Abdul Rasul Sayyaf, a big affable-faced radical fundamentalist xenophobe with a beard you could hatch a California condor in. "Journalists should not do divisive things," he said and cited an Afghan proverb about "trying to find hair in a bowl of dough"—as apt a description of the profession of journalism as I've heard lately. Interesting, seeing spin control from guys dressed in pajamas and sandals with tablecloths wrapped around their heads and bandoliers of ammunition across their chests and almost as many guns as wives. Other aspects of the *mujahideen* worldview, however, weren't so familiar. "One thing the *shura* must do," they told us at the press conference, "is decide the fate of one and a half million martyrs in Afghanistan." I didn't even want to know what that meant.

During the Q-and-A period each foreign reporter was given a media kit containing, among other things:

A booklet in Dari, a language understood by none of the foreign
    reporters
1 business card in Pashto, another language understood by none of
    the foreign reporters
1 business card in English giving the times and frequencies of
    mujahideen radio broadcasts in Dari and Pashto
A pocketknife
A lapel button bearing the symbol of the Alliance, which is a
    whole bunch of hands clasping each other in pregame

basketball-team fashion and which bears an eerie resemblance
to the seven-headed cobra symbol of Patty Hearst's
Symbionese Liberation Army
2 books of matches with colorful matchbook art depicting Russians
being stabbed, Russians with fangs, Russians being stepped
on and a Russian bear getting stuffed into a bottle
A genuine adjustable Unity of Afghan Mujahideen Alliance ring

The ring was not, unfortunately, of the decoder variety.

It will come as no surprise to students of past U.S. foreign policy that
the Alliance party with the greatest hatred for Western civilization and the
worst reputation for brutality is the party that got the most American
money. This was the Hezb-e-Islami, run by Gulbaddin Hikmatyar, a fellow
with a kisser to make the late Ayatollah Khomeini look like Gidget. Hikmatyar is supposed to be notso-hotso at fighting Russians but real good at
killing fellow *mujahideen*. He's also been accused of murdering a free-lance
cameraman who took pictures of Hezb-e-Islami internecine atrocities and
of blowing away Dr. Sayd Majrooh, Afghanistan's foremost (not to say only)
intellectual and so forth. Hikmatyar received a pig's share of U.S. aid
because he was a favorite of the Pakistani intelligence service, the ISI,
which was a favorite of the American intelligence service, the CIA, because
the ISI helped the CIA talk Pakistan into being the duck blind for American
potshots at Soviet expansionism. What the ISI saw in Hikmatyar is more
of a mystery. Hikmatyar is a fundamentalist kook, and so are some ISI
people. Maybe that was it. Or maybe the ISI thought it owned Hikmatyar
(although, personally, I think they would have been better off having a gila
monster in their sock than this guy in their pocket). Or maybe it was just
that Hikmatyar is an asshole and a divisive influence. Pakistan has no
interest in a strong, united Afghanistan, whether run by Sovs or *muj* or
what-you-will. The Afghans have a bad habit, every generation or two, of
descending on the plains of Punjab and Sind for recreational pillage.

At the sunny end of the political spectrum was the National Islamic
Front of Afghanistan, NIFA, headed by Syed Ahmed Gailani who is a pir,
a hereditary Sufi saint. Gailani lives in London part of the year. He and
his supporters are prosperous, sophisticated, well dressed and articulate

and enjoy discussing such things as the Rights of Man and political plural-
ism. It will come as no surprise to students of journalism that the foreign
reporters had made NIFA a laughingstock and called it the Gucci Front.
Journalists worship authenticity the way governments worship expediency.
The Gailani troops weren't dirty and incomprehensible enough to be *real*
Afghan freedom fighters.

The rest of the Alliance parties fell somewhere in niceness between
Hezb-e-Islami and NIFA, and the *shura* elected the weakest party leaders
to head the provisional government—impuissant royalist Sibgatullah
Mojadedi as president and the aforementioned goof Abdul Rasul Sayyaf
(one of whose wives is rumored to be an American Black Muslim) for prime
minister. This is a time-honored political gambit, the same one used by
America's Democratic party when nominating Michael Dukakis and Walter
Mondale. Weak leaders give everybody more latitude to wring each other's
necks, which the *muj* proceeded to do for the entire month of February
while nothing happened over the border.

Of course, hundreds of journalists had been sent to Peshawar. Their
editors wanted them all to be on hand for the fall of Kabul, which the editors
had scheduled for ten minutes after the Soviet pullout. Unfortunately, the
editors had done their scheduling without consulting anyone but the U.S.
State Department. Nobody actually in Kabul knew the city was supposed
to fall. The journalists were left sitting in the lobby of the Peshawar Pearl
Continental Hotel in a country where liquor is illegal and women are
covered with tarpaulins and the only available excitement is being popped
on the head by angry Muslim bookworms.

All the journalists could talk about was getting *"inside."*

"I'm trying to get *inside.*"

"I think I'll be getting *inside* soon."

"I can't seem to get *inside.*"

"I was *inside* two months ago."

I remember this conversation from high school, except it was about
girlfriends and underpants. The very least the editors wanted, if Kabul
wouldn't fall, was an "Inside Liberated Afghanistan" dateline. This meant
the reporters were supposed to go about ten yards up the Khyber Pass

wearing somebody's front-hall rug over their shoulders in the immortal manner of Dan Rather, who is still remembered in these parts as Gunga Dan. But there were too many "Banana Republicans"—as the old hands called the newcomers—and the *muj* were heartily sick of hacks in general. They'd already dragged enough flabby, whiny, chain-smoking news info-tainers through the slush, mud and rocket attacks. What was in it for them now? They had their Stinger missiles. They'd seen the backs of the Soviets. And every aid agency, charity and public-service organization on earth, with the possible exception of Trout Unlimited, was coughing up succor and cash.

The only journalist not frantically trying to get *"inside"* was me. This was because I'd been drinking at the American Club (the only place on the North-West Frontier where you can legally obtain both liquor and pork chops) with an American Special Forces team sent to help the UN train Afghan refugees how to disarm Soviet mines. It seems there are about thirty-eight varieties of these mines, ranging from four-inch widgets called butterfly mines, which look like they were manufactured by the Whammo Corporation and flutter down from Russian helicopters in the manner of maple-tree seedpods, to MON-100 humongous motherfucker command-detonated directional-fragmentation mines containing 450 steel shrapnel fragments embedded in five kilograms of plastic explosives with a lethal range of a hundred yards. The Soviets and their Afghan allies had planted up to thirty million of these mines in Afghanistan, and I figured that worked out to fifteen million per each one of my large, clumsy feet to step on. Whereas if I stayed in Peshawar, I could go shopping.

I suppose I ought to feel guilty for shopping when I should have been trying to fathom American foreign policy by trudging through minefields, shivering in Kabul or hanging around the *shura* in Islamabad. But if you look around this part of the world, you realize there's nothing here *but* shopping. The Hindu Kush Mountains—the "Killer of Hindus"—produce some runty livestock and not much of that. Down on the plains are the same mud-fort houses that were here when the Aryan hordes arrived in 2000 B.C. with the Bronze Age equivalent of swastikas and beer-hall songs. The peasants grow just enough wheat and rice to keep most of the peasants alive some of the time. There's not even firewood. House walls are decorated with circular cow patties being dried in the sun for fuel. From the valley of the Indus to the plateau of Iran, from the Baluchistan desert to Samarkand in the Soviet Union, absolutely nothing is manufactured. And it's not a service economy. And it certainly isn't a hotbed of ideas and intellect—adult literacy in Afghanistan is about 8 percent. What makes this place important, what makes it exist at all, is shopping, though you can call it "trade" if you want to sound important.

All the trade routes of humanity cross here, with silk from China, furs from Russia, spices from the Indies, silly religions from India, slaves from Africa, art from Persia and guns from Europe passing to and fro. For four thousand years this has been Outlet City, Planet Earth. Of course, in an age of UPS and electronic fund transfers, it's pretty dumb to risk WWIII over the Khyber Pass. But tell that to the U.S. State Department.

The bazaars of Peshawar's Old City are the history of mankind as K mart. Everything ever made is on sale in a dirty puzzle of streets too narrow for a 1970s necktie and more crowded than a hockey-game fight. There's Street of the Tinsmiths, Street of the Gold Sellers, Street of the Bird Sellers, Street of the Storytellers and a whole street lined with huge images of false teeth. You can buy a new car here, antibiotics, opium, a Russian refrigerator, a fax machine, a wife. The money changers, squatting in a row on a stone shelf along the filthy Chowk Yadgar Square, keep telephones behind their rolled-up prayer mats so they can call Hong Kong for the latest exchange prices. If you go forty kilometers south to the bazaar at Darra in the so-called tribal areas (tribal areas are what the Pakistanis call the parts of Pakistan that Pakistan has no control over), you can buy a brand-new Moscow-issue AK-47 still in its shipping grease, an entire ack-ack gun, a shoulder-fired anti-tank missile or landing wheels off a shot-down MIG— useful, the locals say, for making a smooth-riding ox cart. At the tobacco stalls in the Saddar Bazaar in the British colonial section of Peshawar I held up a box of fancy Cuban cigarillos I'd bought in Europe. "Two days," said a tobacco seller, and two days later the cigars were there costing less than they cost in London.

I may not have been learning much about foreign policy, but I was learning something about free trade and quite a lot about Second Amendment benefits. Unlike every other place in Asia, there's only a modicum of begging on the North-West Frontier, and that very dignified. There's no wheedling or importuning at all, and never a flutter of street-urchin fingers in your wallet pocket. The only cheating is that ancient and mutual kind known as business. "An armed society is a polite society," said Robert Heinlein.

Besides, the main thing to be learned about foreign policy in this part of the world is that a wise foreign policy would be one that kept you out of here. There are some things you ignore at your peril, but you pay attention to Central Asia at the risk of your life. The people who dominate these mountains, the Pathan tribesmen and their urbanized cousins, are Caucasians, similar to ourselves in appearance and violent looniness. And shopping toughens the breed. The Pathans have made their living for millennia on what might be called a Value Subtracted Tax on everything that crosses their turf. Nobody gets through unscathed, as the British learned in 1842 during the First Afghan War (one of three Afghan wars the British would lose) when they sent an army of forty-five hundred into Kabul and exactly one British soldier made it back alive. Even Alexander the Great didn't emerge in one piece. The "warlike Paktuike," as Herodotus called the Pathans, gave Alexander the toughest fights of his campaign, shot him in the lung with an arrow and saddled him with a termagant Afghan wife, Roxanne.

I was looking through a grammar of the Pathan language, Pashto, written by a British army officer in the nineteenth century and still in print as a textbook in Pakistan. Included in the "useful phrases" section at the back of the book were:

Khodokhelo dwī pa charo pa tūro tote tote kawul.	Men of the Khodokhel tribe cut them to pieces with knives and swords.
Shpa aw wradz lagiyā jang kawī.	They are continually fighting, night and day.
Rāghai, zir shah, guzār pre wukā.	He is come, make haste, fire at him.
Chara lāla rāka chi halāl e kawam.	Give me a knife that I might cut his throat.

As for recreation, the national sport of Afghanistan is something called *buzkashi*, a kind of horse-mounted rugby with a dead calf for the ball. A *buzkashi* match is held in an ill-defined open space at least the size of a city block. Any number can play. There were about forty horsemen involved in the game I saw. The players are divided into two teams. The field has a flag at one end and three large circles chalked into the dirt at the other. The two outside circles are goals for the respective teams, and the middle circle is where the calf is put after its head is chopped off. The point of *buzkashi* is to lean out of your saddle, grab the calf, ride like hell around the flag at the far end of the field and come back and make a veal drop in your team's circle. The twist is that *buzkashi* is played for cash prizes, and the money goes not to the scoring team but to the individual scorer. Therefore, everybody on the other team is trying to take the calf away from you, and so is everybody else. *Buzkashi* says so much about Central Asian politics that reporters call going to a *buzkashi* match "being put on metaphor alert."

I went to have a look at the dead calf before the game started. I couldn't lift it with both hands. But the *buzkashi* riders cock a leg around a saddle horn and whisk the carcass away like a lady's handbag. Then the real fun begins—part Tatar horde, part horse Cuisinart—with hooves and boots and whips and fists flying and the whole barbarian stampede riding headlong into the spectators.

Dignitaries watch *buzkashi* from a mud platform with rugs and awnings and boys to bring lemonade. But real *buzkashi* fans get right down on the field and mingle with the crazed horseflesh. It's exciting. I tried using a French photojournalist for protection, but he was too skinny to absorb the impact of a runaway horse and I got a nasty fat lip off the back of his skull when his face was smashed into his camera. People were trampled all over the place, and bodies were pitched in the air and the crowd was laughing its pajamas off. It's all part of the terrible Central Asian bravery surplus. There's so much death around here that I guess the idea is to die in the most interesting possible way—rooting for a *buzkashi* team or reading novels or whatever. It's that or go shopping.

The *buzkashi* match was at one of the largest of the Afghan refugee camps and was held in honor of U.S. Ambassador to Pakistan Robert

Oakley and Senator Daniel Patrick Moynihan, who'd come to Peshawar on what the staff at the consulate called the "Frontierland Tour." That is, the senator was trotted around for a "grip and grin" with the *muj,* given a quick peek at the border of Afghanistan (a country that was either soon to be liberated from Communist oppression or had been already, depending on who you talked to) and shown some items of local cultural interest, such as a dead cow being dragged all over the map.

I don't think American foreign policy was making a very good impression just at that moment. First the match was held up. The ambassador was almost an hour late because "lunch ran long." Senator Moynihan didn't show at all. He was "too tired." And Oakley arrived dressed to go bass fishing. The Afghans were all in their finest. The *buzkashi* riders were less than ecstatic about the rewards our ambassador handed out after the match. I could see a single red hundred-rupee note in most of the prize envelopes. One hundred rupees is $5. The riders got in a fist fight about this later.

Ambassador Oakley invited the various journalists standing around to come to the Peshawar consulate for an "impromptu briefing," although when we got there, maps and visual aids had been laid out in spontaneous readiness.

The briefing was about humanitarian aid—food, medicine, educational materials—that the U.S. had been smuggling into Communist-ruled Afghanistan, about $200 million worth to date. This program was kept virtually secret while America was shouting from the housetops about the arms and anti-aircraft missiles it was sending the *muj.* In matters of inscrutability the U.S. foreign policy gives nothing away to the mysterious Orient.

The ambassador was going on about what a perfect aid program this had been and how the Pakistanis hadn't diverted any of the humanitarian aid to their own purposes and none of the *muj* had stolen any of it from other *muj* and no food or medicine ever wound up back in the bazaar in Peshawar and the whole thing was "nonpolitical" to boot, while the more experienced gentlemen of the press made "oh, sure" and "I'll bet" faces.

I wasn't paying much attention to the briefing. After all, I wasn't a real foreign correspondent, I was stretched out on a consulate sofa sipping a cold beer and watching Senator Moynihan padding around the front hall in bathrobe and bedroom slippers, giving every appearance of being completely lost. Sort of like U.S. foreign policy. Talk about metaphor alert.

"How come this particular U.S. aid program has been so astonishingly trouble free?" one of the genuine reporters wanted to know.

"The success of our military and humanitarian aid in Afghanistan is the result of the United States' not being intrusive," said Oakley, "unlike Vietnam, where Americans were doing everything everywhere."

"Have any Americans 'gone inside' with this humanitarian aid?" asked another genuine reporter.

"If we sent a flood of Americans in there," said the ambassador, "we might muck it up."

So I took the next plane home.

DEFENSE POLICY

Cry "Havoc!" and Let Slip the Hogs of Peace

A̲uthor's Note: The following chapter has been—to use a favorite government phrase—O.T.B.E.'ed, "Overtaken by Events." The "Defense Policy" section of this book was originally written in the spring of 1990. It was revised in the fall of that year, after the Iraqi invasion of Kuwait. But, at that time, I assumed Saddam Hussein would turn tail and scuttle back to Baghdad. I was wrong, though not as wrong as Saddam.

It is now the middle of February 1991. Half a million American troops are in the Mideast for the duration. (So am I, for that matter.) We can guess, but not know, how the Gulf War will turn out. And this book has to go to press.

Another revision would be pointless, so I'll leave the chapter as it is, only injecting here a few addenda and I-told-you-so's:

The extreme concern about limiting civilian casualties and "collateral damage" in Iraq is prefigured in the fight for Panama City described below.

I assume that a "non-linear" battle, such as Operation Just Cause was, will be fought—on a much larger scale—in Kuwait and Iraq. And I assume it will meet with the same quick success.

The 1989 press hysteria about the usefulness of the Stealth fighter was, indeed, hysterical.

I was right about Russia getting horrible again.

My pride in American technology, as exemplified by the Aegis Missile Cruiser USS Mobile Bay, *proved to be better founded than I ever could have hoped.*

My host aboard the Mobile Bay, *Captain David Bill III, is now an Admiral and the commander of the battleship USS* Wisconsin, *whose guns are, as I write, blowing immense holes in Iraqi defenses in Kuwait.*

I don't know the whereabouts of Colonel Mike Snell, who commanded Task Force Bravo in Panama, but I'm sure he's over here someplace, and I'm sure the Iraqis will soon wish he weren't.

I have seen the well-trained, well-motivated "young, clean-cut and polite" sailors of the USS Mobile Bay *duplicated thousands of times in every branch of the service here in Saudi Arabia.*

There's only one glaring error that I find in rereading this chapter. My budget calculations are wrong. Adding up the cash contributions we are receiving from Saudi Arabia, Kuwait, the United Arab Emirates, Germany, Japan and elsewhere, I see that, if we play our cards right in the Gulf War, we might even make a profit.

—P.J. O'R.
Dhahran, Saudi Arabia

A nation with a goofy foreign policy needs a very serious policy of defense. But for much of the post-Vietnam era we haven't had that either. Then, in the fall of 1989, the Soviet bloc collapsed, and we were left truly confused about what to do with our guns.

For a while in 1990 there was talk about a "peace dividend." We were going to take our war-making resources and turn them to tranquil ends. Even some usually sensible politicians thought this made sense. And maybe they were right. From what I can see of modern kids, the M1A1 Abrams tank is well suited to providing day-care needs. And I can understand how some people might want to retarget our Polaris missiles at the high-crime areas of America's cities—the mayors' offices, for instance.

Defense is the traditional whipping boy for budget cutters, and understandably so. Defense spending is immensely wasteful. Even if defense spending were managed by honest, clairvoyant geniuses (and this is not the case), it would still be immensely wasteful. All forms of defense—national, personal and even biological—are wasteful. The body's immune system is a real waste—big, sprawling old white blood corpuscles floating around all over the place doing absolutely nothing to earn their keep, not even lending paper cuts a festive hue—until the body gets sick. By the same token soldiers and weapons do nothing unless there's a war. And, in 1990, there were about to be a lot fewer American soldiers and weapons doing that nothing. There's no telling what might have happened to our defense budget if Saddam Hussein hadn't invaded Kuwait that August and set everyone to gearing up for World War II½.

Can we count on Saddam Hussein to come along every year and resolve our defense-policy debates? Given the history of the Middle East, it's possible. But we ought to do at least a little thinking for ourselves. How do we go about conducting brief, highly specific, military operations in minor trouble spots? What do we do with elaborate and expensive weapons systems designed for a geopolitical reality that no longer exists? In the future, with any luck, these will be more important questions than whether to carpet bomb Baghdad.

I went to Panama two months after the U.S. military removed Manuel Noriega from power and found a country at peace. The night I arrived in Panama City, some political terrorist chucked a grenade into a bar full of young women and off-duty GIs. The popularity of "low-intensity conflicts" can make it hard to tell war from peace in the late twentieth century. But if a bunch of *lambada* dancers get hurt in a terrorist attack, this usually indicates peacetime.

One American soldier was killed, and all the others were restricted to base. This left the whole J Street red-light district and all of its nudie bars full of procurers, pickpockets, B-girls, strippers, drug pushers, bilko artists and fat, tattooed Colombian prostitutes with a paying clientele of me and one drunk wire-service reporter.

The girls in our particular nudie bar might have looked OK in the middle of a real war, when a man's blood is running hot and every experience is seasoned with fear's piquant relish and heaven knows what the morrow might bring, etc. But this was peacetime, as I pointed out, and no, *gracias, señorita,* I don't care to see how the Last Supper is illustrated across your bottom with Judas Iscariot in the middle.

After Operation Just Cause, Panama City was filled with trash, disorder, devastated housing, human suffering—and the parts of the city that had been fought in looked pretty bad, too. There's been a lot of squeaking and belching among journalists and other members of America's professional bed-wetting class over what happened in Panama. If you watched enough network TV reporting about security snafus and Stealth fighters missing their targets, read enough *Newsweek* exposés about U.S. deaths from friendly fire and listened to enough Jesse Jackson on the subject of civilian casualties, you might not realize that Operation Just Cause was a victory. Like modern war and peace, modern victory and defeat can be hard to distinguish. But let's apply a rule of thumb that is perhaps too unsophisticated for use by the national media and call something a victory if it was victorious. I was in Panama in 1987, during Noriega's blossom days. None of the fire was friendly then. The streets were filled with rioting riot police. Members of such wild-eyed subversive groups as the Panama City Chamber of Commerce were being heaved into jail. And the nation's drunks and thugs had been given guns and formed into "Dignity Battalions" to scare the piss out of anybody who wore a necktie or owned two pairs of shoes. Believe me, Operation Just Cause was just that. Maybe it violated international law, but when was the last time the UN ticketed you for jaywalking?

Jesse Jackson wasn't the only one complaining about civilian casualties during the U.S. incursion; Panamanians were complaining, too. They were complaining that there weren't *enough* civilian casualties—because American soldiers wouldn't shoot looters. Panama City's best shopping district, a mile-and-a-half stretch of the Via España, was destroyed, and none of it by military action, all of it by looting.

Flory Saltzman, an elderly woman with a little shop selling *mola* embroideries made by the Cuna Indians, wasn't insured. She lost her stock and furnishings and had just used all her savings to start over. "But," said Mrs. Saltzman, "if they told me today that they were going to come take Noriega and loot my store again, I'd say it was worth it."

I couldn't even find a kind word for Noriega in his old stronghold, the Chorrillo slum where the Panamanian Defense Force was headquartered and the Dignity Battalions were recruited. "We got rid of a crazy guy," said a street vendor. Chorrillo caught fire during the fighting—was probably set on fire by the Dignity Battalions—and most of it burned, leaving thousands of people without homes. "It was a lousy neighborhood anyway," said one woman with a shrug.

I asked a group of refugees, "Was the U.S. invasion right or wrong?"

"We got rid of that man," said one of them. Then they all complained that they hadn't gotten any U.S. aid money yet.

Operation Just Cause was well fought. There was no sign in Panama City of that kind of wild firing that has left every window, doorway and building corner in Beirut chipped concave. There were fewer bullet holes visible in Panama than in downtown Manila or parts of Washington, DC. Some anti-American activists, such as the Ramsey Clark–led Independent Commission of Inquiry on the United States Invasion of Panama, claimed that more than three thousand Panamanian civilians died in the fighting. But I was unable to find anyone in Chorrillo or J Street or Via España or any other neighborhood with a missing friend or relation. No inordinate number of candles were burning at any church shrines, nor did I see any of the "HAVE YOU SEEN ————?" and "YOU WILL FIND US AT ————" graffiti that normally appears after episodes of urban chaos. Even the people at Americas Watch, who are so firmly convinced that America bears watching, conceded their estimate of civilian deaths was only slightly higher than the U.S. Army Southern Command's count of 202. Besides civilians, 314 Panamanian Defense Force soldiers and 23 members of the U.S. military were killed. There are places on this earth where you can't hold a soccer match with so few casualties.

I went to see Colonel Mike Snell, who commanded Task Force Bravo, one of the operation's four ground combat groups and the one detailed to take Noriega's Commanceia headquarters and seize control of the central Canal Zone. The three thousand soldiers under Snell's command were in some of the worst fighting of the operation, but only sixty-four were wounded, and only five were killed.

Colonel Snell was my age, forty-two, but with firmer jaw and flatter stomach, and he all but emitted a visible glow of pride in Operation Just Cause. What made Snell so happy, however, was not the brave fighting his troops had done or the modest casualties they'd suffered doing it but something it never occurred to me a professional soldier would prize.

"Where my soldiers fought," said Snell, "their restraint was remarkable." Even in the heat of combat, he said—and the fight for the Commanceia had lasted the whole first night of the operation—his troops had used "proportional response." That is, they didn't soften up positions with mile-wide artillery barrages or huge air strikes. To take out individuals firing at them, they relied on snipers instead of M16 fusillades. They used ninety-millimeter recoilless rifles to punch holes, right where they wanted them, in cinder-block buildings. "Minimum collateral damage—minimum injury or death of innocents," said Snell with the smack of satisfaction a Mongol khan might have used with the words "Built a pyramid of human skulls."

Snell went on to describe how his soldiers had been trained in low-intensity conflict using live-ammunition firing ranges dotted not only with "enemy positions" but with "religious monuments," "noncombatants seeking cover" and "surrendering opposition forces." Snell made sure there were Spanish-speaking soldiers, some of them Panamanian-born, in every platoon and squad. And Snell followed each firefight with a pause to allow bullhorn-carrying psy-op specialists to make eloquent arguments for surrender.

The February 1990 issue of the U.S. Army's *Soldiers* magazine gave a vivid—if not very action-packed—description of fighting the way it was done in Panama:

> Sgt. Edward McCrane of C Co. [was] standing in the back of a five-ton truck, surrounded by about 200 Panamanian civilians. He and two other soldiers had stopped in the middle of an intersection. McCrane stood on the left side of the truck with a raised AK-47, speaking in Spanish. "This weapon is used by PDF. . . ." He continued for about ten minutes, urging the crowd to turn in PDF members and weapons. He also warned children not to play with duds or toy guns or taunt the soldiers.
>
> People applauded and the truck moved on to the next intersection.

The nondestruction of Panama and the unslaughter of its inhabitants was the result of the United States fighting a "nonlinear battle"—concentrating on pre-assigned military objectives and not bothering to conquer territory. The army didn't get around to securing our own embassy for two days because there was no threat to the peace in there (which shows how little the army knows about the State Department).

"We got to know the targets," said Snell. "The captains had books with everything about their targets, even down to what windows to shoot through for fire demonstrations." Thus Task Force Bravo was able to "demonstrate" U.S. artillery strength without unnecessary killing of Panamanians by shelling the Commanceia's dining hall at 1:00 A.M., when it was empty, except for some dead snackers.

This postmodern, neural-net, simul-fought, multiphasic info-vasion kind of war is as dependent as the rest of contemporary life on expensive technology. Six different kinds of helicopters were needed for Operation Just Cause. Without helicopters the battle for Panama City would have been fought building to building with terrible casualties, like the Battle of Stalingrad. Well, let's not overstate the case—like a laid-back, disorganized, tropical Battle of Stalingrad.

A variety of equipment that had not been tried in combat got tried in Panama, including the HMMWV, the High-Mobility Multi-purpose Wheeled Vehicle, or Hum-V, which looks like a giant malevolent basement dehumidifier; the AH-64 Apache and UH-60 Blackhawk attack and utility helicopters; the new Kevlar flak jacket and the Kaiser Bill–ish Kevlar helmet. Only the Stealth fighter and the air force's stealthy manner of not reporting how it missed a target got any coverage in the American press. But the rest of the stuff worked fine, especially the Kevlar, though the helmet is as heavy and awkward as a sack of grass seed and the flak jacket is like wearing your own sauna bath. Of the 347 Americans hit by enemy fire, only 23 died. Of the 438 Kevlar-less Panamanians hit by our fire, 314 died.

The American army needed not only its new equipment but its old equipment, too. The 1960s-era Sheridan light tank is still the only tank we have that can be dropped by parachute and the only tank small enough to fight in the narrow streets around the presidential palace and government buildings in Old Panama City. Colonel Snell said his most valuable weapon was that ninety-millimeter recoilless rifle, which dates back to the Korean

War. Recoilless rifles have been made obsolete by improvements in armor plate. It takes a wire-guided TOW missile to knock out a modern tank. But the Panamanians didn't have any modern tanks. And wire-guided missiles need three hundred yards to get level before they can be accurately aimed. There's no place in Panama City where you can get three hundred yards away from anything. Snell had to order the recoilless rifles out of mothballs five weeks before Operation Just Cause, and only a few old lifer sergeants knew how to use them.

Of course, more important than having brilliant new weapons or proven old weapons is having lots of weapons. And more important than that is having enough transport to get any weapons anywhere. And most important of all is having enough trained men—twenty-six thousand in this case—to use those weapons.

Operation Just Cause was launched at 1:00 A.M. on Wednesday December 20, 1989. The director of operations for the Joint Chiefs of Staff, Lieutenant General T. W. Kelly, said afterward, "Recall that the so-called war status was declared by Noriega on Friday, the marine was killed on Saturday, the [beating of a U.S. naval officer and sexual molestation of his wife] occurred on Saturday. We made a decision, and in almost no time at all we were putting our paratroopers and Rangers on airplanes and sending them down there. I don't know that there's another country in the world that can do that."

There isn't.

Which brings us to the real secret behind the success of Operation Just Cause—money. Giving Manuel Noriega the bum's rush cost about $2 billion. And what makes us in America the big-dog, double-barreled, don't-tell-Mother nation that we are is not how much money that is but how little. Two billion dollars is two thirds of 1 percent of our 1990 defense budget. America has the money to oust 150 tin-pot dictators a year if there are that many dictators left and restore democracy and human rights to 150 countries per annum if there are that many countries that want any. And we're still only spending about a quarter of our federal budget on guns, leaving three quarters for all that butter that isn't good for us.

About 5.5 percent of America's gross national product goes to defense. Wouldn't you be willing to spend 5.5 percent of your income to guarantee the safety of your spouse, kids, house, car, savings, investments and sports and hobby equipment? Not only would you—add up your car-insurance, life-insurance and homeowners-insurance premiums—you *do*. Now show me the insurance company that will come over to your house with AH-64 Apache helicopters, M551 Sheridan light tanks and ninety-millimeter re-coilless rifles if the Bahamas invade Fort Lauderdale.

An America with a fart in a thunderstorm defense budget could still mount an Operation Just Cause. We would send fewer soldiers with worse equipment and less training to Panama, and the only difference would be more dead people, mostly Panamanians. But will an American defense budget from which, like the liver of Prometheus, a peace dividend is regularly torn be sufficient to guard us against all eventualities? What if some large industrialized country that is experiencing extreme national turmoil degenerates into a mad dictatorship, the way Germany did in the 1930s? This is not impossible when a large country has a citizenry half-crazed from standing in line for six months at the only McDonald's in Moscow.

The Soviets, or Russians, or whoever they are these days, still have atomic bombs. I'm glad to hear them say they don't want to use the atomic bombs on us anymore. This is sweet of them. But I suspect the Soviets never did *want* to use those bombs. The most Stalinist of Soviet hard-liners— Stalin, for example—must have realized a nuclear war would be a hard thing to clean up after. Even in their most warlike frame of mind the Soviets preferred to wait until the likes of Ramsey Clark and the Independent Commission of Inquiry on the United States Invasion of Panama won a majority in the U.S. Congress or until the entire fabric of American society was torn asunder by clashes between ACT-UP and People for the Ethical Treatment of Animals.

The point is not whether people want to kill us. Think of all the people who want to kill us—people we used to be married to, people we're married to now, children we just grounded for using our Master Charge to call the Naked Chat Line 900 number, the next-door neighbor whose azaleas we crushed trying to back the boat trailer into our driveway. Who cares? We're not interested in whether they want to kill us; we're interested in whether they *can*. The Soviets can. So can the Chinese. And the French, for that matter. Then there are those countries, some run by complete lunatics, that have a bomb or two or could make one or will be able to make one soon: Israel, South Africa, India, Pakistan, Iraq, Iran, Egypt, Libya, Argentina, Brazil, both Koreas . . . The need for technologically advanced defense programs does not end with Russia throwing in the towel.

The military strength-in-depth needed for an Operation Just Cause, a continuing strategic threat from the dark corners of the globe—these are rational arguments against cutting the defense budget. But to debate government policy using only reason is to ignore a number of important irrational aspects of government.

In the first place, we're not going to save money or eliminate the deficit by reducing defense expenditures. It is a law of governance that democracies have to spend themselves dizzy. Citizens of democracies can, after all, tell their government to give them things. For this reason, defense spending in America is not so much a matter of Americans sacrificing to keep their country safe as it is a matter of Americans telling their government to give them defense contracts and defense-industry jobs. When those jobs and contracts disappear, others will be demanded in their place. Call this a peace dividend if you like, or call it turning the pork barrel over and starting to eat from the other end. The deficit won't be affected, because the same citizens who can tell their government to give them things can tell that government "no new taxes." (This being more, you'll note, than the president can accomplish.)

If we do our deficit spending on weapons, at least we get weapons. Then if we need the weapons, we have them. If we don't need them, no harm is done. The weapons lie around in warehouses somewhere emitting just enough radioactivity to keep life interesting for the Friends of the Earth. But if we do our deficit spending on social programs, we create things that are far more dangerous and terrifying than Friends of the Earth.

Social-program spending is spending done directly on the public rather than for the public's benefit. Note the mental image evoked by the very word *public:* public school, public park, public health, public housing. To call something public is to define it as dirty, insufficient and hazardous. The ultimate paradigm of social spending is the public rest room. In a democracy if we don't spend an enormous amount of money on defense, we will have to spend it on vice, bad smells and alarming graffiti.

Then there are the beneficial spin-offs from defense research to be considered, all the wonderful products that we use every day that were originally developed for military applications—guns, for instance.

Defense spending also gives people with military-type personalities jobs in the military rather than in other fields of endeavor, such as psychotherapy, to which they might be less well suited:

LIGHTS ON IN YOUR HEAD, YOU NEURASTHENIC MAGGOT. I WANT THAT OEDIPAL
CONFLICT RESOLVED BY O-NINE-HUNDRED HOURS.

But the best and final argument against cutting defense spending cannot be put into words. It's visceral, hormonal. It is that excitement in the gut, that swelling of the chest, the involuntary smile that comes across the face of every male when he has a weapon to hand.

I traveled from the Mayport Naval Station in Florida to Charleston, South Carolina, on board the Ticonderoga Class Aegis guided-missile cruiser USS *Mobile Bay*. The *Mobile Bay* is armed with the MK-41 Vertical Launching System, a pair of magazines—one in the forward deck and one in the aft—in which a total of 122 missiles are standing on their ends like bottles in cartons of booze. All kinds of missiles are in there: anti-aircraft missiles, ship-attack missiles and, no doubt—though the navy is always coy on this point—Tomahawk cruise missiles with A-bomb warheads. The *Mobile Bay* is also armed with fully automated five-inch guns, quad-canister harpoon missile launchers, torpedo tubes, four fifty-caliber machine guns, two Phalanx close-range anti-missile miniguns and two SH60B helicopters hangared onboard with torpedoes and guns of their own. If all else fails and something out there is still alive, there are two small, pulpitlike structures on either side of the main deck, where sailors can stand and fire hand-held Stinger missiles. All this armament is tactically integrated—guided, informed, managed and targeted by the electronic wonders of the Aegis Weapons System. And the whole thing only cost a billion dollars, less than half of our annual foreign aid to Egypt. And Egypt can't even blow itself up, let alone anything else.

The *Mobile Bay* is 567 feet long, almost four times as long as the Statue of Liberty would be if the Statue of Liberty were lying on its side and floating in the water (which makes no sense, but there are professional-writer bylaws requiring comparisons of this type whenever anything very large is being described). The *Mobile Bay* is 55 feet wide, displaces 9,516 tons of seawater, is manned by a crew of 409 and has four 80,000-horsepower gas turbine engines, essentially the same kind that power a DC-10. The top speed is so top that it's a military secret. The navy will admit to "in excess of 30 knots" (34¼ mph), but crewmen told me that at full power the *Mobile Bay* stands up out of the water like a Cigarette boat, maneuvers like a wind surfer and can come to a dead stop from full throttle in two ship lengths.

The *Mobile Bay*'s "Welcome Aboard" pamphlet was full of Statue-of-Liberty-on-its-side-style information. Building the ship "required enough steel to fabricate 4,000 cars, aluminum sufficient to produce 26 million soft drink cans, over 200 miles of electrical cable . . ." There is enough fuel on board, the pamphlet said, "to run the family car nearly 25 million miles." I always wish the people who figure these things out would just keep going: "The hawsers and bowlines carried aboard the *Mobile Bay* are long enough to hang every Democrat elected to Congress since Roosevelt's second term. The synthetic rubber in the fire hoses would make enough prophylactics to allow every business executive in Japan to visit Manila. The ship's bilge pumps could drain all the ecologically significant wetlands in Oregon in 24 hours." And so forth.

The *Mobile Bay* is not, however, very impressive to see. It has a tall, boxed-in, blank-sided superstructure that gives it a floating-car-barn look. And the only immediately discernible weapons, the two dinky five-incher gun turrets, would not make for dramatic Liberty Bond poster art.

Modern naval warfare is an indoorsy thing. There are almost no portholes on the *Mobile Bay*. The captain had to have one custom-fitted in his stateroom so he could keep an eye on the foredeck without going to his battle-command post and watching it on TV. Once off the deck in the *Mobile Bay*, you might as well be in a submarine or a factory basement. Only on the bridge—with its helmsmen and lookouts and its officers perusing navigational charts—is there any sense of being at sea.

The night before we sailed, I went for a drink with the *Mobile Bay*'s commander, Captain David Bill III. In a bar by the docks we ran into one of Captain Bill's former chief petty officers, now retired, a big man with an important gut, a variety of tattoos and graying hair cut the length of toothbrush bristles. My father was a chief petty officer, and so was my uncle, and I know the type. And I know the navy has changed for certain because, after a couple of beers, Captain Bill turned to me and said, "This is one of the best chiefs I ever had on the *Mobile Bay*—you ought to see what this man can do with a computer."

In the morning the *Mobile Bay* left the Mayport Naval Station and steamed—that is, gas-turbined—out to sea. The departure was so smoothly effected and the engines so quiet in their puissance that I was having breakfast in the officers' mess and didn't know I was gone. I spent the next two days wandering through this repository of my tax dollars trying to discover what defense spending buys.

It buys complexity. The *Mobile Bay* is the most complex thing I've ever been in, not counting love. All the spaces of the ship are filled with nests of valves and switches and transversed by ganglia of pipes and wires. To attempt any real understanding of how it all works is to slide into that mood of childish despair at having taken the alarm clock apart. Defense spending also buys cleanliness. The *Mobile Bay* is unnaturally clean, cleaner than anything ever is in civilian life. Every crease of every corner of the ship is tended every day. And not only is there incessant scrubbing and mopping but eternal chipping and brushing besides, so that in the course of a two-year cycle all surfaces, however inaccessible, and every rivet, nut and bolt head will have been repainted. Each of these items is also numbered. Every hatch, pipe, bulkhead, gangway, locker, compartment and nameless do-funny has a number stenciled on it, and that number tells an adept just what the object is and where, exactly, its proper place is within the ship. The *Mobile Bay* is so clean and organized as to mock God for the frowsy quantum-physics universe he created.

The crew of the *Mobile Bay* lives in tiny and drab (but clean and organized) quarters. The men, petty officers and junior officers sleep in triple-deck bunk beds that look like something you'd organize your CDs in.

I tagged along with the executive officer, the ship's second in command, when he went to brief a group of enlisted men in the crew mess. The mess was not a very martial place. It had a cute name—Patriot's Landing—a salad bar, hanging plants and fake carriage lamps over fast-food-restaurant-style tables for four. Nor were the sailors traditional. They were young, clean-cut and polite. The *Mobile Bay* was soon to head out on an extended tour of duty in the Pacific, and the executive officer was telling the men what to expect. When the time came for questions, the sailors didn't ask about the whore houses of Thailand or what kind of tattoos to get or how many Hong Kong wharf rats a Yankee swab could be expected to whip in a fair fight after consuming fifty beers on shore liberty. They wanted to know how many phone calls home they would be able to afford per month and details of health care and housing allowances for dependents.

After the briefing I went to the aft deck to watch the helicopters land and take off. Here, at least, was some of the noise and excitement that practicing for war should have. The helicopters were trying out their RAST—Recovery Assist Security Transfer—systems, which can bring a chopper down in one piece in the worst of weather. The helicopter hovers above the ship and dangles a cable onto the deck. Then two brave or, anyway, dutiful sailors run out and hook this cable to another cable, which is attached to what is basically an enormous motor-driven spin-casting reel. The helicopter is then hauled down and landed like a giant air bass. Still, the RAST, and the helicopters, too, seemed more ingenious than bellicose. Like the fighting in Panama, the operation of the *Mobile Bay* has more to do with intelligence, training and technology than with plain, straightforward murder.

The largest part of the *Mobile Bay* is given over not to guns or men but to electronics. It is the huge, flat, octagon Aegis radar antennae that determine the missile cruisers' chest-of-drawers shape. And in the upper middle part of that chest of drawers, about where the dress shirts and good handkerchiefs would be, is the *Mobile Bay*'s reason for being. This is a single windowless space, huge by shipboard standards, maybe thirty feet deep by forty feet wide, called the Combat Information Center. The room glows with the graveyard light of cathode tubes beaming data blips at the solemn faces of military technicians, and the only sounds are the snicking of computer keyboards and the low buzz of speech into headset microphones. The CIC is so complex that it moves the uninitiated beyond confusion to catatonic awe. No science-fiction movie set design can capture the sheer inexplicability of science fact—which partly can't be explained for security's sake and partly just can't be explained to someone who was a college English major. (The high-school-educated navy enlisted men who run all this, however, understand it completely, which leads me to believe that the "failing American educational system" is mostly failing those Americans who think they are too smart to pay attention in school.)

The Combat Information Center is the command post for the Aegis Weapons System. And what the Aegis Weapons System is is the shield of Zeus, for which it was named. The *Mobile Bay* uses a kind of radar—phased array—that sends out multiple pulses capable of tracking hundreds of targets at once. The phased-array radar is combined with sonar, magnetic detection devices and various other types of sensors to create a five-hundred-mile-wide bubble of electronic protection around the ship. The MK-41 vertical Launch missiles can then destroy anything within that bubble.

The Aegis radar can detect a basketball 150 miles away and a high-altitude bomber a thousand miles off. The Aegis computers receive information not only from the *Mobile Bay*'s own sensors, but from those carried on its helicopters and onboard all the other ships in its fleet. The *Mobile Bay* is also linked, by satellite, to the computers in the Pentagon. The resulting monstrous in-pouring of real-time data is filtered, distilled and channeled at the individual video monitors in the Combat Information Center and then flashed up on four bay-window-sized green LED displays arrayed along the CICs port side.

Here, in front of these screens, seated like four judges on the bench, are the captain of the *Mobile Bay*, the admiral of the fleet and their respective aides (the aide being especially important to the admiral, because people who are old enough to be admirals have no idea how to work a computer keyboard). From these great seats of authority—actually, government-issue padded-Naugahyde swivel chairs—war can be fought across a large portion of the earth, and large parts of that large portion can be destroyed by nuclear attack. The screens show schematic maps centered on the position of the *Mobile Bay*. The scale of the maps can be changed at the touch of a keyboard from continentwide to 6 inches = 1 mile. On these maps are shown every airplane, surface ship and submarine within the Aegis bubble—ultralights, cabin cruisers, Jacques Cousteau and all. Friendly aircraft are indicated on the screens with the top half of a circle; friendly undersea objects, with the bottom half of a circle; and friendly surface ships, with a circle itself. Similarly, diamond shapes indicate hostiles and squares indicate unknowns. At another punch of the keyboard the Aegis system can be left to think for itself, and all the little diamond shapes will be automatically blown to no shape at all.

"Any questions?" asked the junior lieutenant who was showing me around. But no question I could think of seemed big enough to do the Aegis justice.

"Does it work?" I said at last. And a strange expression came across the mild and pleasant features of the young lieutenant's face. "It works as advertised," he said with an evil grin.

Actually, it works too well. It was an Aegis guided-missile cruiser, the USS *Vincennes*, that obliterated an Iranian airbus full of civilians over the Persian Gulf in 1988. But then again, we're talking about a peacetime weapons system here, and there are a lot more airbuses than strategic bombers in the air during peacetime.

"The *Mobile Bay* can launch all 122 of its missiles in two minutes, though 16 in the air at one time is really the practical limit," said the lieutenant, mild and pleasant again. That is, in less time than it takes to count the dollars in the U.S. defense budget by billions, this one boat can loose more military power on the world than mankind used in all its history from the first australopithecine flint-tossing spat in the Olduvai Gorge until Hiroshima.

I went down to the foredeck and meditated on the thoroughly uninteresting visible part of the Vertical Launching System. Each missile has its own corrugated-metal canister within the magazine, and each canister has a square lid on the ship's deck, a sort of yard-wide solid-steel version of the lid marked SIFT on a can of Durkee's ground black pepper.

I couldn't talk the captain into firing a missile for me, but he gave me a videotape of a test firing, and I watched this in the VCR-equipped fleet admiral's stateroom. Even in slow motion there was nothing slow about the missile launching. The flip lid whips open, and for a moment you see a bald top of something emerging in light and smoke, a high burlesque of a jack-in-the-box; then the ship's deck is covered by a tower of blast and dazzle blanketing one bright, rising, white, fiery column—hell's own hard-on.

This is the way to waste government money.

SPECIAL INTEREST GROUPS: THE ORIGINAL BARREL OF MONKEYS THAT NOTHING IS MORE FUN THAN

In the Big Rock Candy Mountains
You never change your socks,
And little streams of alcohol
Come a-trickling down the rocks.
The box cars are all empty
And the railroad bulls are blind,
There's a lake of stew and whiskey, too,
You can paddle all around 'em in a big canoe,
In the Big Rock Candy Mountains.

—Mac McClintock

AMONG THE COMPASSION FASCISTS

The National March for Housing Now!

On October 7, 1989, I went to see the National March for Housing Now! on the Mall in Washington. The demonstrators seemed sincere in their desire to solve the various habitation-cost and dwelling-availability problems we have in the United States. The organized-labor contingent carried banners calling for a uniform national building code, increased factory mass production of modular homes, stricter Taft-Hartley anti-featherbedding regulations and a federal right-to-work law. Homeless advocates, community activists and welfare-rights organizers led the crowd in chants of

> *Apartments, yes!*
> *Shelters, no!*
> *Rent control has got to go!*
>
> *Quit your whining,*
> *Stop your dithers,*
> *Sell public housing to the highest bidders!*
>
> *We're sick of living in a ditch,*
> *Give real estate tax breaks back to the rich!*

while thousands of homeless men and women waved signs reading "JAIL US, WE'RE DRUNK" and "WE ARE CRAZY. PUT US IN MENTAL INSTITUTIONS, PLEASE."

The actual National March for Housing Now! didn't have thousands of homeless men and women or even hundreds, as far as I could see. At the pre-march rally beside the Washington Monument I did hear one woman say she was homeless. She was a big, resentful woman—the kind who's always behind the counter at the Department of Motor Vehicles when you go to renew your car registration. She was co-chairhuman of something or other, and she was declaiming from the podium: "I've got five kids! We live in one room! We're homeless!" No, ma'am, you're not. Your housing may be as bad as your family planning, but you're not homeless.

We usually think of "special interests" as being something out of a Thomas Nast cartoon—big men with cigars conspiring over a biscuit trust. But in fact, a special interest is any person or group that wants to be treated differently from the rest of us by the government. Every charity is a special interest. So is the League of Women Voters, the Episcopalian church, *Consumer Reports* magazine and anybody who threatens to write to his congressman. A special interest may be humble. It may be (this happens) worthy. It may even be morally correct about its need for special treatment.

Politics would not exist if it weren't for special interests. If the effect of government were always the same on everyone and if no one stood to lose or gain anything from government except what his fellows did, there would be little need for debate and no need for coalitions, parties or intrigue. Indeed, when some great national item appears on the governmental agenda, something that involves every person in the country—World War II or the interstate highway system—government turns apolitical (at least until the defense and paving contracts begin to be handed out).

Traditionally American special interests have been frank about their political goals: They want money and privileges that other Americans don't get. The agriculture lobby of a few chapters back is a good example. Farmers argue that they, as a special interest, should receive special treatment because they're special—they feed us (or did until we started importing all our fast food burger meat from Argentina). Veterans make the same kind of claim—they risked their lives to protect the rest of us, so they should get funny hats to wear on Memorial Day and some cash. But recently special interest groups have begun dressing themselves in the clothes of altruism. And some of these groups have become so well costumed that it's hard to tell what their special interest is, let alone what's so special about it.

Aside from the big, resentful woman with the five kids, the rest of the Housing Now! demonstrators seemed to come from normal homes, that is, the kinds of homes that demonstrators normally come from—homes where they had sufficient resources to become half-educated and adequate leisure to hate their parents. They were all present and accounted for:

World Council of Churches sensible-shoe types who have
    self-righteousness the way some people have bad breath
Angry black poverty pests making a life and a living off the
    misfortunes of others
Even angrier feminists doing their best to feminize poverty before
    the blacks use it all up
Earnest neophyte Marxists, eyes glazed from dialectical epiphanies
    and hands grubby from littering the Mall with ill-Xeroxed
    tracts
College bohos dressed in black to show how gloomy the world is
    when you're a nineteen-year-old rich kid
Young would-be hippies dressed exactly like old hippies used to
    dress (remarkable how behind the times the avant-garde has
    gotten)
And some of those old hippies themselves, faded jeans straining
    beneath increasing paunches, hair still tied into a ponytail in
    the back but gone forever on the top

Together these people constitute America's loudest special interest (and only true, permanent underclass)—the Perennially Indignant. As always these days, they were joined by greedy celebrities who aren't contented with fame and money and want a reputation for moral goodness, too.

The labor unions were also on hand, but their members stood away to one side in well-pressed sport clothes and snappy nylon windbreakers embossed with the names of their locals. The United Auto Workers; American Federation of State, County and Municipal Employees; Steelworkers and various building trades each had neat stacks of professionally made picket signs. The International Brotherhood of Electrical Workers even brought along its kilted bagpipe band. The plump, scrubbed union folk, enjoying a subsidized bus trip with their softball buddies, were as out of place as yarmulkes on a motorcycle gang. And more power to them. If government is going to fling money at homelessness, I'd like at least some of the money to land on people who hold jobs.

That morning as I was going out the door of my own housing—which is handsome, spacious and frankly underpriced due to the District of Columbia Housing Act of 1985, which in the name of keeping DC homes "affordable," instituted rent ceilings that have led to the destruction of rental stock in the less affluent sections of the city while providing a cost-of-living subsidy to rich, unfeeling conservatives like myself. But I digress. . . . As I was going out the door, my wife said, "Will there be lots of people from South Carolina at the housing march?"

I said, "Huh?"

"You know," she said, "where Hurricane Hugo just destroyed everybody's house." My wife, like many wives, is under the impression that mankind is as rational and pragmatic as wives are. I had to explain that there wouldn't be any people from South Carolina in the march demanding houses from the government because the people from South Carolina were too busy building houses for themselves.

The big, resentful woman I mentioned earlier went on to extol a group of what appeared to be just plain street bums called the New Exodus Marchers who had walked to DC from New York. When the New Exodus people arrived in Washington, they promptly got into a fistfight at the Center for Creative Non-Violence. The fight had to do with the disposition of royalty proceeds from the sale of HOMELESS T-shirts. (I am not making this up.) Ms. Big Resentful said, "Five babies died on the walk from New York City! The mothers miscarried but they kept on walking! This was amazing! This was supernatural!"

This was grounds for arrest.

Over on the other side of the crowd I heard somebody shouting through a bullhorn that they were from Alliance, Ohio. "And you may not believe this," they shouted, "but even in little Alliance, Ohio, we have two hundred people in our shelter." I didn't believe this. I'm from Ohio. Alliance is a pleasant, semirural town in the northeast of the state. On Monday I called the Alliance town office and was put right through to Mayor Carr, who sounded puzzled. "The figure is new to me," he said. "I'd never heard the two-hundred figure. Our shelter was put up for people whose houses burn down, things like that. We haven't thought of it in terms of the homeless."

Around noon the demonstrators traipsed down Constitution Avenue and came to a halt, standing dully before a large sound stage near the Reflecting Pool. It was a crowd numbering—as NBC News, with TV's keen eye for hard facts, put it—"between 40,000 and 250,000 people." The marchers packed themselves into the Mall between Third and Fourth Streets (packed themselves very tightly, if we accept the 250,000 figure). They were then regaled by the moderately famous: Richie Havens, Martin Sheen, Dick Gregory, Olatunji, Mary Wilson. There was a fenced-off area beside the stage, a sort of celebrity pen, where additional fairly well-known people were being kept. Demonstrators pressed in to catch a glimpse of Casey Kasem, Susan Dey, Rita Coolidge, Jon Voight and to try to figure out which one of them was which.

The crowd was addressed with much bruiting of homelessness numbers, three million being the favorite. Since this is 500 percent more than any serious estimate, housing advocates seem, rather than ameliorating homelessness, to have created 2.4 million cases of it. A lot of equivalency was in the air. "For the price of one B-2 bomber . . ." began most if not all the speeches. (As if there were a redemption center someplace where you could make a straight up trade of social progress for national defense.) The savings-and-loan bailout has replaced the moon shot as the Perennially Indignants' pet if-then theorem. "If the government can find $500 billion to . . ." But, of course, the government *couldn't* find $500 billion and ended up taking it from you and me.

The only break in the day's smug outrage and furious self-congratulation was a round of catcalls for Washington Mayor Marion Barry. I don't know why these people were mad at Barry. He advocated more federal money for housing and everything else. But Mayor Barry had been accused of taking drugs, and I guess the homeless wanted those drugs back.

Coolly considered over lunch (a pheasant-under-glass-and-caviar sandwich with a six-pack of Dom Perignon, because I mean to spend this money before it all goes to build flophouses), the most prominent feature of the Housing Now! march was its beggary. The march organizers weren't even pretending that the members of their special interest were deserving or that spending tax dollars on them would be useful, wise or fair. Nor were any definite programs proposed. The message of the Housing Now! demonstration was simply and entirely "give me some money."

The Perennially Indignant have, of course, good reasons for not putting forth definite programs. First, the homeless problem isn't what they say it is. Homelessness is not the result of a lack of warm, dry abodes in the United States. It's the result of mental-patient deinstitutionalization, de facto legalization of drug use, elimination of vagrancy laws, destruction of urban neighborhoods through infringement on property rights and a lot of other things that the Perennially Indignant themselves hold dear. Listening to people advocate programs to solve a problem caused by the programs those people advocated—this would be as absurd as, oh, I don't know, letting lawyers make laws.

Second, the Perennially Indignant don't want homelessness to go away (though I'll give them the benefit of the doubt and say that they aren't conscious of this). In our prosperous, peaceful and happy era, homelessness is one of the few undeniable (and telegenic!) social injustices left. No matter what somebody has done to himself or others, he doesn't deserve to freeze in the gutter is the Indignants' almost reasonable argument.

For the Perennially Indignant homelessness is a fine rallying flag where they can all gather and show off how much they care. Homelessness is also a splendid way to indict the American system and, while they're at it, all of Western civilization and its individualism and freedom. Of Thomas Paine's "natural and imprescriptible rights of man . . . liberty, property, security and resistance to oppression," the Indignants believe only in security. They would replace the democratic paradigm of government as a free association of equals with the totalitarian paradigm of the state as family.

Fortunately, few people in government take the Housing Now! kind of special interest lobbying seriously. Actual policymakers (we're not talking about liberal Democrats here) are familiar with the real homeless-population estimates generated by Dr. Martha Burt for the Food and Nutrition Service of the U.S. Department of Agriculture—the only nationwide probability-based study that's been done on the subject. Policymakers know about Thomas J. Main's and Dr. E. Fuller Torrey's investigations of the psychiatric and behavioral problems of the homeless. They have seen or at least heard about William Tucker's regression analysis showing the causal relationship of rent control to housing shortages. Et cetera. Et cetera.

The facts are simple. A government house-building orgy won't work because one third of the homeless are crazy and will jump out the windows and one third are screwed up on drink and drugs and will sell the plumbing. The rest have primarily economic problems, but we can keep giving them free housing forever, and it won't help. The law of supply and demand tells us that when the price of something is artifically set below market level there will soon be none of that thing left—as you may have noticed the last time you tried to buy something for nothing.

But the Perennially Indignant don't care if a policy works. In many ways it's better for them when a policy fails. What's a family for?

I went back to have another look at the demonstration, passing a number of homeless on the way. Despite a sizable protest on their behalf just around the corner, they remained at their posts, cadging change. One fellow was sitting athwart the sidewalk on Twelfth Street near the Old Post Office Building. He had an overnight bag with him and a pile of newspapers and magazines. He'd set out a paper cup primed with a few quarters and was listening to his Sony Walkman while he read the *Washington Post.* I went into a store to get my own copy of the *Post.* There was an Asian man, about fifty, behind the counter. He spotted my press tags and said, in compassionate if barely comprehensible English, "Oh, is Saturday, beautiful day—you must work?"

I told him yes, I was covering the housing march. "But you're working on Saturday, too," I said.

"Oh, yes!" He smiled widely. "Seven days!"

I hesitate to even mention these two encounters. Some things are too amazing for fiction. But the Asian and the sidewalk squatter were too real for reportage.

In certain ways the Housing Now! march was a success. Turnout was a heartening 40 percent of the organizers' advance estimates. Press coverage was slavering yet perfunctory. The march got thirty-three column inches in the next day's *Washington Post,* but in the Section-D metro pages, not with the real news. The network news broadcasters made sympathetic noises but mostly en passant on the way to the day's meatier stories.

It's hard to imagine anyone who got a close look at the Housing Now! demonstration ever voting for a social program again. It was as though we as a nation had made the mistake of feeding the dog at the table. Now Spot won't leave us alone and is going to have to be tied out in the yard.

A few mainstream politicians paid lip service to the aims of the march, but they kept an arm's length between themselves and the chief Housing Now! organizers, who were Donna Brazile, the former Dukakis campaign aide who accused George Bush of having a girlfriend, and Mitch Snyder, the perennial homeless advocate and incessant protest-faster who would commit suicide a few months later, thereby obtaining an eternal home, and a warm one at that.

Best of all, there were hardly any beautiful women at the rally. I saw a journalist friend of mine on the Mall, and he and I pursued this line of inquiry as assiduously as our happy private lives allow. Practically every female at the march was a bowser. "We're not being sexist here," my friend insisted. "It's not that looks matter per se. It's just that beautiful women are always on the cutting edge of social trends. Remember how many beautiful women were in the anti-war movement twenty years ago? In the yoga classes fifteen years ago? At the discos ten years ago? On Wall Street five years ago? Where the beautiful women are is where the country is headed," said my friend. "And this," he looked around him, "isn't it."

"By the way," I said, "where *are* the beautiful women?"

"Well, we know where two of them are," said my friend. "One is married to you, and one is married to me, and they're *home.*"

DIRT OF THE EARTH

The Ecologists

Six months later, on April 22, 1990, I did *not* go to see the Earth Day demonstration on the Mall. Instead, I spent the day calling up environmentally minded friends and asking them, "If the outdoors is so swell, how come the homeless aren't more fond of it?" I wanted to be the one person to say a discouraging word on Earth Day—a lone voice, not crying in the wilderness, thank you, but chortling in the rec room.

Thus, while everybody else was engaged in a great, smarmy fit of agreeing with themselves about chlorofluorocarbons, while *tout le* (rapidly losing plant and animal species) *monde* traded hugs of unanimity over plastic-milk-bottle recycling, while all of you praised each other to the (ozone-depleted) skies for your brave opposition to coastal flooding and every man Jack and woman Jill told child Jason how bad it is to put crude oil on baby seals, I was lying on the couch at home, snacking high on the food chain and talking on the cellular phone.

The Perennially Indignant special interest groups have another lobbying technique besides altruism. When an appeal to overweening self-righteousness isn't enough, the Indignants will argue that their special interest isn't special after all; it's general. If the government does what Indignants want, *everyone* will benefit, they claim. Or, better yet, everyone will die if the government doesn't. The Indignants thereby attempt to turn their special interest into a mass movement.

But can any decent, caring resident of this planet possibly disagree with the goals and aspirations embodied in the celebration of Earth Day? No.

And this is what bothers me. There's a whiff of the lynch mob or the lemming migration about any overlarge concentration of like-thinking individuals, no matter how virtuous their cause. Even a band of angels can turn ugly and start looting if enough angels are unemployed and hanging around the pearly gates convinced that succubi own all the liquor stores in heaven.

Whenever I'm in the middle of conformity, surrounded by oneness of mind with people oozing concurrence on every side, I get scared. And when I find myself agreeing with everybody, too, I get terrified.

Sometimes it's worse when everybody's right than when everybody's wrong. Everybody in fifteenth-century Spain was wrong about where China was and as a result, Columbus discovered Caribbean vacations. On the other hand, everybody in fifteenth-century Spain was right about heresies. They're heretical. But that didn't make the Spanish Inquisition more fun for the people who were burned at the stake.

A mass movement that's correct is especially dangerous when it's correct about a problem that needs fixing. Then all those masses in the mass movement have to be called to action, and that call to action better be exciting, or the masses will lose interest and wander off to play arcade games. What's exciting? Monitoring the release into the atmosphere of glycol ethers used in the manufacture of brake fluid anti-icing additives? No. And sex, drugs and rock and roll won't do much for the fringe-toed lizard. But what about an odium? An enemy? Someone to hate?

Mass movements need what Eric Hoffer—in his book *The True Believer,* about the kind of creepy misfits who join mass movements—called a unifying agent.

"Hatred is the most accessible and comprehensive of all unifying agents," said Hoffer. "Mass movements can rise and spread without belief

in a God, but never without belief in a devil." Hoffer goes on to cite historian F. A. Voigt's account of a Japanese mission sent to Berlin in 1932 to study the National Socialist movement. Voigt asked a member of the mission what he thought. He replied, "It is magnificent. I wish we could have something like it in Japan, only we can't, because we haven't got any Jews."

The environmental movement has, I'm afraid, discovered a unifying agent, a devil, a . . . (I can't say "scapegoat." Scapegoats are probably an endangered species. Besides, all animals are innocent, noble, upright, honest, fair in their dealings and have a great sense of humor.) The environmental movement has found its enemy in the form of that ubiquitous evil—already so familiar to Hollywood scriptwriters, pulp paperback authors, and all the dim-bulb Democrats in Congress—big business.

You might think big business would be hard to define in this day of leveraged finances and interlocking technologies. Not so. Big business is every kind of business except the kind from which the person who's complaining about big business draws his pay. Thus the "Rock around the Rain Forest" crowd imagines record companies are a cottage industry. The Sheen family considers movie conglomerates to be a part of the arts-and-crafts movement, something like Morris dancers. And Ralph Nader thinks the wholesale lobbying of Congress through huge tax-exempt advocacy groups is similar to being a migrant farm laborer.

This is why it's rarely an identifiable person (and, of course, never you or me) who pollutes. It's a vague, sinister, faceless thing called industry. The National Wildlife Federation's booklet on toxic chemical releases says, "industry dumped more than 2.3 billion pounds of toxic chemicals into or onto the land," and, "industry pumped more than 1.5 billion pounds of toxic chemicals into the land via deep-well injection." What will "industry" do next? Visit us with a plague of boils? Make off with our first born? Or maybe it will wreck the Barcalounger. "Once durable products like furniture are made to fall apart quickly, requiring more frequent replacement," claims the press kit of Inform, a New York-based environmental group that seems to be missing a few sunflower seeds from its trail mix. But even a respectable, old, establishmentarian organization like the Sierra Club is not

above giving a villainous and conspiratorial cast to those who disagree with its legislative agenda. ". . . For the past eight years this country's major polluters and their friends in the Reagan administration and Congress have impeded the progress of bills introduced by congressional Clean Air advocates," said the Sierra Club's 1989–90 conservation-campaign press package.

Business and industry and "their friends in the Reagan administration and Congress" make easy and even appropriate targets. Nobody squirts sulfur dioxide into the air for a hobby, after all, or tosses PCBs into rivers as an act of charity. Pollution occurs in the course of human enterprise. It is a by-product of people making things, things like a living. But whatever is required to clean up the environment people are going to have to make that, too. If we desire, for ourselves and our progeny, a world that's not too stinky and carcinogenic, we're going to need the technical expertise, entrepreneurial vigor and marketing genius of every business and industry. And if the Perennially Indignant think pollution is the fault only of Reaganites wallowing in capitalist greed, then they should go take a deep breath in Smolensk or a long drink from the River Volga.

Business and industry—trade and manufacture—are inherent in civilization. Every human society, no matter how wholesomely primitive, practices as much trade and manufacture as it can figure out. For good reason. It is the fruits of trade and manufacture that raise us from the wearying muck of subsistence and give us the health, wealth, education, leisure and warm, dry rooms with Xerox machines that allow us to be the ecology-conscious, selfless, committed, splendid individuals we are.

Our ancestors were too busy wresting a living from nature to go on any nature hikes. The first European ever known to have climbed a mountain for the view was the poet Petrarch. That wasn't until the fourteenth century. And when Petrarch got to the top of Mount Ventoux, he opened a copy of Saint Augustine's *Confessions* and was shamed by the passage about men "who go to admire the high mountains and the immensity of the oceans and the course of the heaven . . . and neglect themselves." Worship of nature may be ancient, but seeing nature as cuddlesome, hug-a-bear and too cute for words is strictly a modern fashion.

The Luddite side of the environmental movement would have us

destroy or eschew technology—throw down the ladder by which we climbed. Well, nuts (and berries and fiber) to them. It's time we in the industrialized nations admitted what safe, comfortable and fun-filled lives we lead. If we keep sniveling and whining, we may cause irreparable harm to the poor people of the world—they may laugh themselves to death listening to us.

Contempt for material progress is not only unfair but dangerous. The average Juan and the average Chang and the average Mobutu out there in the parts of the world where every day is Earth Day, or Dirt and Squalor Day, anyhow, would like to have a color television, too. He'd also like some comfy Reeboks and a Nintendo Power Glove and a Jeep Cherokee. And he means to get them. I wouldn't care to be the skinny health-food nut waving a copy of *Fifty Simple Things You Can Do to Save the Earth* who tries to stand in Juan's way.

There was something else keeping me indoors on April 22. Certain ecological doom-boosters are not only unreasonable in their attitude toward business; they're unreasonable in their attitude toward reason. I can understand harboring mistrust of technology. I myself wouldn't be inclined to picnic nude at Bhopal. But to mistrust science and deny the validity of the scientific method is to resign your job as a human. You'd better go look for work as a plant or a wild animal.

For example, here we have the environmentalists howling like wild animals because President Bush asked for more scientific research on global warming before we cork everybody's Honda, ban the use of underarm deodorants and replace all the coal fuel in our electric-generating plants with windmills (which don't burn very well anyway). The greenhouse effect is a complex hypothesis. You can hate George Bush as much as you like, and the thing won't get simpler. "The most dire predictions about global warming are being toned down by many experts," said the science page of the January 29, 1990, *Washington Post.* And the science section of the *New York Times* from the same week claimed a new ice age was only a thousand or so years away.

On the original Earth Day in 1970—when the world was going to end from overcrowding instead of overheating—the best-selling author of *The*

Population Bomb, Dr. Paul Ehrlich, was making dire predictions as fast as his earnestly frowning mouth could move. Dr. Ehrlich predicted that America would have water rationing by 1974 and food rationing by 1980, that hepatitis and dysentery rates in the U.S. would increase by 500 percent due to population density and that the oceans could be as dead as Lake Erie by 1979. Today Lake Erie is palatable, and Dr. Ehrlich still is not.

Ecological problems won't be solved by special interest groups spreading pop hysteria and merchandising fashionable panic. Genuine hard-got knowledge is required. The collegiate idealists who fill the ranks of the environmental movement seem willing to do absolutely anything to save the biosphere, except take science courses and learn something about it. In 1971 American universities awarded 4,390 doctorates in the physical sciences. After fifteen years of youthful fretting over the planet's future, the number was 3,551.

It wouldn't even be all that expensive to make the world clean and prosperous. According to the September 1989 issue of *Scientific American*, which was devoted to scholarly articles about ecological issues, the cost of achieving sustainable and environmentally healthy worldwide economic development by the year 2000 would be about $729 billion. That's only $14 per person per year, or—to translate that into Perennially Indignant terms—less than three quarters of what the world spends on armaments.

The earth can be made an earthly paradise, but not by legislative fiat. Expecting President Bush to fix global warming (or nuclear winter, if you're still worried about that) by sending a bill to Congress is to indulge yourself in that ultimate totalitarian fantasy of a law against bad weather.

With the environmentalist movement, as with the homeless advocates, we see a special interest group more interested in marrying an evil than curing it. Cures for environmental problems might even endanger the environmentalist fad. Improved methods of toxic chemical incineration, stack scrubbers for fossil-fuel power plants and sensible solid-waste-management schemes lack melodramatic (not to mention fund-raising) appeal. Nobody is going to come to a big demonstration thanking General Motors for developing an electric car.

The beliefs of many environmentalists have little to do with the welfare of the globe or the well-being of its inhabitants and a lot to do with the parlor primitivism of the Romantic movement. There is this horrible idea, beginning with Jean-Jacques Rousseau and still going strong in college classrooms, that natural man is naturally good. All we have to do is strip away the neuroses, repressions and Dial soap of modern society, and mankind will return to an Edenic state. Anybody who's ever met a toddler knows this is nonsense. (Though Rousseau may not have—the five children he had by his mistress Thérèse Levasseur were sent to orphanages at birth.) Neolithic man was not a fellow who always left his camp site cleaner than he found it. Ancient humans blighted half the earth with indiscriminate use of fire for slash-and-burn agriculture and hunting drives. They caused desertification through overgrazing and woodcutting in North Africa, the Middle East and China. And they were responsible for the extinction of mammoths, mastodons, cave bears, giant sloths, New World camels and horses and thousands of other species. Their record on women's issues and minority rights wasn't great either. You can return to nature, go back to leading the simple, fulfilling, harmonious life of the hunter-gatherer if you want, but don't let me catch you poking around in my garbage cans for food.

Then there are the beasts-are-our-buddies type of environmentalists. I have a brochure from the International Fund for Animal Welfare containing a section called "Highlights of the IFAW's History," and I quote:

> 1978: Campaign to save iguanas from cruelty in Nicaraguan market-places—people sew animals' mouths shut.

In 1978 Nicaragua was in the middle of civil war. This means that while the evil Somoza was shooting it out with the idiot Sandinistas, the International Fund for Animal Welfare was flying somebody to besieged Managua to check on lizard lips.

The neo-hippie-dips, the sentimentality-crazed iguana anthropomorphizers, the Chicken Littles, the three-bong-hit William Blakes—thank God these people don't actually go outdoors much, or the environment would be even worse than it is already.

SETTING THE CHICKENS TO WATCH THE HENHOUSE

The Savings-and-Loan Crisis

A government that met the demands of the Housing Now! or Earth Day demonstrators would be doing a profound moral and intellectual disservice to the nation. Usually when the government caters to special interests, the results are less serious and much more expensive.

For example, the U.S. government is in the process of spending $500 billion to bail out the savings-and-loan industry. You know savings and loans, they're pretty much like banks, except banks do business in large, architecturally impressive buildings and won't cash your check, whereas savings and loans do business in places that look like 7-Elevens and won't cash your check, and you can't get a six-pack of beer there either. Savings and loans are the ones with the signs out front that go "56°F/3:00 PM" and, if they are very fancy savings and loans, also go "JOIN OUR 1998 XMAS CLUB" and give a pep-rally message to the local high-school football team: "ROLL THOSE TROJANS."

Well, the savings-and-loan industry screwed the pooch. People deposited money in savings and loans expecting that the savings and loans would do something safe and intelligent with the money the way banks do, such as loan it to Argentina. Instead, the savings and loans invested in fur-bearing trout farms and jackalope ranches. Now all the money is gone, and the United States government is spending $500 billion to preserve the nation's electric time-and-temperature signs.

This is five-zero-zero, zero-zero-zero, zero-zero-zero, zero-zero-zero smackeroos out the blowhole.[1] We are talking about the combined annual profits of GM, Exxon, Ford, IBM, GE and AT&T plus the Department of Education's budget for the next five years plus the gross national products of Sweden and Brazil. But we members of the general public have yet to get as upset about the savings-and-loan crisis as we get about, say, a proposed income tax hike of a couple of hundred bucks.

The S&L bailout is just another case of the government giving money to jerks, and we're all used to that. Somebody gets himself addicted to heroin. He's a jerk. The government gives him money to take methadone. Somebody else owns a corporation that makes rocket boosters that don't work. He's a jerk, and the government gives him money to build more. Then there are the people with the pervert-photo-exhibit grants from the National Endowment for the Arts, those jerks. Not to mention all the jerk nations that our government buys new tanks for every time their old tanks get sticky between the treads from running over civilians. The government gives so much money to jerks that giving money to jerks must be—like giving the power to set the national agenda to network TV—one of the basic, constitutionally mandated purposes of government:

> We the people of the United States, in order to form a more perfect Union, establish justice, insure domestic tranquility, provide for the common defense and give money to jerks . . .

Then there's the matter of the five-hundred-billion number. We have become inured to government figures with vapor trails of zeros behind them.

---

[1] Five hundred billion dollars is only a rough estimate. Members of the press and most politicians (especially nonincumbents) have settled on this figure because it is a big, fat, round one. Other, more exactly calculated estimates of the total cost to the taxpayers of the S&L fiasco range from $325 billion (overconfident Republicans in the Office of Management and Budget) to $1 trillion (gloating Marxist economics professors) to more money than you can shake a stick at plus the stick (the author's best guess).

Certain harmless newspaper humorists have made careers out of inventing funny-sounding names to lampoon big government spending: scungillion, quadra-smellion, ding-dong-dillion. A sum like $500,000,000,000 doesn't ring our doorbell anymore.

But consider how much money that is. Five hundred billion dollars is enough money to pay for a New York City cab ride from Earth to the planet Uranus and back ten times, including tip (unless the driver spots you for a tourist and takes you via the Brooklyn Belt Parkway). It is enough money to send every member of America's high-school graduating classes of 1991, '92 and '93 to Harvard for four years. (Though God knows why we'd want to—they'd probably all go into government.) Five hundred billion dollars is enough to buy a commercial building for each of America's homeless persons so they can sleep on their own steam grates instead of somebody else's. It's enough to get every welfare mother a new double-wide mobile home in your suburb. We could even use the money to do something about the country's drug problem, such as buy 2.5 billion one-ounce lids of high-grade sinsemilla and never have a problem with running out of drugs again.

The Marshall Plan that saved the whole of Western Europe from Communism after WWII only cost $12 billion, that's about $50 billion in today's U.S. Dollars Lite. This means that for what the S&L bailout is costing, we could have saved Western Europe from Communism *and* sent forty-five million Americans on all-expense-paid European vacations. Then, when the forty-five million vacationing Americans realized how arrogant, rude and noisome Europeans are, we could have paid the Communists to take them back and still had enough money left over to save the Chrysler Corporation from bankruptcy, which only cost $1.2 billion.

The Financial Institutions Reform, Recovery and Enforcement Act of 1989 will end up costing every man, woman and child in America $2,000. Except it won't. Because not every man, woman and child in America pays taxes. Babies don't pay taxes. Old farts don't pay taxes. Rich shitpokes with high-hat tax lawyers don't pay taxes, and neither do those high-hat tax lawyers if they're any good. Welfare chiselers don't pay taxes, nor do drug addicts, drug dealers and people whom drug dealers have shot dead in the street. Corporations are famous for not paying taxes. Churches don't have to pay taxes. And no taxes are paid by our unemployed, lay-about brothers-in-law, bum cousins, noodle-brained sisters who give all their money to EST and crazy uncles who are forever losing their shirts in business ventures such as "CHAT-EAU—the catnip flavored blush wine for your cat." That leaves you and me. We're about the only people in America who pay our taxes. So when all's said and done, this savings-and-loan bailout is going to cost us $250 billion apiece.

No doubt you have various questions about the savings and loan industry and the nature of its financial difficulties and the type of legislation necessary to remedy the current problems and prevent their recurrence.

Q. WHAT THE FUCK, HUH?! I MEAN, WHAT THE FUCKING FUCK?!

A. Let me see if I can answer that as succinctly as possible. There are all sorts of different federal banking rules and regulations resulting in all sorts of different banks, including commercial banks and savings banks and—for all I know—five-ball-in-the-corner-pocket bank shots. Among these various types of banks are savings and loans. Savings and loans are a kind of nitwit populist creation of the Depression era. Back then a lot of nitwit populists believed that an international conspiracy of Elders of Zion or Bavarian Illuminati or some such was running the financial world and that regular dumb guys from the sticks didn't stand a chance, bank-wise. Savings and loans were designed to be a kind of bank that regular dumb guys from the sticks could run, no problem. In return for making some home-mortgage loans to other regular dumb guys from the sticks, savings and loans were permitted by federal legislation to borrow money cheaply from the U.S. Treasury, get plenty of tax breaks and be regulated by a group of bank examiners consisting of three schoolchildren and a tame mouse.

This arrangement worked better than you'd think for forty-odd years. Savings-and-loan executives adhered to the "3-6-3 rule": Pay S&L depositors 3 percent interest; charge S&L mortgage borrowers 6 percent interest; play golf at 3:00. Then another nitwit populist creation of the Depression era, Jimmy Carter, got into office, and the economy started to look like an election in Haiti, and interest rates went on that taxi ride to Uranus that we talked about earlier. S&L owners—who are, after all, just a bunch of dumb guys from the sticks—were left with nothing to make money from but 6 percent mortgages that they couldn't get rid of for thirty years. Meanwhile, S&L depositors didn't think 3 percent interest was a very good deal anymore and were taking all their money out of savings and loans and investing it in one gallon of unleaded gasoline. S&Ls started losing money with both hands.

Q. Tough luck. If S&Ls are losing money, let them close up shop, give people back their savings and be done with it. Why should me and PJ have to pay through the nose for it?

A. Unfortunately, that's not how banking works. At some subconscious level—even though we know better—we all have an image of banks as being like Scrooge McDuck's money vault. We put our money in banks, and the bankers put that money—all those ones and fives and nickels and dimes and fifty-cent pieces—into a great big safe, where they rub it and dust it and stack it in piles, and sometimes, late at night, the bankers take off all their clothes and roll in the stuff and yell, "Whee!"

In fact, banks don't keep any money—just a couple of Susan B. Anthony dollars and a stack of twenties with an exploding dye pellet inside that they give to bank robbers. This is why banks will never cash your check. Federal laws require banks to keep only 6 percent of their assets ("their assets" is a technical term for "our money") in what's called reserve capital, which is what you and I would call what I've got on me right now. And, until recently, savings and loans didn't even have to do that. S&Ls needed only 3-percent reserve capital, and that wasn't cash. They were allowed to count their 7-Eleven buildings and their electric time-and-temperature signs as part of the 3 percent. Another part of the 3 percent could be made up of "subordinated debt," which is money that the S&L borrowed from somebody else, maybe you. Therefore, the money you had deposited in an S&L could be backed up by money that the S&L owed you in addition to the money the S&L owed you if you withdrew the money you had deposited in it. You can see how three kids and a pet rodent would have trouble keeping this straight. Furthermore, yet another part of that 3-percent reserve capital could consist of something called goodwill. Goodwill is that warm, cozy feeling that you get when you think about your local savings and loan. This goodwill is very valuable. That's why you can go into any grocery store and fill up a grocery cart with beer and steaks and little cans of smoked oysters and go to the checkout counter and, instead of giving money to the cashier, say, "Whenever I think about my local savings and loan, I feel warm and cozy."

Savings and loans can't just close up shop and give people back their savings, because savings and loans don't have any money. The money is all out at the fur-bearing trout farms, and we can't get money back from the trout because trout don't have pockets.

Q. OK, all right, so the S&Ls are Tap City, and people with savings accounts at S&L's got boned in the ear. Why does that skin my cut? This ain't no hippie commune.

A. Ha. Ha. Ha. It is if you own a savings and loan. You see, there's this thing called deposit insurance. Every federally chartered S&L savings account is insured up to $100,000 by something called the Federal Savings and Loan Insurance Corporation. FSLIC, or Fizz-Lick (as professionals in the stupid acronym business call it), is a government corporation owned by we the taxpayers but that we the taxpayers can't sell or give away or even kill by hitting on the head with a brick. The extra-nitwit, double-populist idea behind Fizz-Lick is that people such as ourselves should scrimp and save and sacrifice to build up a little nest egg to have in case of emergencies, such as needing to buy a jet ski, and Fizz-Lick is there to keep our little nest egg from being lost during depressions or nitwit populist presidencies.

The $500 billion savings-and-loan bailout is, therefore, a $500-billion bailout of ourselves. You may find this a bit mysterious if you have $20 in your savings account, the way I do. So the real reason we have to pony up is that the legislation that created Fizz-Lick says S&L savings accounts are backed by "the full faith and credit of the United States government."

When the United States government makes a promise, that promise is
. . . Well, just ask the people of Southeast Asia, whom we promised to save
from the North Vietnamese. No, the really real reason we have to submit
to this wallet hoovering is that if we don't, our moms and dads are going
to lose some portion of the life savings that they're always fretting about,
and this will completely panic the old feebs, and they'll sell their retirement
condo in Naples, Florida, and move in with us. Come to think about it, $500
billion is a small price to pay.

Now let's find someone to blame. If we're going to have to come up
with billions and billions of dollars, let's at least take them out of somebody's hide. The Second World War was expensive, too, but at least we got
to shoot Nazis.

We can start by blaming the people everybody blames everything on:
Reagan, Carter and the Arabs. They caused the Penn and Teller economy
that savings-and-loan bankers have had to live with for the past decade and
a half. The Arabs gave us an oil boycott, then an oil glut and now an
oil-price surge. Carter let them. And Reagan was the blind, deaf referee at
the subsequent deregulatory wrestlemania match. But Reagan has to spend
the rest of his life with Nancy. The Arabs have a Gulf War to worry about.
And Jimmy Carter has turned into a pathetic coot who spends his days
hammering on poor people's housing, causing the poor people to run
outside and yell, "Knock it off! Our housing is bad enough already without
you hammering on it!" God has taken care of these people for us.

So let's blame the shag-nasties in the savings-and-loan industry. Common sense tells us that no matter what's happening with interest rates,
nobody just "loses" $500 billion. I mean, did these guys look under the
couch?

Don Ray Dixon, proprietor of the Vernon Savings and Loan in Vernon,
Texas, for instance—Don Ray had the Vernon S&L buy a $2-million beach
house in Del Mar, California, where Don Ray lived rent free. Don Ray
carried $5.5 million worth of "lonesome cowpoke" type western art as an
"asset" on the Vernon S&L books. And Don Ray and his wife, Dana, toured
France by private plane and Rolls Royce on a Vernon-S&L-funded "market
study" of world-class restaurants. Federal bank regulators—who were slow

to catch Don Ray because they had to clean their room and mow the lawn before they were allowed out to go regulate banks—now estimate that this particular good-ol' boy did $1 billion in damage to the S&L industry single-handed.

Another such was Herman K. Beebe, Sr., of Shreveport, Louisiana. Herman leveraged his way into a network of some forty banks and S&Ls, which he proceeded to use much as a pig uses a wallow, so that his home, his jet plane, his duck-hunting vacations and all his personal business scams were "assets" of one of his financial institutions.

Hundreds of Hermans and Don Rays were out there using a splendid variety of gyps. There were "back-scratcher loans," where if you and I each controlled a savings and loan, I'd loan you $100 million because you're cute, and you'd loan me $100 million because I'm kind to animals. Then we'd "forget" to pay each other back. And there were "land flips," where I would, on paper, sell you a worthless acre of swamp for one grand and you'd "sell" it back to me for ten grand, and I'd "sell" it to you again for one hundred grand and so forth until we'd established that this acre of swamp was worth millions. Then we'd go to our S&Ls and get millions in loans using the swamp as collateral, and we'd default, and, darn it, lose our 4,840 square yards of muck.

But it's not much use getting mad at the cash-machine cowboys who pulled this stuff. They're criminals, and you know the rules of American cultural anthropology. They'll be folk heroes before you can say, "Financial Institutions Reform, Recovery and Enforcement Act of 1989." Look for Kevin Costner to star as a likable scamp of a Texas S&L swindler in a major studio Christmas season release.

In fact, it would be more useful and accurate to blame *all* the people in the savings-and-loan industry, especially the law-abiding ones. These are the guys who are standing around with the "Who farted?" look on their face, saying things like, "We ran an honest shop. You can't blame us. We hardly even knew Don Ray Dixon, and we never went on any fancy-restaurants-in-France tours with him, and the food wasn't that great anyway."

While a combination of weird economics and flaming muck bills were destroying the thrift business, honest savings-and-loan executives were not exactly screaming for more regulatory oversight and a beefed-up Fizz-Lick insurance fund. The law-abiding members of the savings-and-loan industry are the little boys who cried, "Sheep."

"Hey, wait a minute. Baa, baa, baa," say law-abiding members of the savings-and-loan industry. And they have a point. Savings-and-loan executives are now dealing with a bunch of customers who would rather change their money into singles and use it to economize on Kleenex than deposit it in an S&L. The new Fizz-Lick legislation soaks thrifts for as much as they can stand without going belly-up some more and starting the bailout all over again. And that legislation adds a lawyer's fortune of regulations to what's already one of the most regulated livelihoods this side of child pornography.

All sorts of fools—Marx, Shakespeare, Hitler, Oliver Stone in his movie *Wall Street*—have used finance as a paradigm of cutthroat, capitalist free enterprise. But the enterprise of banking is not free. Bankers kiss more asses than they cut throats. And—if you'll recall the discussion of reserve capital—banking isn't even very capitalistic. Finance is not like selling drugs or real estate or owning galleons full of spices the way Antonio did in *The Merchant of Venice*. The savings-and-loan industry is at the mercy of something more powerful than market forces. The great slime engine of government holds the S&Ls in orbit.

If we want somebody to blame who can stand the blaming, let's look to the jacklegs in Congress. Beginning in the late 1970s savings-and-loan lobbyists produced a bloody flux of political-action-committee funds and other influence effluvia, and members of the House and Senate stood by like toilets with the lids up.

Lately public anger has been focused on the so-called Keating Five. In return for campaign contributions and other largess, U.S. Senators Alan Cranston, Dennis DeConcini, Donald Riegle, John Glenn and John McCain came to the aid of Charles H. Keating, one of the worst egg suckers in the S&L business, a man whose criminally irresponsible investment schemes at California's Lincoln Savings and Loan are costing the public $2 billion. The senators should be ashamed to even know, let alone take money from, the likes of Charles Keating. But, in fact, all the Keating Five did for their cash was get together and tell Edwin Gray, former head of the Federal Home Loan Bank Board (that is, boss of the previously mentioned three school-

children and a tame mouse), to lay off their pal. "And if you don't, we'll
. . . we'll tell you again," they said, or something like that.

In the annals of congressional S&L malefaction, the behavior of the
Keating Five barely rates a complete sentence. It is nothing compared with
the mischief done by Congressman Fernand St. Germain, a Democrat from
Rhode Island, who in 1980 oversaw the raising of the Fizz-Lick insured
deposit ceiling from $40,000 to $100,000. This gave us regular folks with
$20 saved toward a jet ski increased protection and peace of mind, of
course. And, by the way, it also gave the S&Ls huge chunks of federally
guaranteed money to play bank with. Professional dollar jockeys put together $100,000 packages of cash and moved the packages from bad S&Ls
to worse. The most horrible savings and loan in the world, one with no
assets at all except a box of those rubber thumb things that you use to count
money, could get endless new deposits by the simple method of offering
savings-account interest rates that would make a garment-district loan shark
blush. Depositors didn't care because the money was insured, and S&Ls
didn't care because, what the heck, it's only money.

In 1982 St. Germain teamed up with another Port-o-San, Senator Jake
Garn, a Republican from Utah, to pass the Garn–St. Germain bill allowing
S&Ls to do something called direct investment. No longer were the thrifts
limited to relatively conservative methods of throwing money away, such
as loaning that money to people with jackalope ranches. Now an S&L could
buy its own jackalope ranch and spend millions cross-breeding antelopes
with jackrabbits and marketing the eggs in local supermarkets.

St. Germain eventually got so covered in S&L-lobby pocket lint that
even the voters noticed, and he was unelected in 1988. But in one of those
miraculous career comebacks for which Washington is justly famous, St.
Germain reappeared in DC as—who could have possibly guessed it—a
savings-and-loan-industry lobbyist.

There were plenty of congressional dirt slurpers to take St. Germain's
place, such as ex–Speaker of the House Jim Wright. In 1986 the S&L mess
was "only" a $15-billion problem. The Reagan administration came out of
regulatory coma for one brief moment and proposed a bill that would have
refinanced Fizz-Lick with the S&L's own money. The S&L lobby had kittens. Jim Wright stalled the Reagan measure and made sure the sum

involved was too little as well as too late. The idea seemed to have been to let the disaster grow until only the taxpayers could afford to pay for it. Wright also attempted to intervene with regulatory authorities on behalf of several Texas S&L human crap sacks of at least as bad a type as Charles Keating. And he helped to spread rumors that Joe Selby, one of the government's few effective thrift regulators, was gay.

There is not room in this book for a complete list of elected offenders. There are 535 members of the House and Senate; as many as a dozen of them are blameless. And even those few aren't really innocent. All the senators and representatives and all the citizens of the United States who voted for them are guilty of forgetting one basic rule of business and life: When buying and selling are controlled by legislation, the first things to be bought and sold are legislators.

GRAFT FOR THE MILLIONS

Social Security

The great danger of special interests is not, however, that a minority of some kind will get fat at our nation's expense. The great danger is that our nation will discover a special interest to which a majority of us belong. When that happens, there will be no end of robbing Peter to pay Paul, of famishing you to feast me, of the general picking of our own pockets.

The senior-citizen lobby seems to be approaching this frightful proportion. I mean, what's with these old people? Where'd they come from? All of a sudden there are geezers and duffers and biddies and fusspots everyplace you look. Not a highway in the nation is safe from Florida-bound codgers swaying lane to lane at 52 mph in their Cruise Master motor homes with the novelty license plates bolted to the front: "RETIRED—NO JOB—NO PHONE—NO EXCUSE FOR LIVING." Every Sun Belt plane flight has its aisles jammed to impassibility with blue-rinse wide loads and their carry-on cat boxes. Fogies crowd shopping centers in mall-walking packs and swamp the ten-items-or-less supermarket checkout lanes with case-lot purchases of Campbell's soup for one. Turn on the television, and the ads are all for bran, Pepto-Bismol, hemorrhoid medications and high-fiber this and that. *Sic transit* the Pepsi generation. Everyone in commercials is over seventy and has something wrong with his butt.

There didn't use to be this many old people. I remember when it was just the occasional coot on a porch rocker waxing nostalgic about President McKinley and outdoor plumbing plus Grandma in the kitchen baking cookies, and that was it. Now they're all over the place—arteriosclerosising around on the racketball courts, badgering sky-diving instructors for senior-citizen discounts, hogging the Jacuzzi at the singles apartment complex.

The number of fuddy-duddies and mossbacks in the United States has increased by 5.5 million in the past ten years. There are now more than thirty-one million "older Americans" (the term preferred by run-to-seed specimens age sixty-five or more). They outnumber teenagers. They outnumber blacks. They outnumber people who remember being at Woodstock. And they're very well off.

Between 1967 and 1987 oldster households received a 52.6-percent increase in real, inflation-adjusted, income. This versus a 7-percent increase for everybody else. Even though the elderly produce little except complaints about what's on TV, their poverty rate is below the overall poverty rate and has been since 1982. At least the rest of us are generating small Mario Brothers addicts and large VISA bills to keep the economy stimulated, but we have an average net worth of $32,700, and that's counting the yard-sale value of little Jennifer's Barbie wardrobe. Old folks have an average net worth of $60,300. Nearly a third of them have a net worth of more than $100,000. And 83 percent own their homes free and clear.

How'd these rusty customers get to be worth a fortune? By costing me one. Ninety-two percent of the nation's mortuary bait gets a Social Security check. A typical current retiree's yearly take is $8,674. In order to pay for this, the Social Security withholding tax on those of us who look at a Victoria's Secret catalog with more hope than regret is now up to as much as $3,855.60 a year. And if we have the bad luck—as this one of us does—to be self-employed, the bite is doubled: $7,711.20. That means some old doll whom I don't even know is pestering her daughter-in-law with querulous long-distance calls, littering her front lawn with plaster ducks, overfeeding her toy fox terrier and haunting the bingo parlors—on *my* dime.

Now some people might say I have a bad attitude toward the golden oldies. But let's stop and consider exactly who the people turning sixty-five these days are. This is the original blowed-in-the-glass generation of dry holes and mullet heads—our parents. They were born too late to have any good stories about bathtubs full of gin and flappers. We had to spend our whole childhoods listening to how darn poor (but cheerful and optimistic) they were during the Depression. As soon as they'd finished spoiling the New Deal for everybody with their relentless attitude of cheery optimism, they went off to World War II and were relentlessly cheery and optimistic about that—death camps, fire storms, atom bombs and all. In fact, our parents had such a good time during WWII that they absolutely insisted, when the time came, that we have a war of our own—Vietnam. Anyway, Mom and Dad got back from "the big one" and set about inventing a popular culture consisting of Levittown, television quiz shows, pole lamps and "How Much Is That Doggie in the Window?" Then they got all huffy and hurt-acting when we rebelled. Finally our parents reached the apogee of their professional and intellectual powers in the 1970s, wrecked the economy with wild inflation and elected Jimmy Carter. Now we've each got to pay $3,855.60 a year to keep these chuckleheads in Gelusil and Mercury Marquises.

Remember the battle between the generations twenty-some years ago? Remember all the screaming at the dinner table about haircuts and getting jobs and the American dream? Well, our parents won. They're out living the American dream on some damned golf course, and we're stuck with the jobs and haircuts.

About 30 percent of the American government's budget is now spent on grizzled frumps. If we put a strictly monetary value on things (and sooner or later we have to—as anybody who ever tried to give American Express a hug in place of a credit-card payment knows), this means we care as much about denture breath as we care about national defense. Two percent of the federal budget goes to education, so all those people Ed McMahon has to talk to real slow in the insurance commercials are fifteen times as important to us as our children's future. (And never mind that I cut all the education spending out of the federal budget back in the beginning of the book. We're talking odious comparisons here.) One half of one percent of the budget goes to pollution control; thus, as far as we're concerned, what the Eskimo left on ice floes and the Fiji Islanders made into bouillabaisse is sixty times as meaningful as the fate of the planet.

And it's going to get worse. The antediluvian population continues to grow. The over-fifty-fives are the only age group in the country that will get significantly larger in the next century. By 2030—the year in which the last of the baby boomers will enter dotage—a fifth of the nation will be old, and lots of the old will be ancient. The Census Bureau says that the eighty-five-plus bunch is the fastest growing segment of the nation's population. There are almost twenty-three times as many of these fossils as there were in 1900. There will be fifteen million of them by the mid-2000s, and some demographers think it will be twice that.

Though they may be alive, they won't necessarily be doing much living. Last year a Harvard Medical School research project examined thousands of geriatric Bostonians and found double the previously estimated incidence of Alzheimer's. Nearly half of those over eighty-five had signs of the disease. Medicare already costs taxpayers $100 billion per annum, with 30 percent of that money spent on treatments in the last year of patients' lives.

If all that weren't frightening enough, there's one more terrifying fact about old people: I'm going to be one soon. All the signs are present—I've got the gray hairs, the paunch, and as you may have noticed, I'm grouchy as hell. I'm more worried about gum disease than STDs, and all the music recorded since 1980—except Linda Ronstadt's big-band albums—sounds like somebody tipped over the china cabinet.

The baby boom is turning into the senescence swell. Those of us born between 1946 and 1964 constitute one third of the total U.S. population. And we're even worse than our parents. We're the most vapid, puling, screw-noodled, grabby and self-infatuated generation in history. Imagine what we'll be like—wearing roller skates with our walkers, buying Ralph Lauren cashmere colostomy bags, going to see Jackson Browne impersonators at Atlantic City and grumbling that our heart-lung machines have gone condo. Woe to any youngster in the year 2030 who happens to get cornered by one of us when we start reminiscing about the sixties. "Bring the stun ray quick, Ma, Granddad's going into a Nixon fit again!!!"

Not that that child of 2030 is going to have much time for listening to superannuated hippies. The kid's going to have to have a job and maybe two or three of them. At the moment there are 3.4 people in the labor force for every Social Security beneficiary. By 2030 there will be fewer than two. If the present rate of old-goat entitlement continues, two thirds of the next century's federal budget will be spent on the aged, while that pair of very tired and irritable people who are gainfully employed will pay a Social Security tax of between 25 percent and 40 percent of their earnings.

How can we keep gilding the gramps like this and still have anything left over from the gross national product to invest in machinery for making crude plastic cowboy hats to sell to Japanese tourists (which is what our benefit-beggared economy will be reduced to by 2030)? Well, we could ask our wizened deadbeats to go Dutch, make at least some of the richer ones pay the freight on what society sends their way. This was the idea behind the 1988 Medicare Catastrophic Coverage Act, fragments of which may still be seen among the smoldering ruins of various Washington political careers.

The catastrophic-care bill was intended to protect old folks from being bankrupted by hospital bills. Medicare pays for a lot of hospitalization, but if the frost-tops get a disease that's pumped up and goes the distance, it can exhaust their Medicare benefits, and they can wind up as broke as they are old. "Cat-Health" would have paid for all out-of-pocket wrinkle-puss hospital costs beyond $560 per year, doctor bills above $1,370, half of all prescription costs after the first $600 plus breast-cancer screenings and 150 days of nursing home care. Furthermore, it would have protected the financial assets of people whose spouses were parked for good at the Senility Hilton and given some financial aid to those who keep their dodderers at home. In return for this largess, the old-timers would each have had to pony up a $4 monthly flat fee, and the carriage trade among them would have paid a 15-percent income tax surcharge not to exceed $800 per year. A pretty good deal, you'd say. And so said your elected representatives. Cat Health was passed through Congress like beer through a college student.

The hoar-heads went ballistic. Them? Pay? Pay for something themselves? What do we think they are, fellow citizens with duties and obligations or something? These are the goddamned golden years, and no fuzztail

Johnny-come-latelies are going to cut into their greens fees and Caribbean-snorkle-vacation funds. Senators and congressmen began getting mail in mountainous gobs, phone calls by the caboodle, mile-long swards of angry fax messages, and congressman Dan Rostenkowski, chairman of the House Ways and Means Committee, wound up trapped in his car by an angry mob of ancient constituents using some very modern words to describe their feelings about him, catastrophic health and Congress in general.

Without pesky jobs or annoying responsibilities our elders have plenty of time to tell the rest of us what's what. Seventy percent of them vote (versus 35 percent of people ages eighteen to twenty-four). They form the core support group for big-city Democratic candidates and the principal campaign donor pool for suburban Republicans. Everybody had to rush back into the Capitol building and unpass the cat-health bill quick—99 to 0 in the Senate and 360 to 66 in the House.

Thus the "user fee" concept of old-age benefits died and went to hell. Then what about "prepayment"? What if we charge our healthy, young selves a little more Social Security tax than we need to so that when we get obsolete and greedy, there will be a pile of money saved up and ready for us to spend on LSD Senior with fiber supplement.

This was the idea behind the 1983 Social Security finance reform—advance funding. In fact, it's being done right now. By 1995 the Social Security system will be taking in 32 percent more money than it's spending. In that key year 2030 the Social Security trust fund is expected to have a surplus of $2.3 trillion.

However, there are a couple of problems with advance funding. For one thing, $2.3 trillion might be about what a pack of Freedent gum will cost in 2030. Even assuming that some kind of indexing for inflation compensates for this, it's still difficult for any political institution to hold onto a pile of money. Money is dung to the flies who make their living in public service. At the end of 1989 the state of Pennsylvania had $25 billion sitting in its public pension fund. In order to help Pennsylvania's lagging economy, the state treasurer proposed that the pension fund's managers invest hundreds of millions of dollars "in local real estate, state highways and bridges and new businesses, especially businesses started by women and members of minorities." This is the way that your Social Security payroll contributions can turn into a low-interest loan to the Mrs. Marion Barry Fast-Acting Nose Drop Corporation.

Assuming that, due to the Second Amendment to the Constitution, this won't happen either, we're still left with the "excess" taxes used to create advance funding. Because this revenue isn't needed immediately or ear-marked for any particular pork barrel, it is a perfect target for tax cutting. Tax cutting being a politician's second favorite thing to do after raising taxes. If an oily and cynical politician, such as Senator Daniel Patrick Moynihan, were to muscle in on this issue, he could say, "Wait a minute, the American working person is getting charged all sorts of money for Social Security, but the federal government isn't really saving that money; it's just spending it the same way it spends any other money you give it, and when we open up the Social Security trust fund in 2030, nothing is going to be in there but a note saying, 'I.O.U. $2.3 trillion. XXX OOO The Feds.' " This being approximately what Senator Moynihan has been saying.

And the worst thing about what Senator Moynihan says—the really oily and cynical thing—is that it's true. There's nothing more oily and cynical in politics than telling the truth. Think how oily and cynical the Republicans were to tell the truth about Willie Horton in 1988. Think how truly oily and cynical they would have been if they'd told the truth about Kitty Dukakis.

Anyway, it is the truth. Our federal government can't save up the way an individual can. It's such a commonplace to anthropomorphize govern-ment—"Social Security saves for a rainy day." "The Bush administration leaves the porch light on when nobody's home"—that we forget a democ-racy is not a person or a sentient being of any kind. It can't even act like a legal fiction of a person the way a corporation can.

Everyone assumes the Social Security trust fund is a kind of giant national Christmas club, a great big joint savings account with 250 million names on the passbook. However, when an individual puts money in a savings account, that money gets invested in factories, farms, home con-struction, South American drug shipments or whatever. Those investments make money—or are supposed to—and the money they make pays the interest on our savings. But when the federal government buys South American drug shipments, it has to burn them, which isn't very profitable at all. Nor is it politically feasible for our government to invest in private industry, except in emergency situations, such as when under threat of another Lee Iacocca biography. The only thing the federal government can do with extra cash, such as the Social Security trust fund, is buy federal government securities with it—loan that cash to itself. And once the loan has been made, the government has no legal choice except to treat the proceeds of that loan like any other federal revenues and spend the shit out of them. Our Social Security trust fund isn't being "raided." It was never there in the first place.

Of course, inasmuch as we are a democracy, we can fix this trust-fund problem by legislation. We can pass laws making the federal government invest our $2.3 trillion in the private sector—get government to buy farms, factories and housing developments. There's a name for this economic system. Indeed, the citizens of East Germany, Poland, Czechoslovakia and Romania had some very pungent names for it. On the other hand, we can pass laws privatizing the whole megillah. Though if you propose this out loud in Washington, you'll find yourself being chased down the Mall by men with nets. "Take money away from the federal government?" say deeply shocked politicians. "But if you take money away from the federal government, what will it *do* all day?" And they have a point. Five hundred thirty-five members of Congress, nine justices of the Supreme Court and George Bush would have to get jobs in the private sector. Our economy could be destroyed overnight.

So what are we going to do with our pricey ancestors? I really can't think of anything. Except maybe we could hunt them down and kill them. The government could sell licenses and old-bat stamps. We could go out on opening day and build some granny blinds by the RV hookups in Sun City—hide ourselves in a realistic-looking thicket of Medicare regulations, and when the back numbers hobble over to apply for $100 billion in benefits—POW! This idea has appeal even though I'll be on the receiving end of it not too long from now. Presumably the grizzled parties will be allowed a sporting chance to return fire, and taking out a couple of Sinéad O'Connor fans would definitely enrich my sunset years.

With head full of such fancies, I went to beard the gray-dittos in their very den, the headquarters of the American Association of Retired Persons.

And there I received even worse news about our nation's intergenerational conflict—like the SS trust fund, it doesn't exist.

The AARP has a building of its own on Washington's K Street—"Gravy Train Lane"—where America's most powerful special interest lobbies headquarter themselves. And the AARP is arguably the most powerful of all. It has thirty-two million members, more members than any organization in the United States except the Roman Catholic church, and annual tax-free revenues of $262 million.

Just as the National Highway Traffic Safety Administration's offices were not filled with backpackers, the AARP's offices had no doilies over the backs of the word-processor video screens or cabinets full of things filed under "whatchamacallit." And there were no executives in white patent-leather shoes and matching belts waiting to bend my ear about the days when professional athletes weren't so big for their britches. The people at AARP were the same age as people at places of business usually are, and the surroundings were efficient to the point of austerity.

I was ushered in to see Martin Corey, the AARP's director of federal affairs. Corey—in his small workspace with a C-Span live broadcast of Congress flickering like a votive candle in the background—pulled out charts and graphs and tables to show me that by picking on the derelict frumps and fusty cusses, I was putting myself off the sociopolitical reservation. According to Yankelovich polls conducted for the AARP in 1985 and 1987, 92 percent of Americans think the Social Security system is a success.

Upon consideration, it isn't hard to figure out why. Current retirees are getting three to five times what they paid into Social Security, plus their employer's contribution, plus interest, and most of that is tax free. As of 1986 a married worker who paid the maximum amount of Social Security tax and retired at sixty-five would recover his contribution to Social Security in twenty-one months. A low-income retiree would recover his in as little as twelve months. The Social Security payroll tax may be high, but what an investment. To do this well on our own, we'd have to have bought IBM back when they were trading its stock for cigar bands.

Corey said that 64 percent of Americans would even like to see Social Security payments get larger. And young people are more likely to feel this way than old. Of people ages twenty-one to twenty-nine, 74 percent think the government should spend more on Social Security payments versus only 51 percent of people sixty-two years old or older.

The AARP research material made it clear that it's not just our future we're selfishly thinking about; we're also thinking, selfishly, about our present. Eighty percent of Americans agree with the statement—marvelously straightforward in its callousness—"I'm glad we have Social Security because taking care of parents financially is too much of a burden without it."

So we've won the prize. Social Security is a government program with a constituency made up of the old, the near-old and those who hope or fear to grow old. After 215 years of trying, we have finally discovered a special interest that includes 100 percent of the population. Now we can vote ourselves rich.

AT HOME IN THE PARLIAMENT OF WHORES

Abracadabra, thus we learn
The more you create, the less you earn.
The less you earn, the more you're given,
The less you lead, the more you're driven,
The more destroyed, the more they feed,
The more you pay, the more they need
The more you earn, the less you keep,
And now I lay me down to sleep.
I pray the Lord my soul to take
If the tax-collector hasn't got it before I wake.

—Ogden Nash

Hundreds of miles from the ambitions and deceits of Washington there is a little town in New Hampshire where I live. This town is tucked under the arm of an impressive mountain and is surrounded by resplendent gauds of foliage in the autumn and wreathed in downy coverlets of snow all winter long. Delicate spires of colonial church steeples nick the cloud-chased New England sky, and a pellucid trout stream rolls and chuckles in the shadow of the old woolen mill, now a historical landmark. A mere fifty-one hundred souls make their home here. There's not a stop light or a parking meter to be seen. The whole town could be a Norman Rockwell painting come to life if Norman Rockwell had been better at depicting towns that have convenience stores on half the street corners and are filled with pseudo–Cape Cod tract houses, each with a snowmobile for sale in its front yard.

Still, my little town—let's call it Blatherboro—is as decent a place as you will find in America. In 1989 the Blatherboro Police Department received twenty-nine reports of lost property. In the meantime, town residents turned fifty-nine items of lost property in to the police. The citizens of Blatherboro are decent to the point of defying arithmetic.

The citizens of Blatherboro are also employed. Virtually no one in the town is out of work or stays that way long. The town welfare officer, a very practical lady, has been known to come by people's houses early in the morning and *take* them job hunting. Only sixty-three Blatherboro households required any charity in in 1989, and that charity was, as the word indicates, charity. The $21,000 that the town spent on public assistance was all supplied by private donations.

Blatherboro's residents are educated and sensible—literate enough to support three local weekly newspapers and sensitive enough to their neighbors' feelings to make sure that no very juicy news appears in any of the three. They are a calm, law-abiding lot. Shootings, stabbings, rapes and so forth are unheard of in Blatherboro (though there is a certain amount of discreet wife beating and child abuse, especially during the midwinter doldrums). The last murder of any note took place in 1919 and is still discussed with indignation.

Blatherboro is a nice town, but not so nice as to be eerie. The people of Blatherboro are good people but not dreadfully good. Blatherboro is an uncommonly comfortable place for comfortably common people, like me, to live. It is the economy section of Beulah Land.

The government of Blatherboro is as homey and reasonable as Blatherboro itself. There is a traditional New England town meeting held once a year. Here the business of democracy is disposed of in one sitting. And here I go to do my civic duty and help dispose of it.

There is nothing at all of a Rockwell painting to a real New England town meeting, and nothing of a Robert Frost poem either. "Whose woods these are I think I know. . . ." Hah. Whose woods are whose everybody knows exactly, and everybody knows who got them rezoned for a shopping mall and who couldn't get the financing to begin construction and why it was he couldn't get it. And you'd hardly use our town meeting as a calendar photograph. It's held in the high-school gym, a windowless space barely large enough for full-court basketball, redolent of damp socks and painted two-tone yellow in the two worst tones of yellow ever seen except in terminal jaundice.

This political arena is filled with folding metal chairs of an ingeniously uncomfortable design. The front rows of the folding chairs are occupied by elderly know-it-alls in lime-green blazers—business executives who retired (much to the relief of their respective businesses, no doubt) and moved to Blatherboro to reside in their summer homes year-round. These former items of corporate deadwood spend most of their day basking in the warm glow of New Hampshire tax policy. (New Hampshire tax policy is to not have any taxes—there is no state or local income tax and no sales tax either.) And the rest of the time they devote to thinking up great ideas and swell notions for improving everything in Blatherboro, especially the efficiency of its government.

Sitting in the back rows of the folding chairs and standing around the gymnasium walls are the Blatherboro natives, ranging in type from deer-poaching swamp Yankees to frayed Emersonian Brahmins and including a large number of working-stiff French Canadians. The natives live in fear that the improvements in efficiency proposed by the blow-hard retirees will send the one tax New Hampshire does have, the town property tax, soaring. This property tax keeps soaring anyway, despite the fact that every single person at the town meeting has a plan to reduce taxes.

The Blatherboro selectmen (who are the equivalent of city councilmen, except this isn't a city and there's no council) and the Blatherboro town manager sit at a folding table facing the earnest crowd, and the town moderator stands behind a podium and calls on people. Members of the local Boy Scout troop carry microphones to the orators in the audience, and a combination of bad PA system and typical gym acoustics produces a voice of the people that is more *pox* than *vox populi*.

Despite the minimal nature of Blatherboro town government and, indeed, the minimal nature of Blatherboro, and despite the goodwill, good sense and good New England parsimony of Blatherboro's residents, the result of the annual town meeting is always a stupid and expensive mess.

Much of the stupidity is common to all government. There are certain subjects about which people are incurable boneheads. Humans apparently cannot rationally consider what constitutes a danger to humanity or how likely any given danger is to occur. Thus, Blatherboro has fifteen police officers—the same ratio of police to population as New York City. The annual Blatherboro police budget is $425,000. This in a town that, in 1989, had 520 crimes, of which 155 were minor incidents of teenage vandalism. The cost of police protection against the remaining 365 more or less serious malefactions was $1,164 each—more than the damage caused by any of them.

On the other hand, almost everything in Blatherboro is built out of wood. Half the town is too rural to have fire hydrants, and a lot of the town is too cheap to have smoke detectors. Every home has a fireplace, most have wood stoves and quite a few have wood-burning furnaces, so that in March 1989, for example, there were three chimney fires in four days. But the Blatherboro Fire Department is a completely volunteer organization with an annual budget of less than $50,000.

People are also very stupid about what makes people smart. The local school system, which serves Blatherboro and the nearby town of Quaintford, isn't very bad. But it isn't any good either. The Blatherboro-Quaintford School District Annual Report expounds at length on "competency-based programs," "whole-language instruction" and "curriculum coordination" and devotes a dozen pages to discussing "budget objectives" and listing the various administrators, speech pathologists, special-education consultants and so forth that are thought necessary to modern education. But nowhere does the annual report remark on the fact that the high school's ninth grade has 124 students, while the high school's tenth grade—whose denizens are of legal age to leave school—has 79. This is a 36-percent drop-out rate, about the same as the drop-out rate in most inner-city slums.

The Blatherboro-Quaintford schools have only a total of 1,488 students, kindergarten through twelfth grade, yet there is a complete school-district office with a staff of fifteen people, including a superintendent of schools, an assistant superintendent and a business administrator. And there are an additional twenty-eight principals, assistant principals, counselors, aides and other people who don't actually teach anything on the school-system payroll.

Blatherboro's annual per-student spending is over $5,000—almost three times the national average for state college tuitions. If Blatherboro's parents and taxpayers were as serious about education as they—and every other parent and taxpayer in America—always say they are, they could gather the youngsters into miniature academies of perhaps fifteen students each and hire $75,000-per-year private tutors to teach them. In the academic-infested groves of New England, $75,000 would hire a fine tutor. Alternatively, Blatherboro students could be packed off to the local Catholic schools, where they'd get a better education—and a good, sharp rap on the knuckles if they showed any need for counseling—for less than half the price.

City planning is also beyond Blatherboro's ken. The town has a Planning Board, a Board of Adjustment, a building inspector, a Conservation Commission and a Historic District Commission, and the place still looks like hell. Of course, there are patches of twee and precious prerevolutionary beauty, as there are in all old New England towns. Sections of Blatherboro are so overrun with white clapboard and green shutters that if a man were to unzip his fly in these parts of town, the Historic District Commission would probably make him put green shutters on either side of that, too. But the rest of the place looks like every other piece of overpaved, cheap-jack, fake-front highway sprawl in the nation. I don't happen to mind this sprawl myself, at least not in theory, because in theory I'm a private-property strict constructionist. But I do mind all the boards and commissions and employees of the town wasting my money failing to prevent it.

Besides the ordinary and general kinds of idiocy, the Blatherboro Town Meeting also deals in some witlessness specific (but no doubt not unique) to Blatherboro.

The retired blowhards had gotten together with the Blatherboro elected officials, the members of the Chamber of Commerce and all the other people in town whose method of torturing their neighbors is good citizenship and decided that the town offices were too small. Too small for what was not explained, though the selectmen gave an elaborate presentation, complete with slide show, detailing just how much too small. The proposed solution was to sell the snug and handsome little town hall that sits on the Blatherboro common and sell the Mayberry RFD storefront police department down the street and buy an empty factory building out on the east side of town and put everybody in there. This would cost $1.3 million but would, it was said, save the town money in the long term.

The Town Flake stood up to speak. He is an old and addled gentleman with hair in long, white tangles—WASP dreadlocks. He's been making a complete and utter pest of himself at town meetings for over thirty years. He owns his own mimeograph machine and runs off reams of smudgy philippics accusing town government of incompetence and waste. He knows all the regulations in *Robert's Rules of Order* and uses them until he has to be shushed by the moderator or shouted down by the townspeople. And he is always and invariably right on every issue. "Save money in the long term! Save money in the long term!" said the Town Flake with high scorn. "Government's always full of ideas to *save money in the long term.* Just why is it that government never has a single, solitary idea about saving money *now?*" The Town Flake was shushed by the moderator.

A very old lady wanted to know, if we were going to sell the town office, were we also going to sell the World War I monument on the common? It was patiently explained to her that monuments (or commons either) don't get sold. Whereupon another even older lady asked, if the town office got sold, did the World War I monument go with it? The question would come up twice again in the debate.

Someone else wanted to know why a factory couldn't go in the factory building—and provide jobs and pay taxes. To which the selectmen replied that the economy's a bit slow in New England these days, and no business is likely to buy the factory.

"Well, if no business is likely to buy the factory, who the heck is going to buy the town hall and the police station?" hollered the Town Flake.

The arguments continued for two hours. And these arguments were, in their effect, much more persuasive against democracy than for buying the factory or keeping the town hall. It is remarkable, on close inspection, what a lousy way to get things done democracy is. Not that democracy necessarily makes the wrong decisions. Private enterprise can do this with equal or greater ease. But in a democracy the decision-making process must be listened to. The great thing about the invisible hand of the market is not that it's invisible but that it's silent.

Buying a factory to put the town government in was at last voted down, 241 to 207.

Debate now moved to whether the town should spend $1.7 million to build a new water tank.

The Town Flake pointed out that one reason the tank would be so expensive is that the town intended to build it in a valley with pumps instead of on a hill with gravity. He was shushed by the moderator.

New Hampshire is—with the exception of tropical rain forests (which I hear won't be around much longer anyway)—the wettest place on earth. When the snow melts in spring, there's not a basement in the state that you can't launch a boat in. A summer day without rain is considered something to tell your grandchildren about. You cannot walk half a mile in a straight line anywhere in New Hampshire without drowning in a stream, lake, beaver pond or somebody's flooded cellar. Yet the town of Blatherboro was running out of water. This was a stupidity beyond the range of local talents. Anything as astonishingly dumb as this must have the federal government involved in it somehow. And, indeed, it did. Congress had passed the Safe Drinking Water Act of 1982, which assumed that people in small towns were too far removed from Senate subcommittee hearings and presidential fact-finding commissions to know whether their drinking water was safe. Federal law now mandates that all water taken from surface sources in small towns everywhere must be filtered and chlorinated whether it needs to be or not.

So Blatherboro is obliged to build an entire new water system. The $1.7-million water tank is the first step in a three-phase construction program that will eventually cost the town $6.2 million. Never mind that that's enough money to drill a nice, new, clean, private artesian well for every household in town.

The only thing more depressing than democracy at work is democracy not allowed to. The debate on the water tank had just begun when the town's attorney pointed out that if Blatherboro didn't comply with federal water regulations, the town would be fined $25,000 per day. The water tank was approved by a grudging 251 to 108.

Next was an article "To authorize the Board of Selectmen . . . to apply for, accept and expend any and all Federal or State grants, gifts or funds that may become available during the ensuing year." This was passed overwhelmingly, as well it might have been, with loud shouts of "Aye!"

There followed an hour-long argument about whether to close a small section of the old town road. The blowhard retirees claimed that the road should be closed because the town natives liked to run their four-wheel-drive vehicles through there at all hours of the night, and the town natives argued that the road should be kept open because they liked to run their four-wheel-drive vehicles through there at all hours of the night. The natives won on a voice vote by being able to yell "nay" louder with no teeth than the retirees could yell "aye" with false ones. After that the $4-million town-government operating budget was passed with no debate whatsoever, the reasoning being that the thing had already been debated at public Budget Committee hearings, although no one had attended them. There was one "nay" from the Town Flake.

With these mundane matters out of the way, it was time for the real gist of the town meeting, the big fight everybody was waiting for, the keen excitement and high drama of quarreling about sewers.

It really is impossible to overstate the tedium of government. As boring as civics classes were back in high school, they were a bacchanal compared with civics itself. The next six hours of the Blatherboro Town Meeting were devoted to bickering about whether the Department of Public Works should have exclusive authority to approve sewer-line hookups. Of course, I have used the words *quarrel, fight* and even *bicker* in a strictly poetic sense. I doubt that in the course of the evening's long and brutal fray so much as a voice was raised. A town meeting is tedious with that amazing and inexplicable tedium of a large number of people behaving themselves in public. It is the opposite of a mob or a riot, the flip side of human collective behavior. Taking part in a New England town meeting is like being a cell in a plant.

Nevertheless, there were very strong feelings about effluvian matters in Blatherboro. An article was proposed that, if passed, would require that a special town meeting be convened to approve any expansion of the town sewer system costing more than $50,000. The idea was not to save money on sewers. User fees and hookup charges already reimburse the town for all sewer costs. The purpose of the proposal was, instead, to control growth. Every commercial, industrial or housing development of any size would need to be approved by the town as a whole or wind up swimming in its own waste. Specifically, this article was aimed at stopping a golf course and condominium complex already under construction on the west side of town.

The golf-course developer had been punctilious in meeting the town's Planning Board, Board of Adjustment, Conservation Commission and Historic District Commission requirements and in obeying all applicable state and federal laws. The golf-course and condo-complex owner had needed to obtain forty-seven permits from eleven different government agencies in order to start building his golf course and condo complex. But he had done so. An all-sewage special town meeting was the last possible way to stop the guys in plaid pants and kiltie shoes.

As I mentioned before, I hold private-property rights to be sacred—in theory. Which is like saying I'm rich—in Bulgaria. In theory we're all lots of things: good, kind and, above all, consistent. I hold private-property rights to be sacred in theory, but in practice I had thrown in with the anti-golf-course faction.

To be fair, we weren't opposed to the golf course for any Pals-of-the-Animals, Eco-Stalinist reasons. Most of us play golf. We didn't have any cutesy-artsy objections to seeing trees cut down. It's a lot easier to shoot a deer on a 350-yard par-four fairway than it is in the deep woods. And we weren't opposed to growth itself—in theory. But the sad truth of local government, like the sad truth of national government, is that people are no longer an asset. Humans do not benefit the modern state. Total 1989 Blatherboro town expenditure—including the town's share of county government and school-system costs—was $9.5 million, or about $1,860 per person. Almost all this money was raised through property taxes and automobile registration fees. A typical new family moving to Blatherboro, with a mom, dad and two kids (for families still come in that configuration in New Hampshire), would be buying a town-house condominium with a tax-assessed value of $100,000. The current property tax rate on that condominium is $2,860 a year. If the new family owns two late-model cars, registration fees (which are based on the blue-book value of the automobile) would be about $340. Add in a few miscellaneous levies and charges, and the new family ends up contributing approximately $3,500 per annum to the Blatherboro town coffers. But that is almost $4,000 less than what the town will spend on these people. A family of four must own at least a quarter of a million dollars worth of property to carry its own weight in the Blatherboro town budget.

Theory is important, sure, but it shouldn't get between a man and his wallet. You can't serve theory for dinner. People have a *theoretical* right to do what they want with their property, and people have a *theoretical* right to move into my town. *But . . .*

It was at this moment, in the middle of the Blatherboro sewer debate, that I achieved enlightenment about government. I had a dominion epiphany. I reached regime satori. The whole town meeting was suddenly illuminated by the pure, strong radiance of truth (a considerable improvement over the fluorescent tubes).

It wasn't mere disillusionment that I experienced. Government isn't a good way to solve problems; I already knew that. And I'd been to Washington and seen for myself that government is concerned mostly with self-perpetuation and is subject to fantastic ideas about its own capabilities. I understood that government is wasteful of the nation's resources, immune to common sense and subject to pressure from every half-organized bouquet of assholes. I had observed, in person, government solemnity in debate of ridiculous issues and frivolity in execution of serious duties. I was fully aware that government is distrustful of and disrespectful toward average Americans while being easily gulled by Americans with money, influence or fame. What I hadn't realized was *government is morally wrong.*

The whole idea of our government is this: If enough people get together and act in concert, they can take something and not pay for it. And here, in small-town New Hampshire, in this veritable world's capital of probity, we were about to commit just such a theft. If we could collect sufficient votes in favor of special town meetings about sewers, we could make a golf course and condominium complex disappear for free. We were going to use our suffrage to steal a fellow citizen's property rights. We weren't even going to take the manly risk of holding him up at gunpoint.

Not that there's anything wrong with our limiting growth. If we Blatherboro residents don't want a golf course and condominium complex, we can go buy that land and not build them. Of course, to buy the land, we'd have to borrow money from the bank, and to pay the bank loan, we'd have to do something profitable with the land, something like . . . build a golf course and condominium complex. Well, at least that would be constructive.

We would be adding something—if only golf—to the sum of civilization's accomplishments. Better to build a golf course right through the middle of Redwood National Park and condominiums on top of the Lincoln Memorial than to sit in council gorging on the liberties of others, gobbling their material substance, eating freedom.

What we were trying to do with our legislation in the Blatherboro Town Meeting was wanton, cheap and greedy—a sluttish thing. This should come as no surprise. Authority has always attracted the lowest elements in the human race. All through history mankind has been bullied by scum. Those who lord it over their fellows and toss commands in every direction and would boss the grass in the meadow about which way to bend in the wind are the most depraved kind of prostitutes. They will submit to any indignity, perform any vile act, do anything to achieve power. The worst off-sloughings of the planet are the ingredients of sovereignty. Every government is a parliament of whores.

The trouble is, in a democracy the whores are us.

Put not your trust in kings and princes. Three of a kind will take them both.

—General Robert C. Schenck